****

THE
THIRTEEN
COLONIES
COOKBOOK

****

THE THIRTEEN COLONIES COOKBOOK

★★

A COLLECTION OF FAVOURITE RECEIPTS

FROM THIRTEEN EXEMPLARY EIGHTEENTH-CENTURY COOKS

WITH PROPER MENUS FOR SIMPLE FARE AND

ELEGANT ENTERTAINMENTS

AND SELECTED NOTES OF HISTORIC INTEREST

BEING A GUIDE TO OPEN-HEARTH AND BEE-HIVE OVEN COOKERY

ADAPTED FOR TWENTIETH-CENTURY USE

★★

Written and Illustrated by

Mary Donovan

Amy Hatrak

Frances Mills

Elizabeth Shull

★★

PRAEGER PUBLISHERS • New York

Published in the United States of America in 1975
by Praeger Publishers, Inc.
111 Fourth Avenue, New York, N.Y. 10003

Second printing, 1975

© 1975 by Praeger Publishers, Inc.
All rights reserved

Library of Congress Catalog Card Number: 73-15176
ISBN 0-275-22300-0

Printed in the United States of America

We salute the nation's Bicentennial celebration
and the original thirteen colonies.

★★★

This book is affectionately dedicated to our thirteen children:

Mimi, Mike, and Jane Donovan
Melissa and Christopher Hatrak
Libby, Hilary, Frances, and Peggy Mills
Liz, Amy, Hugh, and Annabel Shull

Contents

Acknowledgments

Searching for the colonial housewife—trying to reconstruct her lifestyle from the meager evidence available today—has not been a solitary task. Many historians have helped us trace this elusive woman and have shared their knowledge of the foods she cooked and served. Without the efforts of the many individuals and groups who have preserved and maintained the houses featured in this book, we could not have presented this glimpse of colonial life.

We are especially grateful to the following people from the various states:

New Hampshire: Jane and Charles Kauffman, collectors of rare books on New Hampshire history and cookery; Ruth Sherburne-Wilson, curator of the Moffatt-Ladd House maintained by the National Society of the Colonial Dames of America in the State of New Hampshire; Mary Lynn Ray of the New Hampshire Historical Society; Dorothy Vaughn, Portsmouth Library; Betty Foye; and Virginia Horner.

Massachusetts: Wilhelmina S. Harris, superintendent of the Adams National Historic Site in Quincy, Massachusetts; H. Hobart Holly, president of the Quincy Historical Society; Wendell Garrett, assistant editor of the Adams papers; Margaret Klapthor, curator of the Division of Political History of the Smithsonian Institution; Stephen G. Callas, Legislative Assistant to Congressman Edward Patten; and William Matheson, chief of the Rare Book Division of the Library of Congress.

Rhode Island: Mary H. Reynolds, executive secretary of the Oldport Association; Theodore Waterbury, director, and Gladys E. Bolhouse, curator of manuscripts, of the Newport Historical Society, which maintains the Wanton-Lyman-Hazard House; and Alice A. Fuller of Wickford, Rhode Island.

Connecticut: Stuart M. Frank, research associate, Robert R. Boulware, assistant coordinator of public affairs, and Sandra Oliver, assistant for interpretation, crafts, and demonstrations for Mystic Seaport, Inc., which maintains the Buckingham House.

New York: Frank C. Baker, chairman of the Colonial Dining Committee; Ralph B. Stever, president, and James Whitford IV of the Sons of the Revolution in the State of New York, which sponsors the Fraunces Tavern Museum; and Helen D. Bullock of the National Trust for Historic Preservation.

New Jersey: John E. Chance, past president, and Ronald C. Perez, president, of the Montclair Historical Society, which maintains the Israel Crane House; Sarah M. Williams; Joyce V. Fuller; Leslie Bunce; and Casper J. Owen.

Pennsylvania: Richard H. Shaner, president of the American Folklife Society, which maintains the Keim Homestead; Eleanor Griesemer Shaner; Alice Trout; Robert S. Walch; Harold Yoder of the Berks County Historical Society; and Gurney Clemens.

Delaware: Horace L. Hotchkiss, Jr., curator of the Corbit-Sharp House, preserved by the Winterthur Museum; Dale Fields of the Historical Society of Delaware; and Helen Turner.

Maryland: Mrs. H. W. Keating, historian, and Ione Glaze, curator, of Mount Clare, which is preserved by the National Society of the Colonial Dames of America in the State of Maryland; Richard J. Cox, curator of manuscripts of the Maryland Historical Society; Mrs. Otho J. Keller III; Mrs. T. R. Dibble; and Mrs. John D. Avirett.

Virginia: P. Russell Bastedo, director of Kenmore, which is preserved by the Kenmore Association, and Charles C. Wall, resident director of Mount Vernon.

North Carolina: Frances Griffin, director of information of Old Salem, Inc., which preserves the Miksch Tobacco Shop; the Home Moravian Church, Winston-Salem; Elizabeth Pagett May; Mae Noble; and Zula Atkins Shull.

South Carolina: Mrs. Edward K. Webb, curator of the Heyward-Washington House, which has been restored by the Charleston Museum.

Georgia: Alan McNab, director, and Isabella Stuart, curatorial assistant, of the Telfair Academy of Arts and Sciences, in which the Telfair kitchen is located; Lilla M. Hawes, director of the Georgia Historical Society; Mary H. Freeman; and Robertine McClendon Philips.

Our very special thanks go to J. Lloyd Berrall, whose graceful drawings of the eighteenth-century homes open each chapter of this book.

Introduction

We invite you into the homes, and especially to the hearths, of thirteen exemplary American cooks—one from each of the original colonies. From the simple dwelling of a North Carolina tobacconist, to an elegant Maryland plantation, to the houses of the renowned Abigail Adams, we have attempted to bring to life the mistresses of these historic houses and the eighteenth-century world in which they lived. By presenting the cherished foods they prepared for family and friends, we have stressed each woman's role as an accomplished cook and gracious hostess.

In colonial America, it was the woman who looked after the larder. Whatever her station—rich or poor—she held the final responsibility for planning the family meals. She saw to the pickling and preserving of fruits and vegetables, the smoking and storage of meats and game, and the drying of herbs from her kitchen garden, which she used for medicinal as well as culinary purposes. She made soap from lard and candles from tallow, and when she was finished, she created potpourri from rose petals, spices, and herbs to scent her home. Whether she was preparing daily fare or presenting a proper collation, the woman had to light the open-hearth fire and manage the three-hour-long fire preparation for the beehive oven. Only an improvident housewife allowed the fire to go out, and when it did, she would reach for her trusty tinderbox to start a new one. Even on simple baking days, she could be found "searching" the flour, "pounding" the sugar, "washing" the butter, and "getting" the yeast.

As we studied the lives of these colonial housewives, we were struck by the variety and breadth of this nation's culinary heritage. Scots in Georgia, Germans in Pennsylvania, French in South Carolina, Africans throughout the South, and Dutch in New York all added their epicurean traditions and skills to America's cookery. Frontier conditions and the large number of unmarried men made taverns an essential part of eighteenth-century life; hence we included among our featured cooks one tavern-keeper whose skill was so extraordinary that he became the steward in George Washington's presidential home.

Most of the "receipts" presented here were chosen and adapted from historical and traditional receipts found in period manuscripts, journals, letters, and cookbooks. Others are from family records and receipt books, often written in the mistress's own hand. Dishes that were originally cooked on the open hearth or in the beehive oven have been adapted and tested for use in modern kitchens. Ingredients and measurements that might be problematic have been clarified—"butter the size of an egg" has been changed to ¼ cup butter; vanilla extract has been substituted for the hard-to-find vanilla bean; receipts that begin with "Take twelve eggs . . ." have been changed because colonial eggs were much smaller than those of today. However, we have held to the leavening agents used by the eighteenth-century cook—yeast, eggs "whipt to a froth," and saleratus (baking soda), which was used in combination with buttermilk or cream of tartar—rejecting the temptation to substitute the nineteenth-century invention baking powder for the saleratus and cream of tartar.

Many of the dishes—unusual and interesting, and perhaps forgotten for generations—represent new ideas in food preparation and deserve a revival. Today's cook will discover Roast Lamb Forced with Oysters, Rosemary Crab Apple Jelly, Chestnut Flummery, and Mushroom Pasty and rediscover regional specialties such as a Rhode Island Clambake, Maryland Crab Imperial, Pennsylvania Chicken Pot Pie, and Georgia Jambalaya. These receipts display the ingenuity of the colonial cook in using the bounty of the new nation.

To help today's hostess plan for a bountiful board in the eighteenth-century manner, we have depicted historic social occasions as described by contemporary observers, and created menus for those events that use the receipts found in the book. By so doing, we hope to indicate how the foods were served in combination.

Imagine, then, a colonial American kitchen. The little cakes are baking in the beehive oven, the chicken is roasting in the tin kitchen, the coriander gingerbread hangs from the crane in the Dutch oven, and the orange cakes hot from their iron pans are on the board, waiting to be glazed with the salamander. Perhaps this is the day Raspberry Shrub will be poured from the noggin, or Mock Clary ladled into little cups from its iron pan warming on the hearth.

Please enter and share with us these tastes from America's past.

★★★★★★★★★★★★

THE
THIRTEEN
COLONIES
COOKBOOK

★★★★★★★★★★★★

Catherine Moffatt Whipple of Portsmouth, New Hampshire

Moffatt-Ladd House

Catherine Moffatt, daughter of Captain John Moffatt, a wealthy merchant and shipowner, lived in the prosperous seaport of Portsmouth all her life. In 1767, at the age of thirty-five, she married her cousin William Whipple, a signer of the Declaration of Independence and a military hero who commanded the First New Hampshire Brigade.

At the time of their marriage, General Whipple had retired from the sea as a successful merchant in foreign trade. The couple moved to the fine three-story mansion Madame Whipple's father had built overlooking the harbor. From the captain's walk on the third floor she could watch the boats on the Piscataqua River and the commerce on the wharves owned by her family.

As William became involved in the pursuit of freedom in the colonies, their home became a center for social and political life. The prosperity of both her father and husband allowed Madame Whipple the privileges of upper-class society, and accounts of the day noted that she "kept open house." She provided good food and a congenial atmosphere for her husband's patriotic activities and soon became an important woman in Portsmouth.

When her husband was elected to the Continental Congress and left for Philadelphia, Madame Whipple stayed behind to manage

1

COURTESY MUSEUM OF FINE ARTS, BOSTON

CATHERINE MOFFATT WHIPPLE

the townhouse and the upcountry properties for her aging father. She oversaw the operation from wine cellar to garret, taking pains to see that all ran efficiently (although not as fashionably or extravagantly as her southern counterparts). The changes she made in the house were for convenience rather than for display, and her achievement was as a successful, capable hostess.

Described as "neither young nor handsome but of a good understanding and gayety," Madame Whipple was a straight-forward and pleasant woman whose stolid New England strength and sense of duty held her in good stead throughout her long life. She was devoted to her father and husband, and she played her part well by William's side in the founding of the new nation.

The Moffatt–Ladd House

The mansion in Portsmouth, built of wood and painted a "pink putty" color, is a treasure of eighteenth-century architectural design. The fine detail inside, the handsomely panelled halls and chambers, and the magnificent, broad entrance hall and stairway—perhaps the finest in New England—reflect the taste of Captain Moffatt, who built the house for his son Samuel.

In 1763, the French and Indian War over, a new feeling of peace and prosperity emerged. Samuel Moffatt had a flair for fashion and furnished the house elegantly. He lived there for only a short time. Due to business failure, he was forced to flee one night through the tunnel to a waiting ship setting sail for the West Indies, and with the threat of imprisonment he never returned to Portsmouth.

Captain Moffatt repurchased the house at auction, and it was then that Madame Whipple became the mistress of the house, where father, daughter, and husband lived in apparent harmony for almost twenty years. More concerned with people than fashion, she was content with the way Samuel had left the house, and inventories show that in twenty years she never moved the furniture from room to room.

Her warming kitchen reflected her simple taste. It was furnished with simple Windsor chairs and tables, which bear signs of red paint. A cupboard with shelves to the ceiling held Canton, Delft, pewter, and earthenware. Wide floorboards and interior shutters give the room an air of dignity. The heavy work in the house was probably

BILL FINNEY

performed by servants in the basement kitchen, with a huge fireplace near the buttery, winery, and root cellar.

The gardens at the Moffatt-Ladd house are among the most beautiful and best tended in New England. The most splendid adornments to the house are the terraced pleasure gardens with abundant bloom and grass steps leading from one level to another. The herb garden remains in its original site by the kitchen door. The pleasure gardens, grape arbors, fruit trees, gooseberry bushes, beehives, an original dove and pigeon cote on the coach house, a counting house, and other out-buildings—all reflect the grace and beauty of this well-tended town-house.

Soups and Savories

GOURD LADLE

Soups appear often in New Hampshire rule books. The cold, damp winter air made them welcome and warmed the bones of Portsmouth sailors and sea captains readying their ships for sail to warmer seas.

Corn Chowder

3 slices salt pork, cubed	1 cup milk
1 large onion, sliced	2 cups corn, scraped from the cob,
4 large potatoes, cubed	or canned creamed corn
2 cups water	1 teaspoon salt
6 large common crackers, or hard	Dash of paprika
crackers *	Pieces of pimento, chopped

* Common crackers are about 2 inches round, hard and crisp, made of white flour. Originally, they were stocked in large quantities for long sea voyages because they did not spoil. Gradually, the wives of seafarers learned to make use of them in cooking as thickening in soups, stews, and berry pies, and served them with chowders. They can still be purchased in New England and they are still called common crackers, but they are fairly uncommon today.

Fry salt pork in saucepan until crisp and lightly browned. Stir in onion and cook in rendered fat until golden. Add potatoes and water, and cook until potatoes are done. Crumble crackers in a bowl and moisten with milk. Add to potatoes, onion, and pork. Lastly, add corn, salt, and paprika. Simmer for 8 to 10 minutes and garnish with pimento. Serves 4. For a hearty Sunday night supper, follow it with Pork and Ham Loaf with mustard sauce, fresh applesauce, biscuits and butter, and hard cider.

East India Soup

2 cans consommé, or bouillon
2 tart apples
2 tablespoons flour
1 large teaspoon curry powder

Pinch of salt
1 cup heavy cream
1 apple, thinly sliced

Cut the apples in quarters, leaving the skin on. Simmer the apples in the consommé until soft. Strain the mixture through a coarse-meshed strainer and set aside. Whisk the flour, curry, and a pinch of salt in the cream and heat in a double boiler. Add strained apples and consommé and heat to just below the boiling point, blending flavors well. Float a thin, unpeeled slice of the whole apple, dusted with curry, in each dish. Serves 6.

Almond Soup

Living in a seaport town, Catherine Whipple was familiar with exotic foods brought back from foreign ports. This soup with its mysteriously delicious flavor may have pleased the cultivated taste of John Adams when he visited his good friend and fellow New Englander William Whipple.

4½ cups chicken broth
1⅓ cups almonds, blanched
6 hard-boiled egg yolks
1 teaspoon coriander
Juice of ½ lemon

2 teaspoons grated lemon rind
Salt and pepper to taste
½ cup heavy cream
Chives, chopped
Slivered almonds, sautéed

Put 2 cups of the chicken broth, almonds, egg yolks, and coriander in the blender. Blend until smooth. Heat 2½ cups chicken broth and add almond mixture gradually. Season with lemon juice, lemon rind, salt, and pepper. Stir in cream and heat until hot but not boiling. Let stand overnight in the refrigerator. Sprinkle with chopped chives and almonds. Serve from a tureen to 6 or 8.

(Adapted from Charles Carter, *The Complete Practical Cook*, 1730)

CANTON TUREEN

Fish, Meat, and Fowl

Creamed Cod

1 pound salt cod	2 cups milk
4 tablespoons butter	Salt and pepper to taste
4 tablespoons flour	

Freshen salt cod by soaking in cold water for 3 or 4 hours. Change the water several times. Drain. In fresh, cold water slowly bring the fish to a boil and simmer for 10 to 15 minutes, or until fish flakes with a fork. To make a cream sauce, blend butter and flour; add milk, salt, and pepper. Add the fish to the sauce. Serve with baked potatoes. Sliced hard-boiled eggs make an attractive garnish. Serves 4.

Portsmouth sea captains, who sailed to many ports, wrote letters home to their wives. Captain James McClure wrote from Tobago on August 21, 1784: "My dear Betsey, Take care of yourself and keep a good fire this winter, many a cold night I shall lay wishing to be along side of you." And from London on May 25, 1785: "I should have sent you more shoes but its being so long a time I had the pleasure of feeling your foot, am at a loss as to the size. I hope they will fit."—manuscript, New Hampshire Historical Society

Curried Lobster Salad

"The river below the town of Portsmouth and for some miles above the same is well stored with codfish, bass, and several other sorts of choice fish. Lobsters they bake in abundance near their wharfs."—James Birket, Some Cursory Remarks, 1750–51

PORTSMOUTH HARBOR

½ cup vinegar
Piece of butter "the size of an egg" (2 tablespoons)
2 eggs
1 teaspoon each salt and curry powder
1 teaspoon dry mustard

¼ teaspoon pepper
Juice of 1 lemon
1 tablespoon sugar
½ cup milk
3 tablespoons cream
1 pound lobster meat
Celery, chopped (optional)

Make a dressing of the vinegar, butter, eggs, seasonings, and sugar and cook until the mixture thickens, whisking briskly. Add the milk and cream last and heat thoroughly. Cool. Mix dressing with lobster meat. Add chopped celery. Store leftover dressing. Serves 4.

The dressing is nice with other fish, such as salmon or tuna.

Pork and Ham Loaf

Butchers often came to the doors of Portsmouth homes selling fresh ham and other meat. "Whose pig was this?" the mistress asked.

1 large onion, chopped fine
3 tablespoons butter
1 cup bread crumbs
1 cup milk
2 eggs, beaten
1½ teaspoons salt (less if ham is salty)
½ teaspoon thyme

Big pinch of allspice
2 cloves garlic, mashed
¼ teaspoon each pepper, cloves, and marjoram
½ cup Madeira
1¼ pounds smoked ham, ground (delicatessen ham will do)
1¾ pounds fresh pork, ground

Sauté onion in butter. Soak the bread crumbs in the milk and add the beaten eggs, salt, herbs, spices, and Madeira. Combine the ground meat and onion with the bread-crumb mixture and put it in a large loafpan (9" x 5" x 3"). Bake slowly at 300° for 2 to 2½ hours. Cut the loaf when cool. It is better if allowed to age for a day.

Take the loaf on a picnic with cold beets in dressing, fresh baked bread, and butter. Bring a large basket with a sampling of sweets—gingerbread, hermits, and Old Portsmouth orange cake. Spread a checkered cloth on the bank near a stream and arrange the food in the center, while children hunt for flat stones to skip across the water.

HERB BASKET

Pork Roast in New Milk—Fit for Company

Pork roast, boned, about 5 pounds
5 cloves garlic
2 or 3 sprigs of fresh rosemary and thyme
2 sprigs of parsley

1 sprig of sage
1 large onion, sliced
4 cups milk
Salt and pepper to taste
1 cup soured cream

Brown the roast in a Dutch oven. Add garlic, herbs, and onion. Add milk to cover the meat halfway. Cover and roast slowly in the oven at 300°, for 3 or 4 hours, or until meat is as tender as "pot roast." To serve, take out the roast and slice it. Remove the excess fat. Taste the gravy and season with salt and pepper. Whisk the gravy in a blender to bind the separated milk. Add soured cream. Maced green beans, curried fruit, a green salad, and tomato-ginger preserves "should be served to eat with it." Serves 6–8.

GINGER JAR

To Stuff a Leg of Lamb with Oysters

Lamb and oysters are an unusual combination today but very common in eighteenth-century cookbooks. Anchovies were often put in meat sauces for a special savory taste (they are still a major ingredient in Worcestershire sauce), and oysters were so abundant that they were added liberally to meat, fish, and fowl dishes.

1 cup bread crumbs
2 hard-boiled egg yolks, mashed
3 anchovies, chopped
¼ cup onion, chopped
Salt and pepper to taste
1 teaspoon each thyme and winter savory

⅛ teaspoon grated nutmeg
12 oysters
2 raw eggs
1 leg of lamb, boned and butter-flied

Mix together breadcrumbs, egg yolks, anchovies, onion, salt, pepper, thyme, winter savory, grated nutmeg, and oysters. Mince the mixture very fine. Add 2 raw eggs to make a paste and stuff the lamb. Roll the lamb up and tie it with a string. Roast it at 30 minutes per pound in a preheated 325° oven. For 4½ pounds, boned weight, roast for 2 hours and 15 minutes.

Sauce

¾ cup oyster liquor
½ cup claret wine
2 or 3 anchovies, chopped
Several gratings of nutmeg

2 tablespoons onion, chopped
6 oysters, chopped (optional)
Pan juices

Take some oyster liquor, some claret, 2 or 3 anchovies, a little nutmeg, a bit of onion, and 6 oysters (optional). Stew all these together. Remove fat from pan juices and add juices to the sauce. Serve in a sauce boat with the lamb roast. Serves 8.

(Adapted from Eliza Smith, *The Compleat Housewife*, 1729)

Broiled Game Bird (Cornish Game Hen)

There was a dovecote on the side of the Coach House at Madame Whipple's house, where 136 pigeons or doves could roost. Carrier pigeons were used to alert Captain Moffatt that his ships were nearing port. Later, the pigeons, which were thought to be nourishing to the young and sick, were bred for the table. Catherine Whipple often carried a stewed bird to an ailing friend. Unfortunately, the wild passenger pigeon and other game birds so common in eighteenth-century New England are extinct, or nearly so. Today, we must substitute Cornish game hen for most varieties of pigeon or dove.

½ bird per person (1 pound,
    2-ounce size)
Butter

Mushroom catsup (available in
    specialty food stores)
Pepper

Thaw the birds completely. With poultry shears, split each bird in half. Rub generously with butter and season with pepper and mushroom catsup. Broil 4 inches from flame, skin-side up, for 7 to 8 minutes. Turn rib-side up, basting well, for 12 to 15 minutes. Turn again, re-baste, and broil for another 10 minutes, or until birds are tender. If birds are browning too fast, finish baking in 325° oven until done. Serve hot butter and mushroom catsup (laced with a little Madeira) in a separate bowl. This dish can be accompanied by broiled mushroom caps, wild rice, cranberry relish, and a green vegetable such as broccoli.

(Adapted from Eliza Smith, *The Compleat Housewife*, 1729)

Roots and Vegetables

"*The better sort of People here live very well and Genteel. They have no fixt market but the Country people come to town as it suits them with such of the Commoditys as they have for Sale by which the town is pretty well Supply'd with Beefe, Mutton, veal, and other Butchers Meat; they have plenty of large Hoggs and very fat bacon. They have also abundance of good fish of different Kinds, And abundance of Garden Culture as Beans, Peas, Carrots, Parsnips, Turnips, Radishes, Onions, Cabages, Colliflowers, Asparagus, English or whats commonly called Irish Potatoes also the Sweet Potatoe.*"—James Birket, Some Cursory Remarks, 1750–51

Yankee Vegetable Hash

A good cook decides on the proper amounts for this dish, depending on her number.

Beets
Cabbage
Cider vinegar

Butter
Salt and pepper to taste

Mix beets and cabbage, chopped and cooked, in about equal amounts. Warm up in a little butter. Pour on a little cider vinegar, and season. Good with corned-beef hash.

Baked Pumpkin

1 small pumpkin, cleaned and scraped (top cut off and set aside)
Milk or light cream
About 3 tablespoons butter

1 medium onion, grated
3 tablespoons honey, brown sugar, or maple syrup
Salt to taste
Freshly grated nutmeg

Fill pumpkin half full with milk and the other ingredients. Put pumpkin top back in place. Bake at 350° until the pumpkin is soft when tested with a fork, about 1½ hours. Set in the center of the table and scoop pumpkin out onto each plate with a wooden spoon. Season with more salt and butter. Freshly grated nutmeg may be added. Other hard-shell winter squash, such as Hubbard, may be cooked in the same way. If smaller than the pumpkin, it will take less cooking time. Test for doneness. Pumpkins were staple fare in early New England.

Pickles and Preserves

Mushroom Powder

Preparing this condiment has long since gone out of fashion. Most eighteenth-century English cookbooks inform the cook that "a teaspoonful will give a very fine flavour to any soup or gravy, or any sauce, and it is to be added just before serving." The black appearance and piquant taste reminds one of truffles and might deceive a gourmet. It deserves a revival.

1 pound mushrooms	¼ teaspoon pepper
2 teaspoons onion powder	½ teaspoon mace
½ teaspoon ground cloves	

Wash mushrooms and put them in a stew pan (without water) with the onion powder, cloves, pepper, and mace. Simmer and shake until all the liquor has dried up, but be careful not to burn. Lay them on tins in a very slow oven (225°) until they are dry. Chop very fine. Store in a closed bottle and keep in a dry place.

(Adapted from A *New System of Domestic Cookery*, 1808)

BELL METAL POT

Rose Geranium Jelly

Wash apples, not too ripe, and cut in pieces without paring or coring. Barely cover with water (2 cups water to 4 cups of fruit) and boil until very soft. Pour all into a jelly bag, or several layers of cheesecloth; hang it over a container and allow to drip overnight. Do not squeeze or the apple juice will be cloudy.

To 2 cups juice add 2 cups sugar and the juice of ½ lemon. Boil until the syrup will jell. Skim. Place two rose geranium leaves in the bottom of each warm jelly glass. Pour in the hot jelly and cover with paraffin.

Breadstuffs

Rye and Indian Meal Bread

"The bread used everywhere in New Hampshire was Rye and Indian. It was eaten morning, noon and night."—The Reverend Henry H. Saunderson, History of Charlestown, New Hampshire, 1876

1 cup emptyings (see page 53)	1 cup bran
1 envelope dry yeast	1 cup cornmeal
3 tablespoons warm water	4 teaspoons salt
¼ cup molasses	1⅔ cups warm buttermilk
3 tablespoons bacon fat	1 tablespoon dill, or caraway seeds
2 cups rye flour	(optional)

Bring the emptyings to room temperature. Dissolve yeast in warm water; add molasses and melted bacon fat. Combine with emptyings and then add remaining ingredients. Stir with a strong wooden spoon for about 3 minutes. Cover the bowl and set in a pan of hot water in a warm place. Let dough rise for 1 hour; punch down and let it rise for another hour. Grease two 9" x 5" x 3" pans and pour dough into pans. Let rise, covered with a towel, in a warm place for 45 minutes. Preheat oven to 400°. Bake loaves for 10 minutes at 400°; then turn heat to 350° and bake 40 to 50 minutes more. One tablespoon of dill or caraway seeds may be added to the dough if desired.

Uncommon Cakes and Pies

Hermits

2 cups sugar	1½ cups raisins, figs, or dates
1 cup butter	3 cups flour
3 eggs, beaten	1 teaspoon cinnamon
6 tablespoons brandy	1 teaspoon baking soda
1 cup nuts, chopped	3 tablespoons hot water

Cream sugar and butter. Add eggs and brandy. Mix nuts and raisins with sifted flour and cinnamon. Blend the butter mixture and dry ingredients. Lastly, add baking soda, dissolved in the hot water, to the mixture. Drop from a spoon onto a greased cookie sheet. Bake at 350° for 12 to 15 minutes. Makes 6 dozen.

Old Portsmouth Orange Cake

1 cup sugar
5 eggs
2 tablespoons orange juice
2 tablespoons water
1 tablespoon grated orange rind
¼ teaspoon orange extract
½ teaspoon mace
2 cups cake flour, sifted

Put sugar and eggs in a "kettle" or saucepan. Stir over the fire until lukewarm. Watch carefully. Do not let the mixture get too hot. Remove from the fire. Add orange juice and water. Beat until "stone cold," about 15 minutes. Mixture should be light and stiff. Flavor with orange rind, orange extract, and mace. Fold in flour lightly. Bake in a 10½″ x 15½″ greased and floured pan. Bake cake at 325° for 30 to 40 minutes. Do not overbake. Cut in small squares and serve at teatime. This lovely cake keeps well and can be frozen successfully.

(Adapted from *Old St. John's Parish Cookbook*, courtesy Mrs. Frank Hulshor)

Grandmother Cutt's Gingerbread

"Waste not, want not"—the bacon fat in this rule is undetectable but lends a nice moist texture.

1 cup sugar
1 cup black molasses
2 eggs
Pinch of salt
½ teaspoon black pepper
8 pinches ground red pepper
1 heaping teaspoon ginger
1 tablespoon cinnamon
1 cup soured cream
1 teaspoon baking soda
⅔ cup bacon fat, strained
⅓ cup vegetable oil
2 cups sifted flour

Combine sugar, molasses, eggs, salt, pepper, red pepper, and ginger. Cover contents of bowl with cinnamon and a generous cup of soured cream. Then add soda and beat until it foams. Finally, add bacon fat, oil, and flour. Pour into a 9″ x 9″ x 2″ pan and cook in a very slow oven (300°) for 1 hour and 20 minutes.

MARKET SQUARE, PORTSMOUTH

Sweet Dishes and Confections

Strawberry Banke was the first name given Portsmouth because of the lush strawberries that grew along the shores of the Piscataqua River. The local citizenry continued to use the name for another century, even after a petition in 1653 changed it officially to Portsmouth, "a name more suitable" and dignified. The strawberries continued to flourish nearby.

Queen of Puddings—An Old Rule

½ cup raisins
4 tablespoons rum
4 cups milk
1 tablespoon butter
2 cups fresh bread crumbs
Rind of 1 lemon, grated

Freshly grated nutmeg
1 cup sugar
4 egg yolks
Strawberry preserves
Meringue

Soak raisins in the rum. Heat the milk and butter and mix with bread crumbs, grated lemon rind, and a little nutmeg. Beat sugar and egg yolks and add to the mixture. Stir in the raisins. Bake the pudding in a greased ovenproof bowl at 375° until firm, about 30 minutes. Spread a layer of strawberry preserves over the pudding and a layer of meringue over that. Brown lightly in a 350° oven for 12-15 minutes. Serves 10.

Meringue

4 egg whites
½ cup sugar
Juice of 1 lemon

Stiffly beat egg whites, sugar, and lemon juice. Spread on pudding.

Mincemeat Put Down for Winter

1½ quarts cooked beef, or venison, chopped
2 quarts water
4 quarts McIntosh apples, chopped
1 quart suet, chopped
2½ quarts sugar
2 cups water
1 teaspoon instant coffee
3 15-ounce packages raisins
1 11-ounce package currants

½ pound citron, chopped
Rind of 1 lemon and 2 oranges grated
Juice of 1 lemon and 2 oranges
6 teaspoons cinnamon
3 teaspoons mace
2 teaspoons ground cloves
1 teaspoon nutmeg
4 teaspoons lemon extract
4 tablespoons salt

Cook the meat in water and save the liquid for later use. Put apples, meat, and suet through a food chopper. Mix in other ingredients. Use a canning kettle and put in a 250° oven. Stir often and cook until apples are softened and top is juicy. Oven cooking prevents sticking and scorching. Seal in 19 sterile pint jars.

Peaches Stuffed with Mincemeat—A Sweet Garnish

Take as many preserved peaches as desired and place in a flat pan. Fill each cavity with prepared mincemeat (see previous recipe). Place in a 350° oven until well heated, about 15 minutes. Arrange on a serving platter as a garnish for turkey, chicken, pork, or ham.

Chestnut Flummery with Chestnut Sauce

In the eighteenth century elegant jellied desserts served in glasses or molds were popular for elaborate dinners, buffets, and evening entertainments. Isinglass, hartshorn, or calf's feet produced the gelatin, which was combined with sweetened fruits, wines, cream, or milk to make jellies, blanc mange, or flummery. The molds took fanciful forms—chickens, rabbits, stars, or geometric shapes. Often vegetable tints were added to color the flummery.

1 15½-ounce can of unsweetened chestnut puree
2 cups milk
½ cup, plus 2 tablespoons, sugar
2 envelopes unflavored gelatin
½ teaspoon vanilla extract
6 egg yolks
2 tablespoons dark rum, or Grand Marnier
1 cup heavy cream

Blend chestnut puree and milk (a blender can be used). Add the sugar and mix in with a wire whisk. Transfer to a saucepan, add the gelatin, and bring mixture to a boil. Stir in the vanilla. Beat the egg yolks in a bowl and slowly pour in a little hot sauce, stirring constantly. Slowly pour the eggs back into the hot sauce, again stirring constantly. Cook until thick, but do not boil. Add dark rum. Refrigerate to cool. Whip the cream and fold into cooled, but not jelled, chestnut mixture. Pour into an oiled mold and chill until firm. Unmold and decorate the top with candied violets. Chestnut Sauce should be spooned over each serving. Perfect for holiday entertainments.

Chestnut Sauce

6 egg yolks
½ cup sugar
Pinch of salt
1 cup milk
1 cup heavy cream
1 teaspoon vanilla extract
5 ounces (½ jar) preserved chestnuts (marrons glacés), chopped
¼ cup liquid from chestnuts

Beat the egg yolks and beat in the sugar and pinch of salt. Scald the milk and cream in a double boiler over hot (not boiling) water. Add the milk very slowly to the eggs, stirring constantly. Return to the double boiler and again cook over hot water, stirring constantly until the custard coats a spoon. Add vanilla, chestnuts, and the liquid from the bottle of chopped chestnuts. The sauce is at its best when thoroughly chilled. Serves 8.

Drams and Punches

Whipt Syllabub

"Whip well and as the froth rises, fill your glasses for use."

Related to egg nog but less potent because no strong spirits were used, Syllabub was considered a ladies' drink and was mild enough even for children. Serve at Christmastime.

3 gills (1 gill equals ½ cup) sweet white wine, or Madeira
Juice of 3 lemons
"Loaf sugar, pounded fine, to taste" (about 8 tablespoons)
Grated rind of 2 lemons
4 cups light cream
3 egg whites, beaten and sweetened
Freshly grated nutmeg

Combine wine, lemons, sugar, and lemon rind. Add the cream and whip to a froth in your punch bowl. Pile egg whites on the top and sprinkle with nutmeg. Serves 12.

(Adapted from *A New System of Domestic Cookery*, 1808)

Hot Buttered Rum in a Single Glass

1 lump of sugar
Cider
1 jigger of rum
1 teaspoon butter
¼ teaspoon cinnamon
Freshly grated nutmeg

Mix sugar and a little hot cider in a mug. Add butter, rum and cinnamon. Stir. Pour in hot cider to fill the mug. Dust with nutmeg. For cool New Hampshire evenings or winter nights anywhere.

A Stately Dinner and Entertainment on Cutts Island in Portsmouth Harbor, 1727

Perhaps Catherine Whipple heard her mother, who was a Cutt, describe a time in 1727 when the colonial Governor Wentworth and other guests came to Cutts Island. A Cutt descendant described the event many years later.

"Our company began to arrive at eleven o'clock. A fiddler and drummer were stationed at the landing to bid them welcome with "God Save the King." It was a gay sight to see the crowd of servants, the barges sweeping up to the wharf, several of them with African crews that were dressed in livery, and the rich costumes of our visitors. . . . Upon entering they were entertained with cake and sack passed round by the servants on silver salvers. They remained seated a short time, gossiping and laughing. Some walked about the island, visiting the stables and barns and still others had a little excursion on the water. At one o'clock the great gong summoned all to dinner in our dining room.

The great table groaned under its weight of delicacies such as it seldom bore. At one end the barbeque (a roasted pig), while roasted chickens and turkeys, boiled hams and tongues were paraded at the other, flanked by pastry of various kinds, and immense plum puddings, with ducks, custards, and fish caught from the water within an hour or so, lobsters, jellies and preserved fruits of several kinds.

They sat for two hours at the table, when chocolate and tea were announced upon the green. . . . Late in the afternoon with an abundance of ceremony, bows and curtsies, the company bade us adieu, and Cutts Island settled once more into its accustomed quiet."

Dinner for Patriots

After the war when Portsmouth was the capital of New Hampshire, William Whipple often held committee meetings at home. Madame Whipple served good food to these men intent upon setting up an enduring democracy.

ALMOND SOUP

STUFFED LEG OF LAMB   BROILED GAME BIRDS

BOILED LOBSTERS

ASPARAGUS   STEWED PUMPKIN

PICKLED BEETS

RYE AND INDIAN BREAD   BUTTER   ROSE GERANIUM JELLY

CHESTNUT FLUMMERY WITH CHESTNUT SAUCE

PORTSMOUTH ORANGE CAKE

PORT   MADEIRA   RUM PUNCH

Potpourri and Sweet Scents

Sherburne Potpourri

The oldest flower in the Moffatt-Ladd House garden is a damask rose, or bride's rose, which was planted when the house was built. Today, potpourri is made from its scented petals.

1 pint dried rose petals
1 tablespoon orris root
½ teaspoon each cinnamon, all-spice, and cloves
1 tablespoon whole cardamon, broken and pounded in a mortar and pestle

Dried rinds of 3 oranges, 3 limes, and 3 lemons
1 handful each mint and lavender, dried
1 small handful sage, dried

Dry the rose petals on a screen in a dry, warm place. (You should use roses primarily, but you may add the petals of other colorful flowers.) Scrape the fruit rinds clean of the white pulp. Cut in strips and dry in a slack oven (225°). Put everything together in a stoneware jar. Stir every day for several weeks. (It is better to stir twice a day). Scented bowls of potpourri should be placed in your rooms and stirred to release the fragrance before company comes.

Rose Water (For Cakes and Puddings)

"Gather the leaves (petals) of roses while the dew is on them, put them into a wide-mouthed bottle, and pour over some alcohol*—let stand till ready for use."—Mrs. Grace Townsend, Dining Room and Kitchen.

* Use grain alcohol or 100-proof vodka.

Abigail Adams of Quincy, Massachusetts

The Adams Birthplaces

Abigail Smith Adams, born and bred in New England, was an articulate and literate woman full of that splendid Yankee spirit, ingenuity, and courage one notes in the men and women who were the bulwark of our early nation. She was born in 1744 to the Reverend and Mrs. William Smith of Weymouth, Massachusetts, and was to become the only American woman to be the wife of one president and the mother of another.

In 1764, when she was barely twenty, she married John Adams. Their initial intellectual attraction for each other grew into a tender passion, and the prolific letters written during the years of their marriage survive today as a tribute to their strong bond of love and devotion.

After they had been married for a year a daughter, Abigail, was born, to be followed by John Quincy, Susanna, Charles, and Thomas Boylston. John, a young lawyer active in Braintree local politics, became impelled by the political issues of the times to support and defend the course of liberty, and in 1774 he left for Philadelphia to represent Massachusetts at the First Continental Congress. That summer he wrote to Abigail from Philadelphia: "I must entreat you my dear Partner . . . to take part with me in the Struggle." And so it was that after ten years of happiness as the wife of a provincial lawyer, Abigail found her household broken up by the struggle for independence. Abigail was tireless—she "could never bear to merely vegetate"—and in 1776, while caring for and educating the children, as well as looking after the 140-acre farm at Quincy, she wrote a remarkable letter to John. Independence was about to be declared when she said: "I long to hear that you have declared independence. And by the way, in the new code of laws which I suppose it will be necessary for you to make, I desire you would remember the ladies and be more generous and favourable to them than your ancestors. Do not put your unlimited power into the hands of husbands. Remember, all men would be tyrants if they could." John, with tongue in cheek, replied: "You are so saucy. . . . Depend on it, we know better than to repeal our masculine systems. . . . They are little more than theory. . . . In practice you know *we* are the subjects . . . we only have the name of masters."

Independence was declared, and the visionary John Adams wrote that "it will be celebrated by succeeding generations as the great anniversary festival." But declaring independence was easier than winning it, and John spent the war years in France, joining Benjamin Franklin in seeking a treaty with the French government. Abigail joined him in Paris five years later, where they dined often with Thomas Jefferson and Franklin, renewed the friendship of General Lafayette, and entertained Americans and Frenchmen of the diplomatic corps. John was

ABIGAIL ADAMS

then appointed to the Court of St. James as ambassador to Great Britain, and Abigail was the first woman from the new American nation to be presented at the royal court. It is thought that during her stay in London, Abigail purchased *The House-keeper's Pocket-book and Compleat Family Cook* by Sarah Harrison of Devonshire, a 1755 cookbook that "teaches how to supply the Deficiency of Wealth, by dressing and disposing all Things in the most elegant Manner." Abigail was to utilize this book and combine the bounty of her Massachusetts farm and nearby waters to provide "an Elegance in Eating no ways Inconsistent with Frugality and good Conduct."

In 1788 John and Abigail returned to America: "I do not regret that I made this excursion, since it has only more attached me to America." She was now the vice-president's wife and she and John moved to Richmond Hill near the capital city of New York, "more sublime than beautiful," Abigail said, and her social obligations began. She not

RICHMOND HILL, NEW YORK, 1789

only attended Martha Washington's levees each Friday evening at 8 o'clock—"my station is always at the right hand of Mrs. Washington"—but also personally entertained all members of Congress and their families, as well as visiting dignitaries. The following year, in 1790, the nation's capital was moved to Philadelphia, where she and John lived at Bush Hill; they then moved to the executive mansion when John became president in 1797. "This city is . . . a General Resort during winter, and one continued scene of Parties upon Parties, Balls and entertainments equal to any European city," she wrote. Abigail's ties to Massachusetts, however, were constant, and she wrote her sister that "I wish to have our winter Apples, pears, Butter, some cheese, Bacon, Tongue &c all from our own state . . . as well as two dozen bottles of Rose water, thirty or forty dozen eggs . . . and six barrels of cider."

In the spring of 1800 the government was moved to its third capital, Washington City. John arrived at the incompleted president's house in late May without Abigail, and that evening he wrote her the prayer now inscribed in the State Dining Room of the White House: "I pray Heaven to bestow the best of blessings on this house and all that shall hereafter inhabit it. May none but wise and honest men ever rule under this roof." Abigail arrived and found "a house on a grand scale" but one that "stood on a desolate bog. There were no bathrooms . . . water had to be carried by hand from a distance of 5 city blocks . . . and the great unfinished audience room [East Room] I made a drying room of." She placed her crimson furniture in the upstairs Oval Room nevertheless, and held her first levee, beginning a tradition for all First Ladies to come.

John Adams was not elected to a second term, and John and Abigail left for Quincy in February of 1801. Surrounded by their grandchildren, family, and friends, they found joy and contentment in being together at "Peacefield," their beloved New England home, which was now filled not only with the furnishings of their first cottage but also with the elegant treasures of their life and travels. When Abigail died at the age of seventy-four, her son John Quincy Adams said, "She was the delight of my father's heart. . . . It was but the last time I saw my father when he told me that in all the vicissitudes of his fortunes . . . the affectionate participation and cheering encouragement of his wife had been his never-failing support, without which he was sure he should never have lived through them."

The Adams Birthplaces

Almost 200 years ago two small, red cottages were built at the foot of Penn's Hill in Braintree (now Quincy), Massachusetts. In one of these houses John Adams, born in 1735, grew to manhood; to the other he took his bride, Abigail, in 1764; and it was here that his son John Quincy Adams and four other children were born and raised. This cottage and its 140-acre farm held poignant memories for John and Abigail Adams throughout their lives. "This little cottage has more heartfelt satisfaction . . . than the most brilliant court can afford."

It was in the kitchen of this cottage that Abigail prepared simple fare for their family and friends, reaping the harvest of their extensive farm, using the large open hearth of the larger fireplace and brick oven in the lean-to. On the mantel stood Abigail's tinder box, hog scraper, and gophering iron amid the horehound, sage, costmary, heliotrope, lavender, and other herbs hanging from the rafters. Near the tin reflector oven on the hearth stood her iron peel, corn sheller, cheese press, and sad irons.

At the north end of the lean-to was the butt'ry, which Abigail had converted to a small closet containing an ingenious cooler, with openings between slats at floor level and a lidded chest above it to keep the crockery food containers cool with the cold air from the cellar below.

ABIGAIL'S
INGENIOUS COOLER

In the old, outgrown kitchen, John opened his first law office, and from its cottage door Abigail was to bid farewell to John when he traveled to Philadelphia for the first Continental Congress in 1774. Alone in Braintree with the family, Abigail managed the farm and wrote John that "we are just now ready to plant, the barley looks charmingly, I shall be quite a Farmeress another year." And John, although comfortably ensconced in Philadelphia, wrote back: "I mourn the Loss of all the Charms of Life, which are my family . . . and All the Amusement that I ever had in Life which is my farm."

From 1788 to 1801 Abigail was to have many other residences—each of them elegant. But from England in 1788 she wrote: "I long to return to my native land. . . . 'Tis Domestick happiness and Rural felicity in the Bosom of my Native Land, that has charms for me." She returned to America, but not to her cottage, for in that same year John Adams, as vice-president of the new nation, bought the mansion on Adams Street in Quincy (now known as the Old House), and on their return they settled there, while simultaneously living in the capitals of New York, Philadelphia, and Washington City. The "cottage" always remained in their memories as they traveled.

The great batten lean-to door with its latch string still stands. The environment that molded two presidents to passionate commitment to the new nation is felt here, and the spirit of Abigail Adams pervades.

Soups and Savories

Winter Squash Soup

3 large onions, chopped
1 cup celery, chopped
1 clove garlic
4 tablespoons butter
3 cups chicken stock
2 cups cooked squash, mashed

1 teaspoon each fresh rosemary
  and savory (½ teaspoon dried)
2 tablespoons parsley, chopped
2 cups heavy cream
Salt and pepper to taste
Nutmeg

Sauté onions, celery, and garlic until golden in 2 tablespoons of the butter. Add to chicken stock with cooked squash, rosemary, savory, and parsley. Bring to a boil; then simmer for 10 minutes. Add 2 tablespoons butter. Remove from heat and add cream. Season with salt and pepper. Dust with nutmeg and serve in a warmed tureen. Serves 8.

Grandmother Quincy's Clam Chowder

From "la chaudière," the huge French copper fish cauldron, we have "chowder," which in early Massachusetts became the classic soup with its essential ingredients of clams, salt pork, and rich country cream.

¼ pound lean slab bacon, cut into
  ¼-inch dice
1 cup onion, finely chopped
3 cups water
4 cups potatoes, cut into ¼-inch
  dice
2 dozen hard-shelled clams (quahogs), shucked and coarsely

chopped with their juice, or
  2 8-ounce cans chopped clams
  (2 cups)
¼ teaspoon thyme
2 cups heavy cream
Salt and pepper to taste
2 tablespoons butter, softened
Paprika

Sauté the bacon until softened; reduce heat, add the onions, and cook together until both are golden brown. Add water and potatoes and simmer until the potatoes are firm but tender; then add the chopped clams and their juice. Stir in the thyme and simmer, covered, for 10 minutes. Heat the cream separately, almost to the boiling point; then pour it slowly into the clam mixture. Season with salt and pepper and stir in the butter. Present in a tureen, dust with paprika, and serve with deep-fried clam cakes and sea biscuits. Serves 8.

Mushroom Pasty

1 pound mushrooms, sliced
⅓ cup butter
2 medium onions, chopped
⅓ cup flour
½ cup light cream
1½ tablespoons sweet sherry
1 teaspoon thyme
Salt and pepper to taste
Piecrust dough for double-crust
　8-inch pie

Trim and slice the mushrooms. In a skillet melt the butter and sauté the onions until transparent. Add the mushrooms and sauté until lightly golden. Sprinkle the flour in the pan and gently stir until blended and golden but not brown. Remove from heat and slowly add cream, sherry, and thyme, stirring until smooth. Replace on the heat and cook until thickened. Season with salt and pepper. Allow to cool. This can be refrigerated overnight.

　Roll out the piecrust and fill it with cooled mushroom filling. Cover with latticed strips of crust or a thin upper crust. Preheat oven to 450° and bake for 20 minutes. Serves 8.

Skillet Cranberries for a Slack Oven

"Arrived at Dr. Tuft's, where I found a fine Wild Goose on the Spit, and Cranberries in the Skillet for Dinner."—John Adams, April 8, 1767

1 pound fresh cranberries
2 cups brown or white sugar
¼ cup brandy

Spread 1 pound of fresh cranberries in an iron skillet. Sprinkle the sugar over them, cover the skillet, and place in a slack oven (250°) for 1 hour. Remove the lid and pour ¼ cup brandy into the skillet. You may take it to the table in a pewter basin or, for a collation table, in a crystal compote. Serves 8.

Fish, Meat, and Fowl

EEL SPEAR

Poached Salmon with Egg Sauce

Noble salmon were never plentiful in New England, but they were readily available when they began to run in eastern waters. Somewhat of a rarity, they were saved traditionally for Fourth of July celebrations and served with green peas and young buttered potatoes.

4- to 5-pound salmon, cleaned and dressed, with its head and tail left on
8 cups of water
¼ cup white wine vinegar
3 sprigs of parsley

1 medium onion, sliced
1 tablespoon salt
8 whole black peppercorns
1 bay leaf
2 slices of lemon, seeded
Fresh dill

Wrap salmon in dampened cheesecloth with the long ends creating lifting handles. Bring the water and all other ingredients except the lemon slices to a boil. Boil for 15 minutes. Place salmon on the rack of a fish poacher or in a kettle. Pour in enough of the hot broth to barely cover the fish and simmer it for 30 minutes, or until it flakes easily. (Add more of the broth as necessary.) While the salmon is simmering, make the egg sauce.

Lift salmon from the broth and lay it on a cutting board. Scrape the brown flesh or gray fat gently to expose the pink meat. Turn fish out of the cheesecloth onto hot serving platter. To serve, spoon the egg sauce over the salmon and garnish with lemon wedges and dill sprigs around the head. Serve the remainder of the sauce in a separate bowl. Serves 6.

Egg Sauce

1 medium onion, finely chopped
3 tablespoons butter
3 tablespoons flour
1¼ teaspoons salt
2½ cups milk

3 hard-boiled eggs, coarsely chopped
4 teaspoons fresh dill, finely snipped
⅛ teaspoon hot sauce

Sauté onions in butter until golden. Remove from heat. Stir in flour and salt; then gradually stir in milk. Return to heat, bring to a boil, and simmer for 1 minute. Stir in eggs, dill, and hot sauce. Thin the sauce with light cream if necessary.

Codfish Cakes

Dry salted cod was such an important staple that a six-foot model of the "sacred cod" was hung in the Massachusetts State House, where it has remained for more than 200 years.

1 pound salt cod
2 pounds potatoes
½ cup butter
3 egg yolks

1½ teaspoons Worcestershire
sauce
1 teaspoon dry mustard
Pepper to taste

Soak cod in cold water for 12 hours, changing water 3 times. Cook in an inch of cold water, simmering for about 20 minutes, or until the fish flakes. Drain, remove skin and bones, and flake with a fork. Boil potatoes and mash to a smooth puree. Add cod, butter, and egg yolks and beat hard with a wooden spoon. Add Worcestershire sauce and mustard. Season with pepper. Beat well again. Form mixture into patties. Fry in hot oil for about 4 minutes, or until golden, and serve piping hot for Sunday breakfast with baked beans. Makes 10 cakes.

Beef Boulli with Horseradish Sauce

5 pounds lean, first-cut beef
brisket
2 medium onions studded with
5 cloves each
3 carrots, chunked
3 stalks celery with leaves

1 turnip (white), chunked
1 parsnip, chunked
½ cup parsley, chopped
2 bay leaves
6 peppercorns
1 tablespoon salt

Place meat in a heavy pot and add all ingredients. Pour boiling water over it to cover. Cover pot closely and simmer the meat until tender, about 3 to 4 hours. When meat can be pierced with a fork, lift it out of the broth. For family fare, place it on a warm platter, laying the vegetables around it. For a collation, place the beef, cold, on a silver dish and take to the table accompanied by Horseradish Sauce. Serves 8.

Horseradish Sauce

1½ teaspoons dry mustard
1 cup freshly ground horseradish
2 scant teaspoons salt

1½ teaspoons white pepper
1½ cups heavy cream, whipped

Mix mustard with 3 tablespoons of cold water and stir until smooth; then combine with horseradish, salt, and pepper. Allow to stand for 10 minutes. Fold thoroughly into the whipped cream. Outstanding with cold meats.

Four-Meat Hotchpotch

3 large onions, coarsely chopped
Bacon drippings
1 pound beef, cubed
¾ pound pork, cubed
½ pound veal, cubed
¼ pound lamb, cubed
Flour for dredging
Salt and pepper to taste

1 bunch carrots, cleaned and cut into halved 1-inch pieces
1 pound fresh green beans, cleaned and snapped
3 pounds potatoes, peeled and quartered
12 small white onions

Sauté the chopped onions in bacon drippings until golden. Dredge meat in flour and salt and pepper. Add meat to the chopped onions and brown, adding more bacon drippings if needed. Transfer to a large pot, cover with water, and bring to a boil. Simmer for 1 hour. Add carrots and beans and continue simmering until meat and vegetables are cooked. In a separate pot boil the potatoes and the whole onions; add salt to taste. Drain potatoes and onions and add them to the meat just before serving. If the sauce needs to be thickened, blend 1 tablespoon butter into a paste with 4 tablespoons flour (*beurre manié*). Swirl the beurre on the insides of the pot and blend into sauce until the desirable thickness is achieved. Correct seasoning. Serve from the pot. Unsurpassable with Spider Cornbread, herbed salad, and cold cider, sweet or hard. Whiskey Apple Pie, hot from the oven, is a fitting ending. Serves 10.

Roots and Vegetables

Mrs. Boylston's Asparagus

"Pray how does your asparagus perform?"—John Adams to his wife, Abigail

1 pound asparagus
2 tablespoons butter
½ teaspoon salt
¼ teaspoon sugar

1 teaspoon fresh mint, or ½ teaspoon dry
½ cup heavy cream
2 egg yolks, beaten

Break off asparagus tips and set aside. Break stems into 1½-inch pieces and cook in 1 cup water for 15 minutes. Drain, saving water. In a skillet melt butter; add stems, salt, sugar, mint, asparagus tips, and cream. Simmer for 10 minutes. Stir a bit of cream into the beaten egg yolks and return mixture to skillet. If mixture is too thick, use asparagus water to thin it. Dust with nutmeg and serve alone or on home-baked white bread, sliced and toasted on the hearth. Serves 4.

Boston Baked Beans

Since no work was done on the Sabbath, the ritual of baking beans in the beehive oven began on Friday evening. Baked beans and brown bread were traditionally served every Saturday evening. Kept warm in the brick oven, they were served again for Sunday breakfast with codfish cakes and green tomato relish.

4 cups pea beans	3 teaspoons dry mustard
1 large onion, studded with 8 cloves	2 teaspoons salt
	1 teaspoon pepper
½ pound salt pork	½ cup dark molasses
1 cup brown sugar	

Soak beans overnight. Drain. Cover with water and cook until the skins burst when blown on. Drain and ladle beans into an earthenware bean pot. Press the onion into the center of the beans until barely covered. Cut salt pork 1 inch deep every ½ inch and splay out to cover a larger surface. Push salt pork slightly below the surface of the beans.

Over pork and beans, pour mixture of ¾ cup brown sugar, mustard, salt, pepper, and molasses. Pour 1 cup of boiling water over the beans; slowly stir with a large spoon. Add enough boiling water to cover the beans. Cover the bean pot and bake at 250° for 4 to 5 hours. Uncover for the last half hour. Sprinkle with the remaining brown sugar to brown and crisp the pork. Add water as needed during baking. Serves 12.

Pickles and Preserves

Madeira Wine Jelly Garnished with Frosted Fruit

"I drank Madeira at a great Rate and found no Inconvenience in it."—John Adams, September, 1774, Philadelphia

4 envelopes unflavored gelatin	6 tablespoons fresh lemon juice, strained
½ cup cold water	
2 cups grape juice	Pinch of salt
2 cups Madeira	¾ to 1 cup sugar

Dissolve gelatin in cold water. Add this to the grape juice, which has been brought to a boil. Stir in Madeira, lemon juice, and a pinch of salt. Add sugar to taste. Pour into a mold. Chill until firm.

For Frosted Fruit use strawberries, green grapes, purple grapes, and strawberry or nasturtium leaves if in season. To frost, dip fruit first in slightly beaten egg whites and then roll in granulated sugar. Dry on a rack overnight at room temperature.

Unmold and garnish Wine Jelly with Frosted Fruit. Arrange fruit and leaves around jelly and serve as a complement to meat, or as a dessert with brandied custard sauce. Serves 12.

Madeira and port are fortified with brandy, thus making them stronger than ordinary table wines. Shipped in the holds of sailing vessels, the wine presumably improved because of the heat below deck during tropical weather. Shippers began sending Madeira as far as India, then back to Europe just for the trip, and East India Madeira was considered the finest—and the favorite of all fashionable folk in the colonies.

To Candy Angelica

"Take the great Leaf-stalks of Angelica, cut them in Lengths, and boil it till it is tender in Pump water, with a very little Butter, keeping it close covered; then take it off the Fire, peel off the Strings from it, and dry it in a Cloth, and to every Pound of Angelica put a Pound of Sugar well sifted; then put your Angelica in a glazed Pan, and strew the Sugar over it, and let it stand forty-eight Hours; then boil it till it is clear, drain it, add more Sugar to the Syrup, boil it to a Height, and put the Stalks and Syrup together in a preserving glass and seal. When ready to use, drain the Syrup and roll the Angelica Stalks in Pounded Sugar, and cut in small pieces for garnishing great cakes and little cakes."—Sarah Harrison, The House-keeper's Pocket-book, 1755

Grapes Preserved Entire (In the French Manner)

"At Madame Helvetius's, We had Grapes, preserved entire. I asked how? She said "Sans Air"—Apples, Pairs etc. are preserved here in great Perfection."—John Adams, April 15, 1778, France

Remove stems and seeds from very ripe grapes. Use a goosefeather to remove the seeds, or a toothpick will do. If you wish, omit this step entirely. Measure half of their weight in sugar. Add ½ cup of water and bring to a boil. Add grapes and boil for 2 minutes. Remove grapes with a skimmer and place in hot clean jars, filling them half full. Boil the syrup down until thick and pour it over the fruit. Fill jars almost to the top. Let the jars stand uncovered for 2 days, before sealing with paraffin.

Breadstuffs

Braintree Squash Rolls

2 packages dry yeast
Pinch of sugar
½ cup lukewarm water
6 cups flour
½ cup sugar
1 teaspoon salt
½ pound winter squash (Hubbard, acorn, or butternut), cleaned, cooked, and pureed. Makes ½ cup puree
1 cup lukewarm milk
¾ cup butter, softened
Melted butter for brushing

Add yeast and a pinch of sugar to lukewarm water and set in a warm place until doubled in bulk. Sift 5 cups of the flour, sugar, and salt into a large bowl and make a well in the center. Pour in squash puree, milk, yeast mixture, and ½ cup of the softened butter. Beat dry ingredients into the liquid until the dough can be formed into a ball. Knead, adding the last cup of flour, until smooth and elastic. Place the dough in a greased bowl, using the remaining butter, and flip over. Cover with a towel and let rise until doubled in bulk. Punch the dough and roll into a rectangle about 1 inch thick. With a biscuit cutter, cut dough into 2-inch rounds. Arrange so the rounds are touching in a well-greased Turk's-head mold or small Bundt pan. Brush with melted butter. Let rise in a warm place for 15 to 20 minutes. Preheat oven to 450° and bake for 12 to 15 minutes, or until golden brown. Makes 2 molds or 36 rolls.

Ginger-Apple Custard

5 cups country bread, chunked
2 cups buttermilk
2 cups milk
3 pounds apples, peeled, cored, and sliced
¼ cup water
½ cup molasses
⅓ cup sugar
4 eggs, lightly beaten
¾ teaspoon ginger
1 teaspoon cinnamon
¾ teaspoon nutmeg
⅛ teaspoon ground cloves
⅛ teaspoon black pepper
¼ teaspoon salt

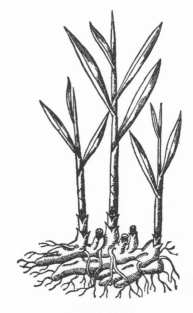

GINGER ROOT

Place broken bread in a bowl and pour the buttermilk and milk over it. Set aside. Place apples and water in a skillet. Cover and cook gently until the apples start to soften but still retain their shape. Cool slightly. Beat remaining ingredients into the soaked bread mixture. Fold in the apples. Pour into a greased 3-quart baking dish or Bundt pan. Bake at 350° for 50 to 60 minutes, or until set. Serve warm with the meat course, or topped with custard sauce for dessert. Serves 12.

Uncommon Cakes and Pies

Brandy Snaps

1½ cups butter
1½ cups sugar
1 cup molasses

1 tablespoon brandy
4 teaspoons ginger
3⅛ cups sifted flour

Heat butter, sugar, molasses, and brandy until well blended. Add the ginger. Remove mixture from heat and add the flour a little at a time, beating after each addition. Drop mixture in half-teaspoonsful onto a greased cookie sheet, allowing 2 inches between the wafers for spreading. Bake for approximately 12 minutes at 300°. Allow wafers to stand for about 2 minutes. Remove each one and roll the wafer over the handle of a wooden spoon. Perfect with wine or afternoon tea. Makes 4 dozen.

THE CHILDREN'S TABLE

Abigail Adams' Pumpkin Pie

1½ cups pumpkin
¾ cup brown sugar, firmly packed
½ teaspoon fresh ginger root,
    grated
1 teaspoon freshly grated nutmeg
½ teaspoon salt
1 cup heavy cream

¾ cup milk
¼ cup dark rum, or brandy
3 eggs, lightly beaten
Pecans
Whipped cream
10-inch pie shell, unbaked

Mix all ingredients together and pour into the prepared pastry shell. Bake at 425° for 10 minutes. Reduce heat to 350° and bake for 40 minutes more, or until a knife inserted in center comes out clean. Garnish with pecans and whipped cream flavored with rum or brandy.

Currant Pound Cake

¾ cup currants	12 eggs
Brandy for plumping	4½ cups sifted flour
2 cups butter	1 teaspoon nutmeg
2 cups sugar	2 teaspoons baking soda

Steep currants in brandy overnight in a tightly covered jar. Cream butter, add sugar, and beat well. Add eggs one at a time and beat until thick. Combine flour and nutmeg with baking soda. Stir into beaten mixture and blend well. Stir in currants, folding lightly. Bake in greased loaf pans or in a large tube or Bundt pan at 325° for 1½ hours.

Sweet Dishes and Confections

Strawberries in Wine

"After walking in the Garden we returned and found the table Spread with 6 or 8 quarts of the large Hudson Strawberry, gathered fresh from the vines with a proportionable quantity of cream, wine and sugar. . . . Our taste and smell were both regaled, whilst ease, sociability, and good humour enhanced the pleasure of the repast."—Abigail Adams, Philadelphia, 1798

Fresh strawberries	Confectioners sugar
Sweet white dessert wine	Whipped cream

Allow fresh strawberries to stand in sweet wine for approximately one hour. Add finely sifted confectioners sugar and mound with whipped cream garnished with small strawberry leaves and dusted with nutmeg. As in the eighteenth century, there is nothing more elegant today than a mounded bowl of fresh strawberries and whipped cream.

"Take some cream, and sweeten it to your taste; then tie a branch of rosemary, and two or three birch twigs together; and whip your cream well with it, still taking off the froth as it rises; do so till you have made all your cream into froth, and lay it high, like a Mountain."—Sarah Harrison, The House-keeper's Pocket-book, 1755

Drams and Punches

Rum-Tea Punch

"We hope to reach Home on fryday of the next week. Will you be so kind as to have some coffee burnt and ground, some Bread and cake made for me. . . . If you should hear of any intention of company . . . Punch must be made by Gallons. You will procure spirit for the purpose, and in a Box in the North cellar which is nailed up is some Jamaica spirit, that with some brandy will answer."—Abigail Adams to her sister, July 29, 1797

2 cups lemon juice	1½ cups amber rum
1 cup strong tea	½ cup brandy
2 cups superfine sugar	2 lemons, thinly sliced and seeded
8 cups cold water	

In a large bowl combine lemonade, tea, sugar, and cold water. Stir until well blended. Add rum, brandy, and lemon slices. More rum, brandy, or lemonade can be added according to taste. Pour over an ice ring in a punch bowl. (To make an ice ring, freeze lemon and orange slices interspersed with mint sprigs in a ring mold.) Makes 2 dozen 4-ounce punch cups.

Punch from the Hindustani "panch," meaning five (referring to the five ingredients then used in the drink—tea, arrack, sugar, lemons, and water), was served in punch bowls by fashionable people to their guests before dinner. The bowl alone was passed and drunk from generally without glasses. At President and Mrs. Adams' Fourth of July celebration, the punch would have been ladled.

Raspberry Shrub

From the Arabic "shurb," meaning drink, a shrub has a fruit base diluted with wine, water, cider, or brandy. Carbonated water was nonexistent, but ginger-root water or ginger wine (forerunner of ginger ale) was popular. It was added to the fruit stewed with sugar and strained to make a syrup.

½ cup lime juice	2 cups apple wine
1 cup raspberry syrup	Ginger root the size of an egg,
3 cups ginger wine	grated

Mix all ingredients. Chill. Makes approximately 10 punch-cup servings. Beloved by all! *Note:* Ginger and apple wine are available in many wine and spirits shops.

Fourth of July Reception at the Executive Mansion in Philadelphia

[This day] *"will be celebrated by succeeding generations as the great anniversary festival. It ought to be solemnized with pomp and parade, with shews, games, sports, guns, bells, bonfires, and illuminations from one end of this continent to the other, from this time forward forevermore."*—John Adams to his wife, Abigail, July 4, 1776

CURRANT POUND CAKE	HICKORY CAKE	CITRON TARTS
Massachusetts	*Pennsylvania*	*North Carolina*
CARROT TEA CAKE	SOFT MOLASSES CAKES	
New Jersey	*Connecticut*	
OLD PORTSMOUTH ORANGE CAKE		
New Hampshire		
COCONUT JUMBLES	KISSES FOR A SLACK OVEN	HOSPITALITY THINS
Delaware	*South Carolina*	*Georgia*
LITTLE SUGAR CAKES	CHARLOTTES	LEMON TEA CAKES
Maryland	*New York*	*Virginia*
RASPBERRY SHRUB	ICED CLARET SANGAREE	DR. SALMON'S PUNCH
Massachusetts	*Maryland*	*Rhode Island*
MADEIRA	RUM TEA PUNCH	PORT
	Massachusetts	

"Dined at Mr. Powells. . . . A Most Sinful Feast again! Everything which could delight the Eye, or allure the Taste, Curds, and Creams, Jellies, Sweetmeats of various sorts, 20 sorts of Tarts, fools, Trifles, Floating Islands, Whipped Syllabubs &c. &c."—John Adams, September 8, 1774, Philadelphia

When President John Adams and First Lady Abigail "dined the Secretaries of State &c. with the Whole Senate," they might have served this Sinful Feast at their home, Bush Hill, in Philadelphia.

A Most Sinful Feast

CRAB CLAWS WITH DILL-MUSTARD SAUCE

SHERRY

WINTER SQUASH SOUP

POACHED SALMON WITH EGG SAUCE

ROAST WILD TURKEY WITH SAUSAGE AND SAGE DRESSING

COLD BAKED COUNTRY HAM   BEEF BOULLI WITH HORSERADISH SAUCE

CLARET

YAMS AND CHESTNUTS WITH PIPPINS   MRS. BOYLSTON'S ASPARAGUS

CARROT PUDDING   MESS OF PEASE

SKILLET CRANBERRIES   WATERMELON PICKLE

MOLDED MADEIRA WINE JELLY

PUMPKIN BREAD   BRAINTREE SQUASH ROLLS

FLOATING ISLAND

TANSY PIE   BRANDIED NECTARINES

CURRANT POUND CAKE

Epergnes Holding

CANDIED GINGER   SPICED PECANS

WHISKEY NUT BALLS   CANDIED PEEL

ANGELICA STEMS   CLUSTER RAISINS

MADEIRA   PORT

BUSH HILL, PHILADELPHIA, 1790

Polly Wanton Lyman
of Newport, Rhode Island

Wanton-Lyman-Hazard House

On July 10, 1780, the French fleet sailed into Newport harbor. All of Newport joined in welcoming their French allies. With all the parties, balls, and teas, it seemed there had never been such a social season! Major Daniel Lyman, aide to General William Heath, conveyed the official welcome to the Comte de Rochambeau and promptly invited him to return for tea to the home of John Wanton, son of a former governor of the colony of Rhode Island. Many an eye must have turned as the splendid French officers in their dress uniforms and swords entered his home. What excitement for the two Quaker maids, seventeen-year-old Polly Wanton and her cousin Polly Bull, who waited inside. The women of Newport, it seems, captivated the hearts of the Frenchmen in their turn. In a public display of affection, one French officer scratched "Charming Polly Wanton" on the windowpane of the Wanton home. Polly, however, lost her heart, not to a gallant Frenchman, but to an American officer, Major Daniel Lyman, who had first greeted the visiting French troops. On February 23, 1782, they were married and moved into the house on Broad Street, which John Wanton deeded to his new son-in-law. Although the Wanton family lived simply, Polly's dowry is an indication of the family wealth. Two beds, six mahogany chairs and table, two dozen china plates, seven dozen silver spoons, and a dozen knives and forks are among the items listed. Daniel Lyman rejoined the American troops and fought until

the end of the war before returning to Polly and his newborn daughter Anna. He practiced law in Newport, was appointed judge and, ultimately, Chief Justice of the Supreme Court of Rhode Island.

Life in postwar Newport was busy and varied for this young mother. Thirteen children were born between 1782 and 1804. Also occupying the Broad Street house were Polly's parents, John and Mary Bull Wanton. Presiding over a large household was no small task for Polly Lyman, although she probably had servants to cook and tend the garden. "My mother made excellent cheese, butter, tho she had always been accustomed to a town life and the greatest indulgence," wrote her daughter Ann Maria many years later. Our lives passed "happy and tranquil," she continued, describing the daily custom of having friends join the family at three o'clock for tea and stay to "spend the evening sociably without form or ceremony."

Busy housewife, avid reader, charming hostess, dutiful daughter, loving wife and mother—scraps of history bring the character of Polly Wanton Lyman to life. In 1807, when daughter Harriet married Newport lawyer Benjamin Hazard, Polly and Daniel Lyman left their house to the young couple and moved to North Providence. With grandchildren who were only a few years younger than her youngest daughter, Polly Lyman could scarcely have retired to a life of quiet and peace. Life in North Providence, too, must have been filled with letters of advice to children at college and state occasions that demanded the presence of the Chief Justice of Rhode Island and his wife. Through such historic gleanings we are able to sketch the life of Rhode Island housewife, Polly Wanton Lyman.

The Wanton–Lyman–Hazard House

Standing close to Broad Street and crowded by its nearest neighbors, the Wanton–Lyman–Hazard House was situated in the middle of early Newport. It provided a perfect location for a busy colonial merchant who could walk to the wharf as he saw the sails of an incoming ship entering the harbor.

Although the house was retrimmed in the mid-eighteenth century, its original structure and framing date from the late seventeenth century. The house is medieval in character, with plank framing supported by a massive central chimney.

Following damages to the house during Newport's bitterest Stamp Act riot, John Wanton, a Quaker merchant, bought the "late dwelling house" in 1765, spending sixty pounds on its repair. The Newport Historical Society, which owns the house, has focused the restoration on both the seventeenth-century construction and the eighteenth-century adornments, thus providing a fascinating example of the evolution of a house.

The roomy kitchen at the back of the house was a part of a story-and-a-half lean-to that was added sometime before 1725. With its wide fireplace and ample hearth, the kitchen is a warm and welcoming room with windows on both sides of the fireplace, which makes it lighter than most eighteenth-century kitchens. The walls are pumpkin colored with an Indian-red diamond design painted over them, a cheery touch indicating the care with which this vital center of family life was furnished.

The New England housewife noted daily items of importance in a journal she commonly referred to as her "rule book." A few yellowed copies of such manuscripts have survived to the present day, the brittle pages filled with homemaking hints, favorite receipts, and remedies, notes of births and deaths, treasured lines of poetry and prose, and the ever-present weather observations.

Soups and Savories

Savoury Winter Soup

This hearty soup, with its distinctive lamb taste, was made during the winter months with the vegetables the colonial cook had stored in her root cellar. The split peas add both body and nourishment to the broth.

1 bone from a leg of lamb roast	2 onions, chopped
3 quarts water	1 cup dried split peas
4 carrots, scraped and sliced	1 tablespoon salt
2 potatoes, peeled and cut into small cubes	1 teaspoon freshly ground pepper
	½ teaspoon thyme
2 turnips, peeled and cut into small cubes	½ teaspoon rosemary
	1 bay leaf
2 stalks of celery, sliced	

Cover the bone with the water. Bring to a boil and simmer gently for 1 hour. Add fresh vegetables, split peas, salt, and spices and simmer for another hour. Remove bone and return any pieces of meat to the soup. Serve hot with freshly baked oatmeal bread and chunks of cheddar cheese. Serves 10.

Consommé au Macaroni

Thomas Jefferson discovered macaroni in Paris and loved to serve it to other Americans after he returned to the United States. It was through contact with the French Army, however, that American soldiers learned to enjoy this dish. English soldiers made fun of the American-French contact with a derogatory little ditty about a country bumpkin who went to war "a riding on his pony." But the Revolutionary soldiers picked up the tune and sang it proudly, and "Yankee Doodle" became the hero of the American Revolution.

4 pounds lean beef, cubed	3 leeks
3 pounds beef knuckle with bone	2 stalks of celery
8 quarts cold water	1 onion
2 tablespoons salt	1 clove garlic
4 carrots	1 sprig of thyme
2 turnips	1 teaspoon macaroni per person, finely chopped
1 parsnip	

Place beef and beef knuckle into a large, heavy stockpot. Cover with the cold water. Bring to a boil; then reduce heat to simmer. Skim the surface of the broth. Add salt, vegetables, garlic, and thyme. Simmer very slowly for 5 hours. Remove from the fire and strain the stock through cheesecloth. Reserve until serving time. Makes 5 quarts consommé. To serve, remove any remaining fat from surface of consommé. Heat 1 cup of consommé per person; when it begins to boil, add 1 teaspoon of finely chopped macaroni per person. Simmer until macaroni is tender. Pour into a heated tureen and serve immediately.

"During a meal one leans against one's neighbor, and one sits with one's elbows on the table while eating. What in France is considered ill-bred is here considered quite correct and universally accepted. The appearance of the American man in general is careless, almost indifferent, and one cannot but be astonished that, with all this apparent indifference, when the occasion presents itself, he fights with unquestioned courage and valor. . . . Another peculiarity of this country is the absence of napkins, even in the homes of the wealthy. Napkins, as a rule, are never used, and one has to wipe one's mouth on the tablecloth, which in consequence suffers in appearance. Also the people, nearly all of them, eat with knives like the English, which are round at the point, and they do not use their two-pronged forks."—from the diary of Baron Louis de Closen, aide-de-camp to Comte de Rochambeau

Fish, Meat, and Fowl

Portuguese Sole with Forcemeat

8 sole fillets	2 tablespoons bread crumbs
2 tablespoons melted butter	1 tablespoon capers
1 teaspoon lemon juice	½ cup beef stock, or bouillon
1 tablespoon parsley, chopped	¼ cup dry white wine (optional)
1 egg, beaten	

Dry the sole fillets; then dip in a mixture of melted butter, lemon juice, and chopped parsley. Spread the fillets with forcemeat, roll them up, and fasten with a toothpick. Place rolls side by side in a Dutch oven or an ovenproof casserole with a tightly fitting lid. Brush with beaten egg and sprinkle with bread crumbs. Add remainder of the egg to beef stock and capers. Pour this mixture over the sole (¼ cup dry white wine may be added if desired). Cover tightly and bake at

350° for 40 minutes, or simmer gently in the fireplace over hot coals until done.

Forcemeat

4 slices bacon	½ cup dry bread crumbs
1 small onion, chopped	1 tablespoon anchovy, chopped
1 small clove garlic, minced	Pepper
1 egg, beaten	Nutmeg

Cut the bacon into small pieces and fry until crisp. Remove from the pan and drain. Add the onion and garlic to the bacon drippings and sauté until limp. Drain. Mix all ingredients together and add pepper and nutmeg to taste. Serves 8.

(Adapted from *The American Domestic Cookery*, 1808)

Homemade Clambake

This is the traditional way Rhode Islanders celebrate the Fourth of July.

Pick over and wash thoroughly 1 bushel of clams and let them stand in heavily salted water for 2 hours; then remove and rinse thoroughly. Sink a large sugar barrel into the ground more than half its height. Fill about half full with hot cobblestones that have been heated to a white heat in a roaring fire for 3 hours. Cover the stones with damp rock-weed and lay a fine wire netting over the weed. Pour the clams onto the netting and cover with more rock-weed. Cover closely with wet news-papers to retain all steam. Bake for about 45 minutes, or until clams open. Serve with melted butter. Corn in season, with a few husks left on the ears or scrubbed potatoes, may be placed on top of the clams. Accompany with sliced onions and cucumbers, and top off with ice-cold watermelon for dessert.

Mussels With Sweet Herbs

24 mussels
½ cup butter
2 tablespoons shallots, chopped
1 clove garlic, chopped
1 bay leaf
¾ cup dry white wine

Salt and pepper to taste
2 egg yolks
½ cup heavy cream
1 tablespoon chives, chopped
2 tablespoons parsley, chopped
2 tablespoons lemon juice

Scrub mussels with a stiff wire brush. Wash in several waters. In a large kettle melt butter and sauté shallots and garlic. Add the bay leaf and wine. Add the mussels, cover tightly, and steam until the shells open (about 2 to 3 minutes), discarding any that remain closed. Discard one shell of each mussel and place mussels on the half shell on a large platter. Keep them warm. Strain broth remaining in kettle through a clean cloth. Season with salt and pepper and heat. Meanwhile, whip egg yolks with cream; then add a few tablespoons of the hot broth very slowly to the cream mixture. Pour this mixture into the broth, stirring constantly until the sauce thickens but does not boil. Remove from heat and add chives, parsley, and lemon juice to taste. Spoon sauce over mussels and serve immediately.

(Adapted from Robert May, *The Accomplish't Cook*, 1660)

Menu for a French Officers' Ball

Grateful for the willingness of Newport citizens to house the French Army officers, Commander Rochambeau entertained the town's leading citizens at a dinner prepared by his French chefs. A "Grand Ball" followed the dinner and the French officers were charmed by the grace of the American women.

Moules Marinières
MUSSELS WITH SWEET HERBS

Vin Blanc Bordeaux

Consommé au Macaroni

Paupiettes De Veau A l'Orange
VEAL BIRDS WITH ORANGE SAUCE

Poularde A L'Estragon Dans Sa Gelée
CHICKEN WITH TARRAGON IN JELLY

Vin Rouge Bordeaux

Quartier de Chevreuil avec Sauce Espagnole
HAUNCH OF VENISON WITH SPANISH SAUCE

Vin Rouge Burgundy

Carottes Glacées du Menthe   Chou-Fleur Du Barry
GLAZED MINTED CARROTS   CAULIFLOWER DU BARRY

La Tarte Bourdaloue
PEAR TART

Brandy   4 Iced Champagne

Fromages
CHEESES

Café Macarons de Nancy
COFFEE MACAROONS FROM NANCY

Mary Hunter's Stewed Beef

"Take two or three pounds of rump steaks, cut thick in square pieces as large as your hand. Put a stewpan on some hot coals with three pints of water, a bunch of sweet herbs, three or four onions chopped fine, a little allspice, a dozen cloves, a teaspoon of cayenne pepper, one of black pepper, and salt to your taste. Cover this close, and let it boil one hour very hard—then put in the beef with half a tumbler of claret or port wine, and a teaspoonfull of good ketchup—and boil it altogether an hour longer—thicken the gravy with butter and flour mixed together— let it boil a quarter of an hour after this last is added."—receipt of Mary Robinson Morton, 1809

Sauce Espagnole (Brown Sauce) for Roast Meat

"In the kitchen were dressers reaching to the wall furnished with pewter, shining like silver, and a jack to roast meat, of whose cheerful noise I am often reminded when I hear young ladies play some fashionable piece of music," wrote Polly's daughter Ann Maria in 1863.

4 tablespoons butter
1 onion, finely chopped
1 carrot, finely chopped
2 tablespoons flour
½ cup dry white wine
Bouquet garni (1 bay leaf, ½ teaspoon thyme, and 3 sprigs of
 parsley, tied in cheesecloth)
2 tablespoons tomato paste
4 cups beef broth
Salt and pepper to taste

In a saucepan melt butter and cook onion and carrot until browned. Stir in flour; then add wine and 3 cups beef broth. Add bouquet garni and simmer for 1 hour. Remove from heat, strain through a clean cloth. Return to the saucepan and add tomato paste, remaining cup of beef broth, salt, and pepper. Simmer for 30 minutes. Serve hot with roast venison, or cool and store in refrigerator. This sauce will enhance the flavor of any roast meat.

(Adapted from Menon, *La Cuisinière Bourgeoise*, 1746)

Chicken with Tarragon in Jelly

"Tarragon gives the flavour of French cookery, and in high gravies is a great improvement; but should be added only a short time before serving."—A New System of Domestic Cookery, 1808

3- to 4-pound plump chicken with Bay leaf
  giblets 1 teaspoon salt
1 veal knuckle Fresh tarragon, or 2 teaspoons
1 onion   dried tarragon
1 carrot 1 egg white
1 stalk of celery ½ cup Madeira

Truss the chicken. Place in a saucepan with its giblets, the veal knuckle, vegetables, bay leaf, salt and 1 sprig of tarragon, or 1 teaspoon dried tarragon. Cover with water and simmer for 1 hour. Cool in liquid; then remove trussing string from the chicken and wipe carefully. Remove fat from liquid; then heat the liquid and strain it through cheesecloth. Lightly whip the egg white with 1 tablespoon freshly chopped tarragon leaves, or 1 teaspoon dried tarragon. Add to the lukewarm stock and bring to a boil; then, simmer slowly for 25 minutes, or until stock is reduced to 2 cups. Remove from heat and stir in ½ cup Madeira. Put several tablespoons of this jelly on the bottom of a serving tray. Chill the tray until the jelly is set. Place the chicken on the jellied tray. Keep remainder of jelly at room temperature. Dip several broad tarragon leaves in the half-set jelly and arrange decoratively over the chicken. Then carefully spoon the half-set jelly over the chicken until it is completely glazed. Place the dish on ice or in the refrigerator until ready to serve. Serves 6.

Veal Birds with Orange Sauce

8 slices of veal (¼-inch thick) ¼ cup currants
  cut from upper leg ¼ teaspoon ground cardamon
Salt and pepper to taste 3 tablespoons butter
1 cup cooked rice ½ cup chicken broth

Flatten the veal slices with a mallet. Season with salt and pepper. Mix the rice, currants, and cardamon. Place a spoonful of this mixture on each slice of veal; then roll them up and tie securely with a string. Heat the butter and brown the veal birds quickly on all sides. Reduce heat to simmer, add ½ cup chicken broth, and cover tightly. Simmer for 20 minutes.

Orange Sauce

2 oranges	½ cup chicken broth
1 lemon	3 tablespoons vinegar
2 tablespoons sugar	1 tablespoon cornstarch

Peel off only the colored part of the orange and lemon rind and cut into thin slivers. Cover with water and boil for 5 minutes. Drain. Sprinkle sugar on the bottom of a heavy pan, heat, and stir until melted and golden brown. Then, slowly stir in the chicken broth and the vinegar. Slice and seed peeled oranges and lemons. Arrange veal birds on a platter with the fruit slices. Pour pan juices into sauce mixture, add lemon and orange slivers, bring to a boil, and add cornstarch dissolved in 2 tablespoons of water. Stir until thickened and pour over veal and fruit. Serves 4. *Note:* 2 tablespoons of Curaçao makes a zesty twentieth-century addition to the sauce.

PEPPERMINT

Roots and Vegetables

Glazed Minted Carrots

1½ pounds carrots (5 cups)	2 tablespoons butter, softened
1½ cups water	2 tablespoons sugar
1½ tablespoons butter	Freshly ground pepper to taste
½ teaspoon salt	2 tablespoons fresh peppermint
1 cup heavy cream	

If baby carrots are used, cut off tops and tips, wash, brush clean, and cook whole. Fresh young carrots should be scraped and halved. Stored winter carrots should be peeled and quartered. Lay the carrots on the bottom of a wide pan that can be covered tightly. Add water, butter, and salt and bring to a boil. Cover and cook slowly until liquid has evaporated and carrots are almost tender, about 20 minutes. Bring cream to a boil in a small pan and pour over the carrots. Simmer slowly, uncovered, until cream has been almost absorbed by the carrots, or until the carrots are tender. Add the softened butter, sprinkle with sugar, and season with pepper. Simmer a few minutes longer. Snip the fresh peppermint over the glazed carrots and take to the table in a pewter basin. Serves 8.

Cauliflower Du Barry

One of many French dishes named for the Comtesse Du Barry, mistress of Louis XV, who was noted almost as much for her taste in food as for her taste in lovers.

1 head of cauliflower	2 tablespoons butter
1 cup mashed potatoes	Salt and pepper to taste
¼ cup heavy cream	1 tablespoon parsley, chopped

Break cauliflower into sections and cook in salted water until tender. Drain well and puree. Mix cauliflower, potatoes, cream, and butter. Season with salt and pepper. Mound on a platter and cover with Beurre Meunière. Sprinkle with chopped parsley. Serves 6.

Beurre Meunière

⅓ cup clarified butter
1 tablespoon lemon juice

Brown the butter in a heavy saucepan until it becomes a rich brown. Add the lemon juice and pour over the cauliflower.

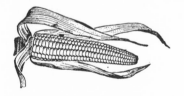

Corn Cakes

Six ears fresh corn, or 1 10-ounce package frozen corn	1 teaspoon salt
2 eggs	1 teaspoon baking soda
⅔ cup buttermilk, or sour milk	½ teaspoon pepper
½ cup flour	¼ teaspoon nutmeg
1 tablespoon sugar	2 tablespoons corn oil

Scrape the corn from the ears, or defrost and drain the frozen corn. Lightly beat the eggs. Add buttermilk, dry ingredients, and corn. (For a smoother cake, whisk ingredients together in a blender. Heat the corn oil in a skillet. Pour the batter like pancakes into the hot skillet (360°). Cook for about 1 minute on each side and serve immediately. Serves 6.

(Adapted from Le Valley A. Inman's rule book)

WOODEN FIRKIN

Pickles and Preserves

Cranberry Conserve

1 large orange	¼ cup honey
4 cups (1 pound) fresh cranber-ries	¾ cup sugar
	1½ teaspoons ginger
1 cup golden raisins	½ cup walnuts, chopped

Quarter the orange and remove seeds. With the cranberries, put through a food chopper. Mix with the remaining ingredients. So that flavors may blend, chill in the refrigerator for several hours. Makes 4 cups.

Pumpkin Chips

1 firm, medium-sized pumpkin	Juice and rind of 12 lemons
1 cup sugar to each 2 cups chips	2 to 3 ounces crystallized ginger

Peel the pumpkin and cut into 1-inch strips; then slice these strips very thin. Measure amount of chips and add half as much sugar to the juice of 12 lemons. Stir well. Add pumpkin chips to the sugar and lemon juice mixture and let stand overnight. Slice the lemon rinds into very thin 2-inch-long strips. Barely cover with water and simmer gently until soft. Drain and refrigerate overnight. The next morning, boil the chips in lemon juice and sugar until the chips are clear and transparent. Remove the chips and boil syrup 10 minutes longer, or until it begins to thicken; then add chips, lemon rind, and crystallized ginger to taste. Bring to a boil. Pour into jars and seal. Makes 6 to 8 pints.

(Kirk family receipt)

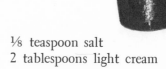

Rhode Island Jonnycakes

1 cup flint cornmeal   ⅛ teaspoon salt
1 cup boiling water   2 tablespoons light cream

Pour boiling water onto the cornmeal. Add salt and enough light cream
to make a cakelike batter. Drop by tablespoonsful onto a hot iron griddle well greased with bacon drippings. Cook over a medium fire until
crisp and brown on one side, about 5 minutes; then turn over and cook
on the other side.

*Every Rhode Island cook has her own receipt for Jonnycakes. An old New-
port receipt uses milk instead of water and calls for 1 teaspoon of sugar in
the batter. A South County receipt adds 1 tablespoon of molasses and 1
tablespoon of butter to the basic cornmeal batter. Means of cooking the
Johnnycakes vary also. Visitors to Smith's Castle, Cocumscussoc, where
Roger Williams once traded with the Narragansett Indians, will see a long,
narrow hardwood board onto which Jonnycakes were poured and then set
before the fire to bake in the reflected heat.*

Aunt Mary's Brown Bread

2 cups sour milk   ½ cup brown sugar
½ cup rye flour   ½ teaspoon salt
2½ cups whole wheat or graham   ½ cup molasses
   flour   2 teaspoons baking soda
2 tablespoons melted butter

Mix ingredients together in the order given. Fill one greased 9" x 5" x 3"
loaf pan, and bake at 350° for about 1 hour. For a steamed bread,
bake in tightly covered pudding steamers, or in loaf pans covered
tightly with aluminum foil. One cup of raisins lightly dusted with flour
may be added to the batter before baking.

(Adapted from a Lyman family receipt)

SOURDOUGH BREADBAKING

Breadbaking was a daily task in the early American kitchen. Although loaves were usually made weekly (so that the oven need only be fired once), quick breads were a part of each day's cooking. Pancakes, waffles, and biscuits were mixed from the starter each housewife kept in a crock on a shelf of the cold pantry. New Englanders called this the "emptyings" crock because the frugal housewife scraped the flour and small bits of dough left on the kneading board back into the crock so as not to waste any of the precious flour.

Cooking with a starter was simple. If pancakes were on the morning's menu, the colonial housewife "set the sponge" by stirring together the starter, flour, and liquid the night before. Next morning, she carefully returned the amount of starter she took from the crock; then stirred additional ingredients into the sponge and poured pancakes onto the sizzling griddle. For the evening's biscuits, she set the sponge in the morning and by evening the dough was bubbling with the natural leavening. In an emergency she could borrow a cup of her neighbor's "emptyings," set a sponge for her own use, and return one cupful of this sponge to her neighbor that very evening.

Today's housewife can fill her own "emptyings" crock and start a family tradition of sourdough cookery.

Starter

1 package dry yeast
2 cups warm water
2 cups white flour

In a large bowl (the starter needs room to ferment), dissolve yeast in warm water, add flour, and stir vigorously. Cover with a cloth and allow this mixture to stand in a moderately warm kitchen for 3 days, stirring occasionally. The mixture will rise, then separate into a yeasty smelling liquid (hootch), and, finally, a heavier flour paste. Don't worry about the dirty gray color of the liquid; just stir it back into the flour mixture.

After 3 days the starter is ready for use. It may be stored in the refrigerator in a glass, ceramic, or plastic container with a lid that is not tightly fastened—the bubbling yeast might explode in a tightly fastened jar.

There are two secrets to using this starter: 1. Always replace what is taken from the crock. This may be done in two ways: Either add equal amounts of flour and water to the starter when some is used, or let the sponge set overnight and replace one cup of the sponge into the crock next morning before adding the other ingredients the receipt calls for. To double the amount of starter, add 2 cups of warm water and 2 cups of flour to the crock and let it sit in a warm spot overnight. 2. Use the starter at least every 2 weeks. Yeast is a living organism that "feeds" on the flour added to the mixture. In a sense, it "starves" if fresh flour is not added. If not used, refresh the starter by adding ½ cup of warm water and ½ cup flour and let it stand in a warm spot overnight.

English Muffins

¾ cup starter	1½ teaspoons salt
1 cup milk	¾ teaspoon baking soda
3 cups flour	2 tablespoons cornmeal
1 tablespoon sugar	

The night before: Set the sponge by mixing together the starter, milk, and 2 cups of the flour. Cover and set in a warm place to rise.

The next morning: Mix sugar, salt, and baking soda with the other cup of flour. Add to sponge, turn out onto floured board, and knead until smooth, about 5 minutes. Roll out the dough ¾ inch thick. Cut with a large, round cutter (an empty tunafish can makes an ideal cutter). Place on a cookie sheet covered with waxed paper and sprinkled with cornmeal. Let rise until light, about 45 minutes. Bake on a hot griddle, lightly greased, over coals in the fireplace for 6 minutes on each side, or bake in a covered electric skillet (350°) for 6 minutes on each side. Makes 12 muffins.

Split and toast these muffins and serve with quince marmalade or apple butter—no finer taste anywhere.

FAMILY AT TEA

Sourdough Bread

1 cup starter
2 cups warm water
8 cups flour
2 teaspoons sugar

2 teaspoons salt
1 package dry yeast
½ teaspoon baking soda

The night before: Set the sponge by mixing starter, water, 4 cups flour, sugar, and salt. Cover and set in a warm place to rise.

The next morning: Dissolve yeast in ½ cup warm water. Stir this mixture into the sponge and add baking soda sifted with remaining 4 cups of flour. Turn onto a floured board and knead until smooth, adding more flour if necessary. Shape into two loaves and place in two well-greased 9″ x 5″ x 3″ loaf pans; or, cook one large round loaf in a 3-quart casserole dish. Let rise until double in bulk, about 2 hours depending on the warmth of the kitchen. Make 3 diagonal slashes across the top of the bread with a sharp knife. Bake in a hot oven (400°) until done, about 45 minutes for two loaves or 55 minutes for a single loaf.

Sourdough bread has a characteristically white crust. For a darker crust, brush bread with a beaten egg white before baking. For crustier bread, brush with water before baking. For a more pronounced sour flavor, allow the sponge to sit for 24 hours before baking.

Uncommon Cakes and Pies

Apple Molasses Pie

Piecrust dough	1 teaspoon cinnamon
6 large tart apples	¼ cup butter
Juice of ½ lemon	1 cup molasses

Cover the inside of a cast-iron Dutch oven with a rich piecrust dough. Pare, core, and slice apples. Cover the bottom of the crust with apples. Sprinkle with lemon juice and cinnamon and dot with butter. Cover with ½ cup molasses. Add another layer of apples and the remaining molasses. Cover with a top crust, sealing edges carefully. Slit crust and brush top with milk. Bake for 2 hours "in an afternoon oven" (325°).

(Adapted from Le Valley A. Inman's rule book)

Glazed Pear Tart

Piecrust dough for a 9-inch shell	6 pears, peeled and quartered
1 cup sugar	1 vanilla bean
2 cups water	

Fill a 9-inch flan (or pie plate) with rich piecrust dough. Prick well and bake until golden brown, about 10 minutes at 425°.

Combine 1 cup sugar and 2 cups water; bring to boil and stir until the sugar is dissolved. Add pears and vanilla bean and simmer until pears are tender, about 30 minutes. Drain and reserve pears.

Custard

½ cup sugar	3 cups milk
½ cup flour	1 vanilla bean
2 eggs, plus 2 additional yolks	3 tablespoons butter

In a heavy saucepan beat egg yolks until fluffy.   Add sugar, then the whole eggs. Add flour, beating well after each addition. In another saucepan, scald milk with vanilla bean. Remove bean and pour milk slowly into the egg mixture, stirring constantly. Place this mixture over the heat and bring to a boil, stirring constantly. Let the custard simmer for 3 minutes until the mixture thickens; then remove from heat and stir in the butter. Cool slightly and pour into the pastry shell. Chill while preparing glaze.

Glaze

1 cup apricot jam
1 tablespoon Kirsch

Heat apricot jam with Kirsch until mixtures comes to a boil. Boil for 1 minute. Arrange pears on top of the custard; then glaze with apricots. Chill for at least 6 hours before serving.

Sweet Dishes and Confections

Newport Orange Meringue

Ships returning from the West Indies brought oranges to delight Newport housewives. Mrs. Lyman looked forward to serving oranges in this elegant manner.

2 cups milk
2 eggs, separated
¾ cup sugar
⅓ cup cornstarch

4 small oranges, peeled, seeded, and sectioned, or 1 12-ounce can mandarin oranges, drained

In a saucepan combine egg yolks, milk, cornstarch, and ½ cup sugar. Bring to a boil over moderate heat, stirring constantly, and cook until quite thick, about 1 minute. Mixture will be very thick and must be stirred to prevent lumping. Cool slightly. Arrange orange slices in the bottom of a 2-quart casserole dish. Sprinkle with remaining ¼ cup sugar. Cover with custard mixture.

Meringue

Beat egg whites with 2 tablespoons sugar until they form stiff peaks. Cover custard with this meringue. Brown in a 375° oven for about 10 minutes. Serves 8.

(Adapted from LeValley A. Inman's rule book)

Irish Moss Pudding

4 cups milk   ½ cup sugar
4 large slices Irish moss, freed   1 tablespoon rum
   from grit (see note below)   ¼ teaspoon nutmeg

In a saucepan combine milk, Irish moss, and sugar. Bring to a boil, stirring constantly, and boil for 1 minute until the mixture is creamy. Flavor with rum and nutmeg. Strain out the moss and pour the mixture into molds. Serves 6.

(Fuller family receipt)

Note: Irish moss is a type of seaweed that grows plentifully in Narragansett Bay. Early Rhode Islanders learned from the Indians that the moss could be used as a thickening agent.

After a storm, the Rhode Island housewife would send her children to gather the sea moss on the beaches. They might find two varieties—a white moss for the finest of puddings or a dark purple-red moss, which is richer in iodine and minerals. The housewife dried the moss and stored it in a pantry basket; when dried it would keep indefinitely.

A handful of the moss crumpled into the stewpot simmering over the fire would thicken the stew as well as add essential minerals to the nutritive content. For over two centuries Rhode Island mothers have claimed that children who have been fed on sea moss puddings and stews are healthier and stronger than children who have not.

Drams and Punches

Switchel

At haying time a jug of switchel hung in every Rhode Island barn. This refreshing mixture both quenched the thirst and renewed the energy of the busy workers. At the end of the day, a jigger of rum and a twist of lemon peel was added to the cup of switchel—to relax their aching muscles.

"3 cups molasses and 3 tablespoons ginger mixed, then dissolved in a quart of cold water. Pour in a 10-quart can and fill with cold well water. Keep can covered with wet blanket and place in shade if possible."—Le Valley A. Inman's rule book

Doctor Salmon's Punch

> *"When Wine inflames, Punch does but cheer,*
> *Nor fuddles like the muddy Beer,*
> *But like the Fountain runs off clear."*
> *—Nathaniel Ames, Almanack, 1764*

2 quarts water
¾ pound sugar
1 pint lime juice

1 teaspoon freshly grated nutmeg
3 pints choice brandy

Boil water and sugar together until the sugar is completely dissolved. Cool. Add lime juice, nutmeg, and brandy and serve well chilled.

Lydia Watrous Buckingham of Old Saybrook, Connecticut

Buckingham House

"Many families have owed their prosperity full as much to the propriety of female management, as to the knowledge and activity of the father."—The American Domestic Cookery, 1808

Lydia Watrous Buckingham's life centered around the great hearth of her simple kitchen, where her five children helped her with the baking, candlemaking, soapmaking, spinning, and weaving. Elegance was not the style of the Puritan housewives of Connecticut. Unlike the landed gentry of the South and the ladies of New York and Philadelphia society, there were no servants to assist with the arduous management of the house and garden.

Lydia Buckingham unquestionably fits the description that St. Jean de Crèvecoeur gave to a good wife in his *Letters from an American Farmer*: "He may work and gather the choicest fruits of his farm; but if female economy fails, he loses the comfort of good vituals. He sees wholesome meats, excellent flours converted into indifferent food; whilst his neighbor, more happy, though less rich, feeds on well-cooked dishes, well-composed puddings. For such is our lot: If we are blessed with a good wife, we may boast of living better than any people of the same rank on the globe."

The world of the Buckinghams was pleasant, simple, and uncomplicated. One can imagine a bustling scene by a roaring fire. Lydia has readied the oven for the day's baking of breads, pies, and little cakes. The irons are heating by the fire for pressing the family's garments. One of the children gathers fresh herbs from the garden. A spicy aroma fills the air as mulled cider heats in an iron pot hanging from the crane, awaiting the arrival of Samuel Buckingham. Husband, children, and home—these were the things of greatest importance to Lydia.

Samuel, who was a veteran of the French and Indian War, earned his living through farming and land investments. Although little is known of Lydia's early years, we do know that Samuel had a distinctive heritage. His great grandfather, the Reverend Thomas Buckingham, was one of the founders of the Collegiate School, which later became Yale University. His scholarly bent was inherited by his son Daniel, who was appointed custodian of the college library. It is believed that the kitchen of the Buckingham House was a portion of the house in which Daniel stored the library. He caused an uproar when Yale College was moved from Old Saybrook to New Haven. In defiance of the sheriff and the governor, he refused to part with his books, and they had to be removed by force.

The five Buckingham children and many grandchildren must have been a source of great pride to Samuel and Lydia. Samuel's namesake

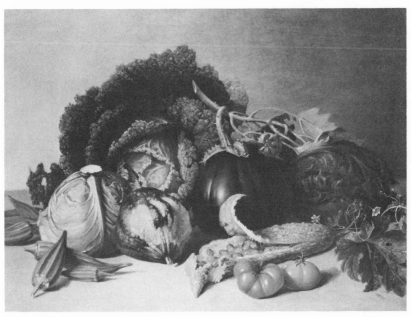

became active in the Connecticut River Fisheries at Old Saybrook. He eventually moved to Lebanon, Connecticut, and his son Samuel Giles Buckingham became a well-known minister. Another grandson, the Honorable William Alfred Buckingham, was a mayor of Norwich, a governor of Connecticut, and a United States senator during the Grant administration. He was baptized in the Buckingham House in 1804, and we know that he often visited his grandparents.

Lydia survived Samuel by eighteen years; throughout the years of their marriage they led an exemplary life devoted to the New England Puritan belief in education and simplicity.

The Buckingham House

Mystic Seaport, founded in 1929, is a reconstructed village that brings to life a nineteenth-century seaport community established by our sea-faring ancestors, who sailed westward from Europe centuries ago.

The Buckingham House was a typical Connecticut dwelling of the pre-Revolutionary middle class. Although we are not certain that Samuel Buckingham built the main portion of the house, which was built in Old Saybrook between 1725 and 1758, it is known that he and Lydia were living in the house at the time of the Revolution. The kitchen ell

OFFICIAL MYSTIC SEAPORT PHOTOGRAPH

was added by the Buckinghams in the eighteenth century and is thought to have been part of a house built in the 1690s. The kitchen has been restored to its original seventeenth-century appearance, the main portion of the house to its appearance during the first four decades of the nation's independence.

A huge central chimney is the focal point of pre-Revolutionary New England architecture and functions as the structural backbone of the house, providing fireplaces for every room. The great kitchen hearth suggests an early date, as does the domed brick baking oven, which is behind the hearth. In later houses the fireplaces were smaller and the oven to one side of the hearth. The oak mantel above the hearth is also an early feature, for later versions were generally constructed of brick.

In the dining room of the Buckingham House are portraits of Ohio relatives. At that time, Ohio was part of the Western Reserve, and Hartford was the capital of both Ohio and Connecticut. Also in the dining room is a set of unusual andirons, which represent the sun and the moon.

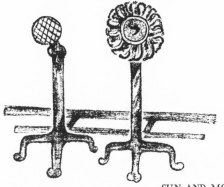

SUN AND MOON ANDIRONS

Soups and Savories

Dutch-Oven Seafood Chowder

1 pound fish fillets (cod, haddock, sole)
1 cup carrots, sliced
1 cup potatoes, cubed
1 cup onions, chopped
1 teaspoon salt
1 teaspoon dill weed
2 whole cloves

1 small bay leaf
1 pound salt pork, chopped
1 cup boiling water
¼ cup dry white wine
½ cup light cream
1 tablespoon flour
1 tablespoon parsley, chopped

Cut the fish into 1-inch cubes. Set aside. Combine carrots, potatoes, onions, salt, dill, cloves, bay leaf, and salt pork in a Dutch oven. Add the boiling water and cover tightly. Bake in a moderate oven (375°) for 40 minutes, or simmer over hot coals until the vegetables are tender. Add the fish and wine; simmer until the fish flakes easily, about 20 minutes. Blend cream and flour together until smooth; stir into the chowder. Heat the chowder but do not boil it. Sprinkle with parsley. Serves 6.

Onion Soup

"All cooks agree in this opinion, no savoury dish without an onion."—The American Domestic Cookery, 1808

1 cup butter	1 large piece of French bread
10 onions, peeled and chopped	2 egg yolks, beaten
2 tablespoons flour	1 teaspoon vinegar
4 cups boiling water, or beef stock	Salt and pepper to taste

Heat butter in a large saucepan until it bubbles. Gently sauté onions for 15 minutes. Add flour and stir in well. Pour in the boiling water or stock and stir well. Add French bread. Season with salt and pepper. Stew for 10 minutes.

Beat the egg yolks and vinegar together. Add some of the stock to the egg yolk mixture; then stir it gently into the soup by degrees. Serve from a soup tureen with crusty bread and butter. Serves 4 to 6.

After-dinner savories were common in colonial days, and they can be equally appealing today served as aperitif accompaniments or for luncheon.

Roast Cheese to Be Carried up After Dinner

Grate three ounces of fat cheshire cheese, mix it with the yolks of two eggs, four ounces of grated bread, and three ounces of butter; beat the whole well in a mortar, with a dessert-spoonful of mustard, and a little salt and pepper. Toast some bread, cut it into proper pieces, lay the paste as above thick upon them, put them into a Dutch oven, covered, till hot through; remove the dish and let the cheese brown a little."— The American Domestic Cookery, 1808

Fish, Meat, and Fowl

Clam Fritters

1 tablespoon onion, chopped	¼ teaspoon salt
2 cups clams	1 egg
1 cup cornmeal	Enough milk to make a thin batter
¼ teaspoon pepper	

Chop onions and clams. Add the other ingredients. Fry as you would pancakes on a greased iron griddle. Serve very hot and accompany the fritters with fresh bread and a salad of greens for luncheon or a light supper. Serves 4.

Codfish and Potato with White Sauce

Tear two pieces of fish about the size of your hand from salt cod. Soak them in cold water, changing the water at least 3 times to wash away the salt. Pare 8 potatoes, cut in half, and place in a wire basket or steamer. Place cod on top of potatoes. Cook in a kettle of boiling water until potatoes are done. Arrange on a platter and cover with white sauce. Serve with fresh garden peas. Serves 6.

White Sauce

2 tablespoons butter
2 tablespoons flour
½ teaspoon salt

2 cups milk
2 hard-boiled eggs

Melt butter; add flour and salt, stirring with a wooden spoon. Add milk slowly as you stir. When mixture is thick, remove from heat and add chopped egg whites. Pour over the fish. Sprinkle sieved egg yolks over the sauce.

   This traditional New England receipt can be used for fresh cod or haddock: Let the potatoes cook for 10 to 15 minutes before adding the fish.

The Frenchman St. Jean de Crèvecoeur wrote in a travel journal during the eighteenth century: "We had entered the province of Connecticut, one of the most productive in cattle, wheat, and every kind of commodity. It is unquestionably the most fertile province in America, for its soil yields every-thing necessary to life. The pasturage is so good here that the cattle are of truly excellent quality. The poultry and game are exquisite. Among the for-mer the turkeys, geese, and ducks are renowned, especially the wild ones."

Breast of Veal Stuffed with Forcemeat

Breast of veal with a pocket for stuffing
1 cup fresh bread crumbs
½ cup onions, chopped and sau-téed
½ cup Virginia or Westphalian ham, chopped
½ cup tongue, chopped

½ cup parsley, chopped
1 teaspoon mace
1 teaspoon salt
½ teaspoon pepper
½ cup beets, chopped
1 raw egg
2 tablespoons melted butter
1 calf's foot (optional)

Remove the thick skin and gristle from the breast and pound the meat with a rolling pin. Make a stuffing with all the ingredients except the calf's foot. A little broth or stock can be added to the stuffing for moisture. Stuff the veal and bind it with string. Brown the meat in butter in the bottom of a heavy roasting pan. Add a little veal stock, or bouillon, and the calf's foot (optional). Cover and roast in a slow oven (300°) for 1½ to 2 hours. When done, remove the string. Place the roast on a warm serving platter. If the breast is to be served hot, a sauce can be made with the pan drippings. Add a little flour to the pan, stir until blended and add a cup of beef or veal stock. Serve with the breast of veal. The veal is excellent served cold for an elegant buffet. Slice the breast so that the multicolored stuffing is visible. Serves 6.

(Adapted from *The American Domestic Cookery*, 1808)

SAUSAGE GUN

A New-Fashioned and Economical Dish

"Prepare two pounds of meat for a pie. (Use leftover roast beef or other meat.) Mash potatoes, and mix them up with milk, salt, pepper and butter. Spread it over the meat in the form of a pie crust and dot with butter and grated cheese, in which situation send it to the oven. Spare your comments until you have made the experiment and tasted."—Nathan Daboll, New England Almanack 1819

Herbed and Spiced Sausage

1½ pounds ground lean pork
½ pound ground fat pork
2 teaspoons salt
½ tablespoon dried sage, chopped or powdered
½ tablespoon dried oregano, chopped or powdered

1 teaspoon freshly ground pepper
¼ teaspoon cayenne
2 teaspoons brown sugar
2 tablespoons parsley, chopped

Mix the ingredients together well and pack into a container with a cover. Place in the refrigerator overnight so the mixture can absorb the flavor of the herbs. The next day, shape into patties and brown well on both sides in a skillet. Serve the sausage for breakfast or for supper with pan-browned potatoes and fried apples. Serves 4.

Calf's Liver Roasted

"A large calves liver. Wash and wipe it; then cut a long hole in it and stuff it with crumbs of bread, chopped anchovy, herbs, a good deal of fat bacon, onion, salt, pepper, a bit of butter, and an egg. Sew the liver up; then lard it, or wrap it in a veal-cawl; and roast it. Serve with good brown gravy and currant jelly."—The American Domestic Cookery, 1808

Pulled Chicken

2 small fryers, boned and skinned
or 1½ pounds boned and
skinned chicken meat
1 cup flour, plus 2 tablespoons

Salt and pepper to taste
Juice of ½ lemon
1½ cups chicken stock
½ cup butter

Pull the skin off the chicken and tear into pieces. Dredge the pieces in 1 cup flour seasoned with salt and pepper and fry them in butter until brown. Remove the chicken from the pan and keep it warm. Gradually stir 2 tablespoons flour into the pan juices. Add the stock, lemon juice, salt, and pepper and stir until smooth. Add the chicken and simmer until heated thoroughly, being careful not to overcook it. Accompany this simple dish with fluffy rice, fresh string beans, and sautéed mushrooms. A perfect company dinner, perhaps served at a family baptismal party in The Buckingham House. Serves 6.

(Adapted from The Experienced American Housekeeper, 1823)

A Three-Day Wedding Feast

In Stonington, Connecticut, in 1726, Temperance Tealleys was wed to the Reverend William Worthington from Saybrook. The Buckinghams may well have been acquainted with the bride and groom.

Because of the large number of guests expected, a two-day celebration was planned. Elaborate advance preparations commenced for the feast. Chairs, tables, dishes, and utensils were borrowed from the neighbors.

Following the marriage ceremony, performed by the groom's best friend and fellow minister, came the reception. The blessing given, tankards of spiced hard cider were passed, and each filled his own mug of glass, pewter, china, silver, horn, or wood. The main course was family-style and consisted of fish or clam chowder, stewed oysters, roasted pig, venison, duck, potatoes, baked rye bread, Indian cornbread, and probably pumpkin casserole. A dessert of Indian pudding studded with dried plums and served with a sauce made from West Indian molasses, butter, and vinegar followed. And they did have coffee. The tablecloths were removed and trays of nutmeats and broken blocks of candy made from maple sugar, butter, and hickory nuts; pipes, tobacco, and brandy; burgundy and Madeira were set on the tables. Outside the front door stood a gigantic punch bowl, hollowed out from a boulder, filled with hard cider combined with West Indian products such as sugar, lemons, and limes. "None became boisterous, though the big bowl was kept well and strongly replenished during the entire three days of the feast."

After the dignitaries and most-honored guests were served on the first day, and after the bride and groom left on horseback for Saybrook, there was a second day of feasting for the second-ranked guests. The third day of feasting was a surprise, for some friendly Mohawks and Pequot Indians appeared—no one knows just why—and more chowder and roast pig were served to them. (Courtesy of Stonington Historical Society.)

Herb Pie

In the charming herb garden behind the Buckingham House, near the kitchen, there are nasturtiums. These can be used in salads, or the buds can be pickled. Lamb's ears, which were used to wrap a wound, and mugwart add an interesting flavor to meats. More traditional herbs such as sage, parsley, thyme, tarragon, and oregano are hung and dried in the kitchen for later use. An herb garden was most important to the eighteenth-century house-wife—she relied upon it for medicines, flavoring for meats, stews, soups, vegetables, and sweets, and also for sweet bags and potpourri.

2 bunches of parsley
1 head of lettuce
1 cup spinach leaves
1 bunch of watercress
A few borage leaves or any other herbs you fancy, such as tarragon, chervil, or summer savory
1 onion, chopped
Butter for sauté
1 large, or 2 small, pie shells, unbaked

2 tablespoons melted butter
1 tablespoon flour
2 cups light cream
1 cup milk
2 eggs
1 teaspoon nutmeg
1 teaspoon salt
½ teaspoon pepper
½ cup mild cheese, grated

Wash the greens and boil them under tender. Press out the water and chop fine. Sauté the onion in butter until golden and place them in the piecrusts. Add a layer of the greens on top of the onions. Make a batter of the melted butter, flour, cream, milk, eggs, nutmeg, salt, and pepper and pour this over the greens. Cover with grated cheese and bake at 350° for 20 to 25 minutes, or until set. Serves 6.

Roots and Vegetables

Bubble and Squeak

"*Boil, chop, and fry, with a little butter, pepper, and salt, some cabbage, and lay it on slices of rare-done beef, lightly fried.*"—The American Domestic Cookery, 1808

Fricassee of Parsnips

"Parsnips are a valuable root, cultivated best in rich old grounds, and doubly deep plowed, late sown, they grow thrifty, and are not so spongy; they may be kept any where and any how, so that they do not grow with heat, or are nipped with frost; if frosted, let them thaw in earth; they are richer flavored when plowed out of the ground in April, having stood out during the winter, tho' they will not last long after, and commonly more sticky and hard in the centre."—Amelia Simmons, American Cookery, *1796*

A trip to the root cellar may have produced this fine accompaniment to a roast of lamb or beef.

1 bunch of parsnips	½ cup cream
1 cup milk	½ teaspoon mace
1 tablespoon butter	Salt and pepper to taste
1 tablespoon flour	1 teaspoon parsley, chopped
½ cup chicken broth	

Peel and cut the parsnips into 2- or 3-inch slices. Simmer them in milk until nearly tender. Melt butter and add flour to make a paste. Gradually stir in broth, cream, mace, salt, and pepper. Simmer parsnips in this white sauce for a few minutes. Sprinkle with chopped parsley and serve. Serves 6.

PIPKIN

Pickles and Preserves

Mushroom Ketchup

Mushroom ketchup appears as an ingredient in many eighteenth-century receipts. It can be used as an excellent sauce for cold meats and fowl. Add a dash to sauces and stews for a delectable flavor.

5 pounds mushrooms
2 bay leaves
4 tablespoons salt
1 medium onion, chopped
½ teaspoon ground cloves

½ teaspoon allspice
⅛ teaspoon cayenne
½ teaspoon grated horseradish
Rind of 1 lemon, grated
½ cup cider vinegar

Trim the ends of the mushroom stems. Wipe the mushrooms, but do not peel or wash them. Chop, and put them in a bowl with the bay leaves and salt. The next day, crush the mushrooms (but not the bay leaves) with a potato masher. Add onion, cloves, allspice, cayenne, horseradish, lemon rind, and vinegar. Bring the mixture to a boil and simmer for 30 minutes. Discard the bay leaves. Puree in a blender, or leave as is, and pack in hot sterilized jars. Makes 2 pints.

(Adapted from *The American Domestic Cookery*, 1808)

Kitchen Pepper

"*Mix in the finest powder, one ounce of ginger; of cinnamon, black pepper, nutmeg, and Jamaica pepper, half an ounce each; ten cloves and six ounces of salt. Keep it in a bottle—it is an agreeable addition to any brown sauces or soups.*"—The American Domestic Cookery, 1808.

Crab-apple Rosemary Jelly

5 cups crab apples (enough to make one quart)
2 cups water

1½ to 2 cups sugar
Fresh rosemary

Gather fresh crab apples. Wash and cut out the ends. Chop in half and measure (there should be 1 quart). Combine apples with water, cover, and simmer until fruit is soft. Drain through 4 layers of cheesecloth. Measure juice into a large saucepan. For each cup of juice add ¾ to 1 cup sugar and boil rapidly to the jelling point (220° on a candy thermometer). As the jelly cooks, swirl fresh rosemary branches in the liquid. Remove jelly from heat and skim off the foam. Fill sterilized jars with jelly, leaving ½ inch of head space. Add one clean sprig of rosemary to each jelly glass. Seal with paraffin. Makes 2 to 4 half-pints.

Curry Powder

Curries were found in kitchens from the deep South to New England, especially in seaport towns. Spices were imported from the Caribbean islands, and the fragrance of their heady mixture imparted a delectable taste that has remained a favorite to this day. Make your own curry powder to keep for cooking, or for an unusual gift.

8 ounces ground turmeric	½ ounce ground cardamon
1 ounce ground ginger	1½ ounces ground mace
4 ounces ground coriander seed	1 ounce cayenne
2 ounces ground black pepper	1 ounce fennel seed
4 ounces ground cumin seed	

Mix ingredients and store in an airtight container.

(Adapted from the receipt book of Dr. B. F. Hayward, Sturbridge Village Library)

Breadstuffs

"The following hint may be useful as well as economical. Bread is now so heavy an article of expense, that all waste should be guarded against."—The American Domestic Cookery, 1808

Baked Rye Bread

3 packages dry yeast	2 tablespoons caraway seeds
¼ cup melted butter	4 cups rye flour
2½ cups lukewarm milk, or water	4 cups white flour
3 tablespoons salt	1 tablespoon cornstarch
6 tablespoons molasses	1 cup water
1 tablespoon vinegar	

Place yeast in a bowl. Stir butter into milk and pour over the yeast, stirring until dissolved. Add salt, molasses, vinegar, and caraway seeds. Add rye flour and 2 cups white flour. Mix well. Add enough of the remaining flour to make a stiff dough. Mix well. Let rise in a warm place in a clean, greased bowl covered with a towel until doubled in bulk. Punch down and place in 2 greased and floured bread pans, or shape as desired. Let rise again. Bake at 325° for 1 hour. Mix cornstarch and water. Boil and brush this glaze on bread while it is still hot.

Uncommon Cakes and Pies

Soft Molasses Cakes

2½ cups sifted flour
2 teaspoons baking soda
1 teaspoon ginger
1 teaspoon cinnamon
¼ teaspoon salt
½ cup butter or margarine,
 softened

½ cup sugar
½ cup molasses
1 egg
¼ cup cold water
1 cup golden raisins

Sift together flour, baking soda, ginger, cinnamon, and salt. Beat butter, sugar, molasses, and egg together until light and fluffy. Add the sifted ingredients alternately with cold water and beat until blended. Stir in the raisins. Drop by rounded tablespoonsful 3 inches apart onto a greased cookie sheet. Bake for 10 to 12 minutes at 350°. The size should be approximately 4 inches across.

STONEWARE JUG

Cranberry-Apple Pie

¾ cup cranberries, halved
⅓ cup sugar
¼ cup raisins
¼ cup brandy
8 large cooking apples, pared,
   cored, and sliced
⅔ cup sugar
1 tablespoon lemon juice
1 tablespoon grated lemon rind

1 teaspoon cornstarch
½ teaspoon cinnamon
1 pie shell, unbaked
Piecrust dough
1 egg
1 tablespoon milk
¼ teaspoon cinnamon
1 cup apricot jam

Mix the cranberries and ⅓ cup sugar and let stand for 1 hour. Plump
the raisins in brandy. Mix the remaining ingredients; then add raisins,
brandy, and sugared cranberries. Turn into a pastry shell, mounding the
mixture high. Cover with an upper crust or latticed pastry and brush with
an egg wash made with 1 egg, 1 tablespoon milk, and ¼ teaspoon
cinnamon. Bake at 425° for 20 minutes; then at 350° for 40 minutes.
Remove from the oven and spread with apricot jam. Serve with Devonshire Clotted Cream or home-churned ice cream. Serves 6.

Sweet Dishes and Confections

Lemon Cream

2 cups heavy cream
2 egg yolks, well beaten
½ cup sugar

Rind of 1 lemon, grated
Juice of 1 lemon
2 egg whites, stiffly beaten

Beat together cream, egg yolks, sugar, and lemon rind. Bring this mixture to a boil, remove from fire, and stir until cool. Put the lemon juice
into a bowl and pour the cream mixture over it, stirring until mixed.
Gently fold in the egg whites. Sprinkle with additional grated lemon
rind. Serve chilled. Pound cake is an excellent accompaniment to this
simple dessert. Serves 6.

(Adapted from *The American Domestic Cookery*, 1808)

Marlborough Pudding

6 eggs, well beaten	Juice of 1 lemon
½ cup sugar	Rind of 1 lemon, grated
6 apples, peeled, cored, sliced, and stewed	3 hard biscuits, pounded *
¾ cup melted butter	1 cup heavy cream

Beat the eggs and sugar together until creamy. Add the stewed apples, melted butter, lemon juice, lemon rind, pounded biscuits, and cream. Put into a greased pudding dish and bake in a moderate oven (300°) for 30 to 35 minutes, or until set. Serve hot or cold with soured cream or heavy cream. Serves 8.

Indian Pudding with Sweet Sauce

4 cups milk	1 teaspoon ginger
3 tablespoons stone-ground yellow cornmeal	½ teaspoon salt
½ cup sugar	⅛ teaspoon nutmeg
½ cup molasses	Pinch of ground cloves
1 tablespoon butter	⅛ teaspoon baking soda
1 teaspoon cinnamon	2 eggs

In a heavy pan scald milk. Gradually sprinkle with yellow cornmeal and bring to a boil, stirring briskly. Stir in sugar, molasses, butter, and all other dry ingredients. Let mixture cool slightly. In a small bowl beat the eggs with a little of the milk mixture and beat the egg mixture into the milk mixture. Pour the batter into a buttered 1½-quart baking dish and bake in a moderately slow oven (325°) for 2 hours. Pour Sweet Sauce over pudding and serve to 6.

Sweet Sauce

Mix 1 cup molasses, 1 tablespoon vinegar, and 2 tablespoons butter. Cook until bubbly and slightly thickened.

---

* Eighteenth-century cooks often used crackers or biscuits to thicken different dishes. The modern cook would use any kind of cracker or hard bread.

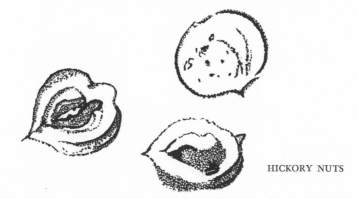

HICKORY NUTS

Nut Sweet

2 cups maple sugar (or brown
  sugar)
¼ cup water

1 tablespoon butter
1 cup hickory nuts, or walnuts,
  broken

In a saucepan combine sugar, water, and butter. Cook over low heat until a candy thermometer indicates 238°, or until the syrup dropped in cold water forms a soft ball. Add the nuts. Remove from heat and stir until the candy is thick. Drop in spoonsful onto waxed paper and let the patties harden.

Drams and Punches

TIN SCONCE

Hot Mulled Cyder

1 tablespoon whole allspice
1 tablespoon whole cloves
12 sticks cinnamon
1 gallon cider
2 teaspoons freshly grated nutmeg

1 cup orange juice
Juice of 3 lemons
Sugar to taste
Baked apples studded with cloves
Fresh mint

Tie allspice, cloves, and cinnamon in a cheesecloth bag. Bring cider, spices, juices, and sugar to the boiling point; then beat for 15 minutes to develop the flavor. Serve piping hot. Float small, firmly baked apples spiked with cloves in the punch bowl. Sprig cups with mint. Serves 20.

Samuel Fraunces of Fraunces Tavern, New York City

Fraunces Tavern

"New York . . . In the beauty of its situation, it surpasses Philadelphia by far . . . infinitely more gay . . . Broad Way is Superb, with very beautiful houses on it . . . Nothing is more cheerful than the part called the Battery . . . an esplanade which gives on to the canal and looks out on Long Island . . . deliciously cool."—1797 Julian Niemcewicz (companion to Kosciuszko) Under their Vine and Fig Tree

"To be sold at the Merchant's Coffee House on Tuesday, the 3rd of April, at noon, by public auction or at private sale any time before. The Queen's Head (Samuel Fraunces') Tavern, near the Exchange, is three stories high with tile and lead roof, has 14 fireplaces, a most excellent large kitchen, fine dry cellars . . . a corner house very open and airy and in the most complete repair, near the new ferry. Further particulars and a good title will be given by Samuel Francis who so far from declining his present business is determined to use ever the utmost endeavors to carry on the same, to the pleasure, and satisfaction of his friends and the public in general." —March 13, 1775, New York Gazette and Mercury

The splendid bay of New York, which was the chief port of entry between the old world and the new, designated the city of New York the queen of commerce, travel, government, and social activity. In such a

78

bustling hub of activity, taverns and houses of public entertainment were a necessity. Fraunces Tavern was one such establishment; it was owned by Samuel Fraunces, a true Delmonico of his day, who provided food, beds, entertainments, and service of superior quality.

In 1664, the very year that New Amsterdam became New York, Colonel Stephanus Van Cortlandt, the son of a wealthy Dutch merchant, was granted the plot of ground upon which Fraunces Tavern now stands. He, in turn, deeded it to his son-in-law Stephen de Lancey, who in 1719 built a hip-roofed Georgian mansion constructed of small yellow bricks brought from Holland, with a Dutch tile-and-lead roof. Beneath its gabled front and five windows on Pearl Street, was the main doorway, and it boasted a back veranda overlooking the bay, with woodsheds, barns, box-bordered flower and vegetable beds, and trees running almost to the water's edge.

The mansion was built well, and was destined to outlast all other buildings of its time, to become Manhattan's oldest restored building today.

It was not until 1762 that the roomy mansion passed into the ownership of Samuel Fraunces, a man of French extraction from the West Indies, who had been a caterer in New York since 1755, selling "portable soup, catsup, bottled gooseberries, pickled walnuts, pickled or fried oysters fit to go to the West Indies, pickled mushrooms, currant jelly, marmalade, etc." The architectural design common to eighteenth-century dwellings easily lent itself to tavern use; the first floor rooms were

SAMUEL FRAUNCES

used for dining, gaming, and lodging, and the upper chambers for housing additional guests. In addition, Samuel Fraunces' newly acquired tavern boasted a 43 by 20-foot Long Room, which was perfectly adapted to grand entertainments and balls.

Presenting his sign, which bore a portrait of Queen Charlotte, the young wife of King George III, Fraunces named his tavern "The Queen's Head," and announced that "dinner would be served daily at half-past one." The tavern was patronized by the best people in New York, not only for food, drink, and lodging, but for auctions, sale of subscriptions, and as a place where one could "Lodge a Memorandum" to a wigmaker, a French instructor, or a marriage bureau. The Long Room was used for the accommodations of banquets, balls, "Polite and Rational Amusement of Philosophical Lectures," citizen's meetings and social clubs. The Boston Post Road started almost at the front door of the tavern, and during the greater part of the year the general stage office was at the tavern, "whence stages left for Albany, Boston, and Philadelphia," taking three days for the trip in summer and four or more in winter.

As the troubles between king and colonies became more serious and demonstrative, the Queen's Head became the headquarters of opposition to the Crown, and a favorite meeting place of active patriots like John Jay, Gouverneur Morris, and Robert Livingston, who argued over the burning question of the day—taxation without representation.

Even though during the Revolution the tavern entertained both British and Americans, Samuel Fraunces was clearly an American patriot; in fact, toward the war's end General Washington cited him for this patriotism. In 1782 he received a vote of thanks and two hundred pounds from Congress, stating that "you have invariably through the most trying times maintained a constant friendship and attention to the Cause of our Country and its Independence and Freedom." It was not until November 1783, that the American troops took possession of the city, following the evacuation of the British. From this date forward, the "Queen's Head" on Queen Street became "Fraunces Tavern" on Pearl Street. On December 4 of that year the tavern's most memorable event took place—Washington bade farewell to his beloved officers in the Long Room.

Washington did not return to New York until six years later, when, on April 30, 1789, he was inaugurated as first president of the United States. In 1785, having owned the tavern for twenty-three years, Fraunces sold it for 1,950 pounds and retired to country life in New Jersey. But within four years he was back in New York where, as "the person best fitted for the office," he was made the steward of Washington's presidential household in New York at 3 Cherry Street.

Fraunces was a man of great ability. He not only performed the duties of the present-day steward but was, as Washington observed, "an excellent cook, knowing how to provide genteel dinners, and giving aid in dressing them, preparing the dessert, making the cake etc." Because of his extravagance, however, Fraunces was dismissed as steward; but he was subsequently re-engaged, continuing with the first family when the capital was moved to Philadelphia. By July, 1794, Fraunces had opened his own home as "an Ordinary and House of Entertainment" at 166 Second Street in Philadelphia. He died in 1795, while his newspaper advertisements were still inviting tavern patrons to his home—a tribute at the age of seventy-three to his extraordinary ability and integrity.

"Throughout America, in private houses as well as in the inns, several people are crowded together in the same room; and in the latter it very commonly happens that after you have been some time in bed, a stranger of any condition (and there is little distinction) comes into the room, pulls off his clothes, and places himself without ceremony between the sheets."—Travels in North America in the Years 1780, 1781, and 1782 by the Marquis de Chastellux

IRON TAVERN POT

Soups and Savories

Black Bean Soup

1 pint dry black beans
3 quarts water
¼ pound salt pork
½ pound stewing beef
1 carrot, sliced
2 onions, chopped
1 tablespoon salt

3 cloves
⅛ teaspoon mace
¼ teaspoon cayenne
3 hard-boiled eggs, sliced
1 lemon, thinly sliced and seeded
½ cup sherry

Soak the beans overnight in 1 quart of the water. The next morning, pour the water and beans into a large soup kettle and add 2 quarts water, salt pork, beef, carrot, onions, salt, and spices. Cover and simmer for 3 to 4 hours. Remove the meat and put the soup through a sieve, or blend in a blender until smooth. Serve piping hot in a tureen garnished with hard-boiled eggs and lemon slices. Add the sherry just before serving. Serves 20.

Pâté Maison Fraunces

6 strips bacon, or salt pork
½ pound pork or beef liver
½ pound pork fat
½ pound sausage meat
1 teaspoon each thyme, marjoram, and parsley
1 clove garlic, pressed
1 small onion, chopped
½ teaspoon each cinnamon, ground cloves, ginger, salt and pepper

½ teaspoon grated lemon rind
2 hard-boiled eggs, chopped
¼ cup brandy
½ pound veal, or game, cut into strips
1 bay leaf
1 teaspoon unflavored gelatin
⅛ cup cold port wine

Line a 1-quart croute or crockery mold with the bacon or salt pork. In a meat grinder, grind the liver and pork fat; mix with sausage meat, herbs, garlic, chopped onions, spices, lemon rind, eggs, and brandy. Put a layer of this mixture over the bacon; then a layer of the veal or game strips; then repeat. Place the bay leaf on top and seal with foil. Cook in a moderate oven (350°) for 1 to 1½ hours in a pan of water. Remove from the oven and drain the juices. Soak gelatin in the cold port wine. Heat the pâté juices to the boiling point, add dissolved gelatin, and stir. Pour over the pâté. Cover and chill until the jelly has set. Unmold and serve.

"New Yorkers alone have, I believe, twenty different ways of cooking oysters. On the bill of fare were the nice little items of 'wild turkey with oyster sauce,' 'wild duck,' 'roast chicken,' 'oyster pye,' 'roast oysters,' 'fried oysters,' 'stewed oysters,' 'scalloped oysters,' etc, etc. etc."—Aristocracy in America

Fraunces' Oyster Pie

2 onions, chopped
1 rib celery, chopped
Butter for sauté
3 tablespoons butter
3 tablespoons flour
1 cup milk
½ cup oyster liquid

Dash of mace
1 pint oysters (1 dozen)
Sherry for thinning
2 tablespoons parsley, minced
Salt and pepper to taste
10-inch pie shell, baked
Piecrust dough

Sauté onions and celery in butter until golden and soft. In the same pan make a white sauce of the butter, flour, milk, and oyster liquid. Add thyme and mace. Stir in oysters and cook briefly until edges curl. Add sherry and stir for proper sauce consistency. Check seasonings and add salt and additional mace if desired. Add pepper and minced parsley. Stir thoroughly. Turn into prebaked pie shell. Cover with pastry and bake in a hot oven (400°) for 20 to 25 minutes, or until pastry is done and pie is bubbly. A lovely complement to baked country ham.

Planked Shad

The arrival of shad in April was always welcomed, and huge catches of fish were recorded in the eighteenth century. A great catch was noted on April 21, 1747: "Last Tuesday morning 9,000 shad were caught in the seines of Mr. Justice Cortelyou at the Narrows."

1 3- or 3½-pound shad	Pinch of salt and pepper
Hardwood plank, greased	Bacon strips
Melted butter	Lemon wedges

Clean and split the shad in half. Place skin-side-down on the greased plank. Nail down 1 strip of bacon laterally at the top section and another strip nearer the bottom. Sprinkle with a pinch of salt (if bacon is not used, more salt is needed) and pepper and brush again with melted butter. Prop up the plank at an outward angle from the hot coals on the open hearth. Place drip pan near the base to catch juices. The shad should be on the hearth for approximately 30 minutes, or until the flesh flakes easily when touched with a fork. Serve with potatoes pureed with 3 egg yolks and ½ cup of butter, and fresh spring asparagus.

THE TAVERN HEARTH

Beefsteak and Kidney Pie

A daily item found on the Tavern Bill of Fare, this traditionally English pie became one of George Washington's favorites.

4 small veal kidneys	1 onion, diced
1 cup claret wine	2 cups water
1 onion, sliced	½ cup celery, chopped
2 bay leaves	½ cup parsley, chopped
Salt and pepper to taste	2 teaspoons marjoram
1½ pounds rump or round steak, cut into 1-inch strips	1½ cups mushrooms, sliced
	Butter for sauté
Flour for dredging	Puff paste or biscuit dough
Bacon drippings	

With a sharp knife separate kidneys and remove fat and gristly membrane. Sprinkle with salt. Cover with claret, sliced onion, bay leaves, and pepper. Marinate for 2 hours. Pound strips of steak and dredge with flour. Melt bacon drippings, add diced onions, and cook until golden. Remove from skillet. In the skillet, brown the steak well. Drain kidneys, reserving marinade; dredge with flour and brown in the skillet, stirring carefully and adding bacon drippings if necessary. Add approximately 2 cups hot water and stir well. Add chopped celery, parsley, and marjoram. Simmer very slowly, covered, stirring occasionally, for about 1 hour, or until meats are tender. Sauté mushrooms in butter, straining the marinade into them. Add mixture to beef and kidneys. If gravy needs thickening, do so with flour and cold water. Pour into a deep pie dish. Cover with a crust of puff paste, or thin biscuit dough, and bake at 400° until brown, about 20 to 30 minutes. Serves 8.

A Made Dish of Chicken Curry

6 pounds chicken breasts	1 teaspoon each salt and pepper
3 large onions	4 firm apples
½ cup butter for sauté	2 tablespoons flour
4 cloves of garlic, minced	¼ cup butter
2 tablespoons curry	2 tablespoons sugar
4 tablespoons flour	1 teaspoon salt
1 cup white wine	4 tablespoons soured cream
2 cups chicken stock	1 tablespoon butter
Bouquet garni (1 bay leaf, 1 sprig marjoram, and 3 sprigs of parsley)	4 tablespoons flour
	3 tablespoons brandy
⅛ teaspoon thyme	2 tablespoons sherry

Parboil chicken breasts in order to remove bones in a quick, clean manner. Remove skins. Chop onions coarsely and sauté in ¼ pound butter until golden. Add boned breasts and sauté briefly until golden but not browned. Remove chicken to a platter. Add garlic to onions and immediately stir in curry and 4 tablespoons flour. Add wine, chicken stock, bouquet garni, thyme, salt, and pepper. Stir-cook until mixture starts to boil. Reduce heat. Add chicken, broken into large pieces, and cook for approximately 20 minutes.

Core but do not peel apples. Chop them into large diced pieces. Coat with flour. Brown in a skillet with ¼ cup butter. Sprinkle with sugar and 1 teaspoon salt. Cook until brown on all sides. Remove chicken and arrange pieces in buttered pudding dish or deep iron pan. Discard bouquet garni. Add cream to sauce. Adjust thickness of sauce with 1 tablespoon butter blended with 4 tablespoons of flour (*beurre manié*) to make a smooth, thick consistency. Arrange browned apples over the chicken. Stir brandy and sherry into the sauce and pour over the chicken and apples. Serves 12.

A statement of Washington's household expenses during three months of the year 1789 may be taken to show the dishes which appeared on the tables of that day. Among its items were butcher's meat, bacon, tongue, geese, ducks, turkeys, chickens, birds, scale fish, lobsters, crabs, oysters, cured fish, eggs, cheese, bread, biscuit, cake, vegetables, butter, ice cream, preserves, fruit, melons, nuts, citrons, and honey. The wine included Madeira, Claret, Champagne, Cherry, Arrack, Spirits, Brandy, Cordials, Porter, Beer, and Cider. Among these, the item for Madeira was the largest, that for beer being next in amount. The teas which he used were hyson and bohea, the expenditure for both of them being less than that for coffee.

Roots and Vegetables

To Ragoo French Beans

"*String and cut them, boil them tender, put a piece of butter worked in flour into your stew pan, in which fry a couple of sliced onions; then put in the beans, with a little nutmeg, pepper and salt, the yolk of an egg beat up with a little cream; stir them a minute or two, and send them to the table.*"   —The Lady's, Housewife's, and Cookmaid's
Art of Cookery, 1778

An Herb Sallad for the Tavern Bowl

*Use all lettuces, sorrel, salad burnet, tarragon, lovage, shallots, garlic
chives, chervil, watercress and parsley*

*To make this condiment, your poet begs, the powdered yellow of two
hard-boiled eggs.*
*Two boiled potatoes passed through kitchen sieve, smoothness and
softness to the salad give.*
*Let onion odours lurk within the bowl, and half suspected animate the
whole.*
*Of wondrous mustard add a single spoon. Distrust the condiment that
bites too soon.*
*But deem it not, thou man of herbs, a fault, to add a double quantity
of salt.*
*Fourtimes the spoon with oil of Lucca crown, and twice the vinegar
procured from town.*
*Lastly o'er the flowery compound, toss a magic soupspoon of Anchovy
sauce.*

Oh green and glorious, oh herbaceous treat.
T'would tempt the dying authority to eat.
*Backward to earth, he'd turn his weary soul, And plunge his fingers in
the sallad bowl,*
*Serenely full, the epicure would say, "Fate cannot harm me—I have
dined today!"*

—Sidney Smith, 1780

SPIDER

Breadstuffs

Spider Cornbread

A long-handled iron skillet with three short legs, or "spider," was placed on the hearth right over hot coals to bake this corn cake. As the coals cooled, they were removed with a long-handled iron "peel," and fresh glowing coals were replaced. In this way, Fraunces could maintain an even cooking temperature for slow cooking without burning the bottom of the bread.

1½ cups white cornmeal (prefer-
  ably water-ground)
1 tablespoon sugar
1 teaspoon salt

1 teaspoon baking soda
2 eggs, well beaten
2 cups buttermilk
1½ tablespoons melted butter

If not cooking on the hearth, preheat the oven to 450°. Put an iron skillet in the oven to warm. Sift together cornmeal, sugar, salt, and baking soda. Add the buttermilk to the beaten eggs; then stir into the cornmeal mixture until smooth. Add melted butter. Pour into the warm skillet, which has been well greased. Bake at 450° for 30 minutes. Serves 8.

New Year's Olykoeks

The tradition of holding open house on New Year's Day originated in New York with the Dutch, who served Cherry Bounce, koekjes, honey cakes, and olykoeks. The ball of sweetened dough was to become the American doughnut. To the Dutch, it was delectable "oily cake."

1 package dry yeast
½ cup warm water
¼ cup butter and lard mixed
1 cup sugar
1½ cups milk
3 eggs
7½ cups flour

1 teaspoon salt
1 teaspoon nutmeg
Citron, raisins, and 1 apple,
  chopped
Fat for deep frying
Sugar for sprinkling

Dissolve the yeast in the warm water. Heat butter and lard, sugar, and milk. Cool until lukewarm. Beat eggs. Add to milk mixture. Beat in 6½ cups of the flour in batches with the salt and nutmeg. Knead the remaining flour in. Place dough in a greased bowl. Cover with a towel and allow to double in bulk (approximately 2 hours). Punch down dough. Pat down dough on lightly floured board. Pinch off and form the dough into small balls with your hand. Place in the center of each ball a bit of raisins, citron, and apple. Allow to rise again, covered, on a floured pie board. Use a well-floured knife to remove, rolling with your hand to make them round again. Fry in deep fat for about 5 minutes, or until golden. Drain and sprinkle with sifted confectioner's sugar, or granulated sugar with cinnamon. Makes about 50 *olykoeks*.

Samuel Fraunces' Cranberry Bread

2 cups flour	¾ cup fresh orange juice
1 cup sugar	3 tablespoons corn oil
1 teaspoon baking soda	1 tablespoon grated orange rind
1 teaspoon cream of tartar	2 cups cranberries, chopped
1 teaspoon salt	½ cup walnuts or pecans, chopped
1 egg, well beaten	

Sift the first 5 ingredients. Combine liquid ingredients. Make a well in the sifted ingredients and pour in the liquids. Mix only to moisten. Fold in cranberries (which can be chopped in a blender), orange rind and nuts. Spoon into a 9″ x 5″ x 3″ greased and floured loaf pan. Spread evenly. Bake at 350° for 50 to 60 minutes. Remove immediately and cool on a rack. Extraordinarily moist and lovely.

A law was passed on March 1, 1788 which made tavern-keepers subject to fine and imprisonment should they allow cock-fighting, gaming, card-playing, dice, billiard tables or shuffle boards in their taverns.—New York in 1789

Crock-preserved Fruits

The hearty appetites of eighteenth-century Englishmen and their relatives in the middle colonies encouraged housewives to put down fruits in brandy or rum. The custom spread until preserved fruits became familiar on butt'ry shelves everywhere.

Take only well-ripened fragrant fruits, each as in season. First, thoroughly wash strawberries and soak them in rum (they will probably float for one day before they sink.) Then add cherries, gooseberries, red currants, raspberries, mirabelle plums, apricots, peaches, and if desired, sliced pears. For an extra touch of flavor, use fresh pineapple. DO NOT use apples, black currants, or blackberries. Use the same weight of sugar as of fruit, and to avoid any fermentation, half the liquid should be rum. Care should be taken to see that the fruits are always covered with liquid and that the jar is airtight. When a new layer of fruit in season is added, add more rum and the weight of the fruit in sugar. It takes 6 weeks for one layer to mature. Do not stir. After adding last layer of fruit, let it rest for 6 weeks. Stir well before you serve fruits. This is very nice with a sugared ham, but is cherished as a holiday dessert with freshly churned vanilla ice cream.

Pineapple Chutney

In New York fruits were cultivated with great assiduity. William Prince, nurseryman, in 1769, listed 28 varieties of plums, 25 of peaches, 23 of apples, and no less than 41 of pears. Still, not content with what their own orchards could supply, New Yorkers imported the fruits of the West Indies, and pineapples were regularly on the market.

2 pounds fresh pineapple, or 1 pound, 13-ounce can, crushed	1 teaspoon salt
2⅓ cups brown sugar	½ teaspoon ground cloves
1 cup dates, diced	½ teaspoon cinnamon
1 cup raisins	½ teaspoon ground allspice
1 tablespoon onion, minced	¼ teaspoon garlic powder
⅛ teaspoon pepper	1 cup cider vinegar
	1 cup almonds, sliced

Mix all ingredients and cook over low heat for 1 hour, or until very thick. Stir occasionally to prevent sticking. Seal in preserve glasses or store in a large crock. Appropriate not only as a meat complement, but for tea or breakfast as well.

Tavern Watermelon Pickle

Rind of 1 large watermelon
1 small bottle calcium hydroxide,
available in drugstores (flake of
lime—#40 Eli Lilly, .04-ounce
size)

1 cup water
1 cup cider vinegar
2 cups sugar
3 inches stick cinnamon
8 cloves

Cut the outer tough green skin and the red meat from the white inner
meat. Cut the white meat in small rectangular strips ½ inch wide.
Soak flake of lime and melon strips in 1 gallon of cold water overnight.
Drain and rinse until water runs clear. Weigh the melon strips. For
every pound of melon use the above quantities of water, vinegar, sugar,
and spices. Place spices in a kettle with the water and vinegar and boil
for 5 minutes. Add the strips. Boil for 30 minutes, or until the strips are
clear. Ladle them vertically into preserving glasses. Cover with the boiling vinegar mixture and seal. The flaked lime gives a crispness that
makes this pickle extraordinary. Best served chilled.

Uncommon Cakes and Pies

Charlottes

1 cup shortening
1 cup sugar
1 cup brown sugar
2 eggs, beaten
3 cups sifted flour
1½ teaspoons baking soda

½ teaspoon salt
2 teaspoons vanilla extract
1 cup dates, chopped
1 cup walnuts, chopped
Granulated sugar for dipping

Cream together the shortening and sugar and beat in the eggs. Sift the
dry ingredients together and add to the egg mixture. Beat until blended.
Add vanilla. Stir in dates and nuts. Blend with a strong wooden spoon.
Form into large flattened balls. Dip flattened tops in granulated sugar.
Place on a greased baking sheet 3 inches apart and bake at 375° for 12
to 15 minutes.

Queen's Cake

POTTERY PITCHER

This cake was named for Queen Charlotte, the wife of King George III, who as a young girl of seventeen had written an essay on the horrors of war, thereby winning the heart of the king. An unusual, uncommon cake.

Pour 1 cup boiling water over 1 cup chopped dates and 1 teaspoon baking soda and let stand while mixing the following:

2 cups sugar	3 cups sifted flour
½ cup butter	2 teaspoons baking soda
2 eggs, beaten	⅔ teaspoon salt
2 teaspoons vanilla extract	

Add this mixture to the dates and pour into a large pan, or a tube or Bundt pan. Bake for 35 minutes in a moderate oven (350°).

Frosting

5 tablespoons brown sugar	Flaked coconut and chopped or
5 tablespoons heavy cream	whole nuts for sprinkling
2 tablespoons butter	

Mix the ingredients. Boil for 3 minutes, cool, and spread on the cake. Sprinkle with flaked coconut and nuts.

Pearl Street Rum-Cream Pie

5 egg yolks	⅓ cup rum
1 cup sugar	1½ cups heavy cream
1 envelope unflavored gelatin	10-inch pie shell, baked
½ cup water	Shaved, unsweetened chocolate

Beat the egg yolks and sugar until light and fluffy. Sprinkle the gelatin into the water in a saucepan and bring almost to a boil until dissolved. Stir the gelatin into the egg yolk mixture. Cool. Add rum slowly, beating constantly. Whip the cream to soft peaks; fold into the gelatin mixture. Cool until the mixture begins to set, then pour into a prepared crumb or paste shell. Garnish with shaved chocolate.

Sweet Dishes and Confections

The ingredients of elaborate dishes were readily obtainable by Samuel Fraunces in the city shops, for the groceries of the day were almost as varied as now. All kinds of spice, candied and dried fruits, preserves and pickles, both imported and native, were procurable, as well as "double and single Refined Loaf-Sugar, Powder and Shop-Sugars, and Sugar-Candy at Reasonable Rates."

Floating Island, or Snow Eggs

Custard

2 to 2¼ cups light cream
4 egg yolks
½ cup sugar
1 teaspoon vanilla extract

Meringue

4 egg whites
Dash of salt
½ cup sugar
1 teaspoon almond flavoring

Caramel

⅔ cup sugar
⅓ cup water

First scald the cream for the custard in a shallow skillet. To prepare the meringue, whip the egg whites with salt until stiff. Gradually beat in ½ cup sugar and almond flavoring. With a large spoon, scoop out egg-shaped portions of the meringue. Smooth with another spoon and drop the eggs into the hot cream and poach for 3 to 4 minutes, carefully turning once. Lift with a skimmer onto a paper towel.

To prepare the custard, beat the egg yolks with ½ cup sugar until fluffy. Add the vanilla. Strain the hot cream, adding enough additional cream to make 2 cups. Add the cream mixture slowly to the egg mixture. Place over boiling water and cook, stirring constantly, until the custard is thick enough to coat a wooden spoon. If the custard comes close to a boil it will curdle. Pour into a serving compote and chill for 3 to 4 hours.

Prepare the caramel half an hour before serving. Combine sugar and water and bring to boil; then simmer for 10 minutes or until the syrup turns tea-brown. Pour into a separate bowl. Assemble the chilled floating meringue islands over the custard and drizzle the lukewarm caramel over the meringues with a small spoon. You may present this as a grand dessert, ladling the meringue onto individual plates and spooning the custard around it.

Pistachio Cream

½ pound pistachio nuts, shelled   2 cups light cream
1 tablespoon brandy   3 egg yolks, well beaten

Set aside some whole nuts for garnish. Grind the rest in a mortar as fine as possible. In a small pan blend together the nuts and brandy. In a separate bowl beat the cream with the beaten egg yolks and stir into the nut and brandy mixture. Cook over low heat, stirring constantly until the mixture thickens. Remove from heat and pour into a glass compote. Cover and chill. Stud the surface with the remaining nuts.

Drams and Punches

The bar was the most interesting furnishing of the tap room, usually made with a portcullis grate, which could be closed if necessary. A broad sign usually hung near the grate reminding patrons to "Mind your P's and Q's"— pints and quarts—an admonition still in use today.

Fish House Punch

A potent, traditional punch originating with the men of The Fish House— a hunting and fishing club formed in 1732. Purportedly, George Washington was a guest at the club, shared the Fish House Punch, and made no entry in his diary for the next three days. Each year on his birthday they drink a toast "to the president."

1 Fifth lemon or lime juice   1 Fifth brandy
1 cup sugar   1 cup peach brandy
1 Fifth water   2 peaches, peeled and sliced
2 Fifths Jamaican rum

In a bowl empty the rum and brandy bottles and use one for measuring the water and lime juice. Dissolve the sugar in the water and stir in the lemon or lime juice. Mix in the other ingredients. Allow the mixture to mellow for a few hours, or overnight, before using. In order to keep dilution to a minimum, chill the mixture thoroughly before pouring it over a good-sized chunk of ice in a punch bowl. Garnish with peaches. Serves approximately 40 4-ounce punch glasses. *Note:* A good rum to use is a mixture of 75 percent to 80 percent Light or Golden Rum, and 20 percent to 25 percent Myers Jamaica Rum. Double the water content if a less potent punch is preferred, but always allow for the melting of the ice.

Cherry Bounce

When New York became the nation's first capital, George Washington held Open House to the public on New Year's Day. Cherry Bounce, which combines spirits with the native American sour cherry, was the New Year's Day drink.

12 pounds cherries, pitted   1 quart each rum and brandy
4 pounds sugar to
   each gallon of juice

Mash the cherries and crack the stones. Place cherries in a large stone crock. Add sugar and spirits; stir well. Cover the crock and let stand for three months, stirring occasionally during the first month. Strain and bottle. Improves with age. Makes 4 quarts.

"Cheap rum at 75 cents or 50 cents a Gallon answers equally as well as the best Spirit for a Bogus or Bounce."

Mock Clary

To 1 gallon claret wine, add enough honey to sweeten considerably. Add several pieces of cinnamon bark or sticks, some whole cloves, and freshly ground allspice. Place in a large pot hanging over the fire or resting on the hearth comfortably close to the fire to warm well. Do not boil or burn. Before it gets too warm, taste for the perfect blending of spices and honey, as it may need more honey. Serve in warmed cups.

Near the tavern fireplace were drawers set for pipes and tobacco, and sometimes the tobacco shelves were in the entry over the front door. Hanging near the tobacco shelf were slender pipe tongs, with which the smoker lifted a coal from the fireplace to light his pipe. Sometimes a comfortier, a little brazier of metal containing hot coals, was passed after dinner for pipe lighting.

Punch for Chambermaids

"Four parts brandy, two parts white wine, one part lime juice sharpened with a little orange juice; sugar to taste."—Cyclopedia, or an Universal Dictionary of Arts and Sciences, 1741

A Yard of Flannel

The passengers and drivers of the stage-coach would have "wrapped" themselves in A Yard of Flannel before boarding at the door of Fraunces Tavern.

"To make a quart of flip—Put the ale on the fire to warm, and beat up three or four eggs with four ounces of moist sugar, a tea-spoonful of grated nutmeg or ginger, and a quartern of good old rum or brandy. When the ale nearly boils put it into one pitcher, and the rum, eggs, &c. into another; turn it from one to another till it is as smooth as cream. This is called a Yard of Flannel."—The Cook's Own Book

Today's fireplace poker was known as a flip-dog or loggerhead in the 18th Century. It was generally found in the hot coals, ready to be plunged into a flip or a "yard of flannel"—or to meet the enemy if need be—hence the term "at loggerheads"

British Evacuation Day
Reception for George Washington and French Ambassador Luzerne
Fraunces Tavern November 25, 1783

More than a hundred generals, officers, and distinguished civilians sat down to table in the Long Room with Governor Clinton and his guests of honor, where a profusion of elegant foods was presented. In addition to an exceeding amount of punch and sprauce, or spruce beer, one hundred and thirty-three bottles of Madeira, port, and claret were consumed, and eight lights, sixteen wine glasses and six decanters were broken. The toasting was robust and there were thirteen toasts in all.

In the evening the Queen's Head was brightly illuminated. Bonfires blazed at every corner, and as their contribution to the general joy, Washington and the French Ambassador superintended a display of fireworks on the nearby bowling green.

It was on this day that the old sign bearing the portrait of Queen Charlotte was taken down and consigned to the rubbish heap, and the new sign "Fraunces Tavern," put up. It stands there still, bearing an image of the inn's most renowned patron—George Washington.

FISH HOUSE PUNCH

CRAB CLAWS WITH DILL MUSTARD SAUCE   PÂTÉ MAISON FRAUNCES

CHEDDAR BISCUITS

FRESH SORREL SOUP WITH SIPPETS

COLD POACHED STRIPED BASS WITH CUCUMBER SAUCE

WHITE WINE

MUSHROOM PASTY   BEEFSTEAK AND KIDNEY PIE

ROASTED LAMB WITH OYSTER FORCEMEAT   BAKED SMOKED COUNTRY HAM

MADEIRA MOLDED WINE JELLY

YAM AND CHESTNUT PIPPINS   A PILAU OF RICE   RAGOO FRENCH BEANS

SKILLET CRANBERRIES

WATERMELON PICKLE   PEAR HONEY

SALLY LUNN MOLDED BUTTER PRINTS

CLARET

CARROT TEA CAKE   TIPSY SQUIRE   TANSY PIE

WHISKEY NUT BALLS   CHOCOLATE TRUFFLES

APPLES   HAZELNUTS   PEARS   ALMONDS   GRAPES

TOBACCO   COFFEE

MADEIRA   PORT

Thirteenth toast: "May the remembrance of this day be a lesson to princes."

Washington's farewell to his officers on the afternoon of December 4, 1783, was his last visit to Fraunces Tavern until he became President. Filling his glass with wine, Washington toasted the 44 war officers present: "With a heart full of love and gratitude, I now take leave of you. I most devoutly wish that your latter days may be as prosperous and happy as your former ones have been glorious and honorable. I cannot come to each of you, but shall feel obliged if each of you will come and take me by the hand." Colonel Talmadge, aide to General Washington wrote, "I do not think that there were ever so many broken hearts in New York as . . . that night."

Fanny Pierson Crane
of Montclair, New Jersey

Israel Crane House

Born just three years before the Declaration of Independence was signed, Fanny Pierson Crane and her husband, Israel Crane, were members of the generation that formed and built the new republic. Both were young children through the revolutionary war years; although they may have seen Continental soldiers marching from New York toward the winter encampment at Jockey Hollow, New Jersey, in 1776 or 1777, as children they could scarcely have grasped the significance of the troop movements they were witnessing.

Fanny Pierson was born in 1773, the daughter of a physician who lived in the small rural community of Doddtown (now East Orange), New Jersey. Even then, New Jersey was a crossroads, and traffic from the bustling Quaker city of Philadelphia had to pass through the state to reach New York City. Doddtown was a prosperous and growing town, and Fanny's father was one of its prominent citizens.

Israel Crane, a student at Princeton University, probably met Fanny at the Presbyterian Church, where both families were members. Israel was the son of a wealthy farmer whose ancestors left England for Connecticut and settled Newark with Robert Treat. Seven generations later, he inherited eighty-six acres at the foot of First Mountain, where the farming village was named Cranetown and was later to be known as Montclair.

He married the engaging Fanny Pierson, and, in 1796 at the age of twenty-two, impressed by the homes of wealthy merchants and ship-owners of Salem and Portsmouth, he built for his new bride an impos-ing Federal mansion more grand than any other dwelling in the village. Although neighbors predicted that "such wanton waste of hard-earned money would drive Mr. Crane to ruin and the poor house, and serve him right," no such disaster occurred, and the Cranes spent all their married life in the house. The young couple with their growing family soon filled the many rooms.

Israel Crane became an entrepreneur—a new breed of men who, af-ter the Revolution, saw the opportunities for developing business and industry in an expanding economy. He was the proprietor of Crane-town's first general store, and he organized the Newark and Pompton Turnpike—the area's first and longest toll road, which linked the port of Newark with the growing towns, farmlands, and natural inland re-sources. His brownstone quarry, which employed 300 men, his cider mill next to his store, and his cotton mills, which utilized the power of the Passaic Falls, contributed to his prosperity to such a degree that his neighbors dubbed him "King Crane."

PHOTOGRAPH BY C. P. OWEN

Conscious of her husband's role as Cranetown's most influential citizen, Fanny Crane herself became a social leader who liked to entertain in a manner befitting her family's prominence. Her sewing circle met regularly for tea in the front parlor, and she often planned formal entertainments and an occasional grand collation. Her greatest pleasure, however, was to prepare cherished foods for her husband, family, and small circle of friends, and she became known as an accomplished cook and hostess.

In spite of his affluence, Israel Crane cared little for material things. Fanny, on the other hand, had taste and cared very much about nice possessions. She selected all the furnishings, and her husband never questioned the resulting expense. Their acres were bountiful, and in the fall of the year—the time for harvesting and hog slaughtering—all the gardenstuffs and meats that were not smoked, preserved, pickled, or stored in the root cellar, were hung from the kitchen rafters to dry. Fanny enjoyed the obvious advantages to being a storekeeper's wife and could have afforded the luxury of imported pins, ribbons, and laces, exotic spices and China teas, the blue-and-white Cantonware, and English tea accoutrements.

Fanny knew much about the curing properties of medicinal herbs. She had a sizable herb garden, and was well known in the village for her herbal teas and infusions. Neighbors came to her for medical advice, although it may have been her sympathetic and confidential manner as much as her curative remedies that attracted their solicitations.

Her main interest throughout her marriage was the loving care she could give her husband and their five children.

The Israel Crane House

Israel Crane's house was a two-and-one-half-story mansion built of wood in the Federal style that became popular in postcolonial America. With a front and back parlor, dining room, and kitchen on the first floor, and four bedrooms on the second floor, the Crane house was the most elaborate structure in Cranetown. Israel's son James, who inherited the house, remodeled it in the early 1840s in Greek Revival style, raising and flattening the peaked roof to make the third floor a full story high. He added a roof-line cornice and an entrance flanked by Ionic columns. Probably earlier, a separate two-story kitchen had been constructed behind the house, linked by a covered passageway. The house was rescued from near demolition in 1965 by the Montclair Historical Society, which moved the building a few blocks from its original site and restored it to its Federal elegance.

Soups and Savories

Scotch Mutton Broth

Leftover lamb bones with some meat still on them, or several lamb shanks
10 cups water (more if needed)
2 leeks, coarsely chopped
2 onions, coarsely chopped
3 stalks of celery, coarsely chopped
1 carrot, coarsely chopped

1 small turnip, coarsely chopped
Salt and pepper to taste
½ cup barley
Bay leaf
2 teaspoons curry powder (or more)
Fresh parsley, chopped

Make a stock with the water, bones, or shanks, and vegetables. Season with salt and pepper. After 1½ hours add the barley and bay leaf. Simmer for another hour. Add curry powder if desired. Twenty minutes before serving, put in some chopped, fresh parsley. The soup should be thick and spicy. Garnish with chopped parsley. Serve with freshly sliced apples, or an apple pie with cheddar cheese for dessert.

(Adapted from A *New System of Domestic Cookery*, 1808)

Mushroom Savories

3 medium onions, chopped
¾ cup butter
2 pounds fresh mushrooms, finely chopped
4 tablespoons fresh thyme, or 2 tablespoons dried

2 teaspoons salt
½ cup parsley, chopped
¾ cup white wine, or sherry
Piecrust dough (make two batches of the double-crust receipt on page 211)

Sauté onions in butter until golden. Add mushrooms, thyme, salt, and parsley. Simmer for 5 minutes. Add wine, or sherry. Simmer until liquid is almost absorbed. Cool.

Roll pastry dough very thin and cut into 2½-inch circles. Place filling on half of each circle. Fold over and crimp. Moisten the edges. Bake on an ungreased cookie sheet in a moderate oven (350°) until golden brown. Makes approximately 200 savories.

Jersey Skillet Apples

"I have seen orchards laden with fruit to admiration, their very limbs torn to pieces with the weight, and most delicious to the taste and lovely to behold," wrote one early New Jersey visitor.—U. P. Hedrick, A History of Horticulture in America

6 large apples, Red Delicious or Cortland	1 cup water
1 cup sugar	1 cup rose-geranium-flavored applejack

Core and peel the top third of each apple. In a large iron skillet combine the peelings with sugar, water, and rose geranium flavored applejack. Boil for 10 minutes, strain, and return to the skillet.

Place a lightly buttered rose geranium leaf in each apple and arrange in pan with juices. Cook the apples over moderate heat, turning them frequently until they are tender but hold their shape. Ladle pan juices over apples as they cook. Serves 6.

Rose Geranium Applejack

To 1 pint applejack add 4 or 5 mature rose geranium leaves, letting the combination steep for 3 weeks. If the aroma and strength are still not suitable, remove the old leaves and add new ones, steeping for another week. This infusion will be most enjoyable added to sliced fruit, compotes, custards, meringue toppings, meat marinades, and basting sauces.

Cheddar Biscuits

½ cup butter	½ teaspoon salt
½ pound sharp unprocessed cheddar cheese, grated	¼ teaspoon cayenne
1½ cups flour	Almonds or pecans, blanched

Cream the butter and cheese and mix in flour, salt, and pepper. Roll into balls the diameter of a half dollar. Chill overnight.

Slice about ⅓ to ½ inch thick. Press half an almond or pecan in the center of each biscuit. Use an ungreased cookie sheet sprinkled lightly with salt. Bake for 7 or 8 minutes at 350°. Makes 6 dozen. These keep beautifully in a closed tin.

Fish, Meat, and Fowl

Baked Elizabethtown Crab

Although not as plentiful as the oyster, crab was nevertheless found in local waters throughout the middle colonies. Here it is utilized in an elegant made-dish.

1 pound white crab meat	4 tablespoons sherry
4 tablespoons butter	½ tablespoon nutmeg, grated
4 tablespoons flour	¾ cup sharp cheese, grated
1 cup cream	½ tablespoon mace
Salt and pepper to taste	Fresh parsley, chopped

Flake the crab meat well. Make a cream sauce with the butter, flour, and cream. Add salt, pepper, and sherry. Remove from fire and add the crab meat and nutmeg. Pour the mixture into a buttered iron pan. Sprinkle with grated cheddar cheese and powdered mace. Bake in a moderate oven (350°) until the cheese melts. Do not overcook. When ready to serve, quickly brown with a red hot salamander or run under the broiler. Serves 4.

Dinner in eighteenth-century New Jersey was described by a visitor, Julian Niemcewicz: "The meal consists of the following. The first course, two or three roast capons with a sauce of butter, cooked oysters, etc., a roast beef, some boiled mutton, some fish or a ham. The second course a Pouding or tart or Custards or blanc-manger and some preserves. The tablecloth is removed and fruits, almonds, grapes, chestnuts and wine are then served. One drinks the health of the President, the Vice-President, and Congress. The ladies retire; the gentlemen remain for hours in order to chat and drink toasts. Finally they join the ladies and take coffee and tea."—Julian Niemcewicz, Under Their Vine and Fig Tree, *1797–99*

Beefe Steake Pudding

1 medium onion, finely chopped
Beef drippings or butter for browning
1 pound top round steak in ½-inch pieces
¾ cup beef broth
¼ cup tomato juice
½ teaspoon Worcestershire sauce
Salt and pepper to taste
1 tablespoon butter
1 tablespoon flour
A few pieces of fresh tomato, peeled and seeded

Cook onion in drippings until clear. Add meat to pan and brown. Pour on broth, tomato juice, and Worcestershire sauce and season to taste. Cover pan and simmer gently until meat is tender. Thicken with butter rubbed in flour (*beurre manié*), and fold in the tomato pieces. Set aside. Prepare Yorkshire pudding batter.

Yorkshire Pudding Batter

1 cup flour
½ teaspoon salt
1 cup milk
2 eggs

Sift flour with salt into the bowl. Make a well in the center and add milk to the well. Then add eggs to milk. Beat vigorously for several minutes until batter is smooth and bubbly.

Cover bottom of a 1½-quart casserole with melted butter or beef drippings. Put in a hot oven until it sizzles. Pour half the quantity of batter into the dish, or about ½-inch deep. Place in a 450° oven and bake until puffed and set, about 15 minutes. Spread meat and gravy mixture on the pudding and cover with the remaining half of batter. Continue to cook in a hot oven for 10 to 15 minutes. The outside should be crisp and golden, the inside soft. Serves 6.

Native Roasted Turkey with Sausage and Sage Dressing

In the New Jersey fields and woods were grouse, quail, passenger pigeon, woodcock, and the bronzed native—wild turkey, which sometimes weighed as much as fifty pounds.

14-pound oven-ready turkey
1½ large loaves of stale country, or French, bread
Milk for soaking
2 large onions, finely chopped
3 stalks of celery, finely cut
Butter for sauté
1¾ pounds fresh country sausage
1 teaspoon salt

1 teaspoon pepper
3 tablespoons fresh thyme, or 3 teaspoons dried
6 large sprigs parsley, chopped
18 ripe pitted olives, cut small
8 sprigs of fresh sage, chopped, or 3 teaspoons dried
Butter and applejack (optional) for basting

Wipe turkey inside and out with a damp cloth. Soak bread in enough milk to moisten it. Sauté onions and celery together in butter until soft but not brown. Pour into a large mixing bowl. In the same skillet slightly brown the sausage; then break it into pieces with a fork. Add all remaining ingredients and stuff turkey. Sew and truss it well. Place in a large roasting pan and cover with several layers of cheesecloth soaked in butter. Bake in a moderate oven (325°) for 5 to 5¼ hours, or until the leg joint can be moved up and down with ease. Baste frequently through the cheesecloth, during the roasting period with butter, natural juices, and applejack. Remove cloth during the last half hour to allow bird to brown. Garnish with fresh sage and small, polished crab apples.

Roots and Vegetables

A salt was placed in the center of the Board. Persons of honor were seated above the salt, others below the salt; thus the expression "Worth your salt."

Maced Green Beans

4 to 6 cups fresh green beans
4 tablespoons sweet butter

Salt and pepper to taste
1½ teaspoons mace

Swish the beans in cold water and snip off the ends. To make them uniform, slice the larger ones lengthwise down the flat side. Drop beans by the handful into 3 quarts of rapidly boiling, lightly salted water. Bring water back to a boil before adding another handful of beans. Boil rapidly for 6 to 8 minutes, uncovered. Test for tenderness, drain, and return to the kettle. Add sweet butter and season lightly with salt and pepper. Sprinkle generously with mace and take to the warming-kitchen table. Serves 8.

TREENWARE SALT

Pickles and Preserves

Tomato-Ginger Preserves

1 pound red tomatoes
1 pound sugar
2 lemons, thinly sliced and seeded

2 ounces crystalized ginger, chopped

Scald, skin, and slice the tomatoes. Cover them with the sugar and permit them to stand for 12 hours. Drain the juice and boil it until the syrup falls from a spoon in heavy drops. Add the tomatoes, sliced lemons, and ginger. Cook the preserves until they are thick and clear. Pack in hot jars and seal. Makes 3 half-pints.

TIN MOLD

Flowers and Fruit in White Wine Jelly

3 envelopes unflavored gelatin
1 cup water
1 cup sugar
1 bottle white wine (4/5 quart)
4 tablespoons fresh lemon juice, strained

3 well-washed damask, rugosa, or moss roses (or deep-red modern roses in full bloom)
Seedless grapes
Rose leaves

Heat gelatin and water in a medium saucepan until dissolved. Add sugar and white wine. Heat until the sugar is melted and the mixture steams. Stir in strained lemon juice. Pour ¼ inch of the gelatin mixture into an 8-inch ring mold. Set in freezer for 10 minutes, or until just softly firm. Press in roses, grapes, and a few rose leaves in a pleasing pattern. Pour a small amount of mixture on top but not too much or the flowers will float. Place in the freezer for another 10 minutes. Then, very slowly pour remaining mixture into mold. Return to the freezer for 10 minutes more. Remove to refrigerator. When firm, unmold on a platter. Serve plain with fish or fowl. Other flowers, herbs, and fruits may be substituted for the roses: Gilly flowers (dianthus) and strawberries; pot marigold, nasturtiums, and lemon balm. Serves 8 to 10.

Wine Jelly

"Take 4 calves feet, and wash them well without taking off the hoofs (or instead of that 1 oz. isinglass, or 1 oz. of deer horns). These feet must be well boiled the day before they are wanted. After taking off the grease put the jelly in a casserole."—early manuscript cookbook

Fruit in Jelly

"Take a bason, put into it half a pint of clear stiff calf's foot jelly, and when it be set and stiff, lay in three fine ripe peaches, and a bunch of grapes with the stalk upwards. Put over them a few vine leaves, and then fill up your bowl with jelly. Let it stand till the next day, and then set your bason to the brim in hot water. As soon as you perceive it gives way from the bason, lay your dish over it, and turn your jelly carefully upon it. You may use flowers for your garnish."—John Farley, The London Art of Cookery, *1811*

Breadstuffs

Crane House Pumpkin Bread

Pumpkins, or pompions as they were called, were grown between corn stalks,
thus utilizing space and balancing the soil. Indians taught the settlers how
to dry and string the pumpkins for winter use.

1 cup corn oil	1 teaspoon nutmeg
4 eggs, beaten	1 teaspoon cinnamon
⅔ cup water	2 teaspoons baking soda
2 cups canned pumpkin	2 cups sugar
3⅓ cups sifted flour	1 cup golden raisins
1½ teaspoons salt	1 cup nuts, chopped

Grease and flour 2 long loaf pans, or 3 8″ x 5″ x 3″ loaf pans. Mix corn
oil, eggs, water, and pumpkin. Add flour, salt, nutmeg, cinnamon, baking
soda, and sugar. To the combined mixture, add raisins and nuts. Bake
for 1 hour at 350°. Will stay moist for days.

Beehive-Oven Apricot Bread

2 cups dried apricots	3 cups flour
1 cup boiling water	2 teaspoons baking soda
4 tablespoons butter	½ teaspoon salt
1½ cups sugar	1 cup pecans, chopped
2 eggs, lightly beaten	

Cut dried apricots into pieces with scissors, cover with boiling water,
and let stand for 1 hour. Cream together the butter and sugar; then add
eggs, apricots, and the water in which the apricots were soaked. Sift
together flour, baking soda, and salt and blend the dry ingredients into
the batter. Add nut meats. Pour into 1 8″ x 5″ x 3″ or 2 small buttered
bread pans. Bake in a slow oven (325°) for 1 hour, or until the bread
tests done.

IRON BREADPAN

Uncommon Cakes and Pies

Rolled Holiday Cakes

½ pound butter
1 cup sugar
3 eggs, well beaten
1 teaspoon mace

⅓ cup brandy
4 cups sifted flour
Almonds, chopped
Sugar for sprinkling

TIN CUTTER

Cream butter and sugar until light and fluffy. Add the eggs and flavorings. Add flour and beat or knead until smooth. Roll the dough into 2 rolls, wrap in wax paper, and chill for several hours.

Using 1 roll at a time, roll the dough out on lightly floured board until ⅟₁₆ inch thick. Cut with cookie cutters. Place the cookies carefully on unbuttered cookie sheets, sprinkle with chopped almonds and granulated sugar, and with a toothpick make a hole at the top for stringing. Candied angelica can be used for eyes and buttons. Bake at 375° until light golden, usually 8 to 10 minutes. Makes several dozen.

Cobblestones

½ cup butter or margarine
1 cup light brown sugar
1 egg, beaten
1 teaspoon vanilla extract
1½ cups sifted flour

1 teaspoon cinnamon
½ teaspoon baking soda
½ teaspoon salt
½ cup white raisins

Cream together the butter or margarine and sugar. Add the beaten egg and vanilla. Sift together flour, cinnamon, baking soda, and salt and stir well into the creamed mixture. Fold in the raisins. Drop from a heaping tablespoon onto a greased cookie sheet 3 inches apart. Bake at 375° for 12 to 15 minutes. Makes 1 dozen 3-inch little cakes.

Maids of Honor

1 cup almond paste	5 tablespoons melted butter
Sherry	½ cup almonds, ground
4 eggs	Rich piecrust dough
1 cup sugar	Red currant jelly, preferably home-
1 teaspoon nutmeg	made, or strawberry jam
4 tablespoons flour	

Moisten almond paste with enough sherry to mix into a medium-paste consistency. Set aside to mellow for at least 1 hour. Butter smallest size muffin pans very well. Beat eggs for 5 minutes; then gradually add sugar and nutmeg mixed with flour. Mix in melted butter, ground almonds, and moistened almond paste.

Line muffin tins with dough. Add ¼ teaspoon jelly or jam to center of each pastry and cover with almond filling. Do not overfill. Bake at 350° for 25 minutes, or until lightly browned on top but not dark in color. Turn out of pans to cool. Makes 2 dozen.

Glazed Orange Cake

Rind of 1 orange, chopped	2 cups flour
1 cup golden raisins	1 teaspoon baking soda
½ cup butter	½ teaspoon salt
2 cups sugar	1 cup buttermilk
2 eggs, beaten	Orange juice for moistening
1 teaspoon vanilla extract	Brandy for flavoring

Combine the chopped orange rind and raisins. Blend butter with 1 cup sugar. Add eggs, vanilla, and chopped mixture. Sift flour with baking soda and salt. Add to the blended mixture alternately with the buttermilk. Turn into a well-greased 9″ x 9″ x 2″ pan, or 2 well-greased loaf pans. Bake at 350° for 30 to 40 minutes.

Moisten 1 cup sugar in orange juice. Flavor with brandy. Spread glaze on warm cake and sizzle with a red hot salamander or peel. If these utensils are not available, place briefly under a high broiler until the glaze sizzles. Slice into small squares and serve warm with herbed tea sprigged with orange mint.

The salamander was the animal in mythology that could go through fire unharmed; thus, the eighteenth-century name given to the glazing tool.

Tipsy Squire

In Fanny Crane's day, this elegant dessert was made with stale cake restored to full flavor with liberal sprinklings of rum. It was served to the squire or parson and honored guests, who became a little "tipsy" after abundant helpings.

3 dozen Savoy or Naples biscuits (lady fingers) or 2 sponge cakes
Rum for sprinkling
1 envelope unflavored gelatin
4 tablespoons cold water
8 egg yolks
1 cup sugar

2 cups milk, scalded
1 teaspoon vanilla extract
1 tablespoon almond extract
2 cups heavy cream, whipped
Toasted almond halves
Freshly grated nutmeg

Line 2 compotes with the Savoy biscuits, or sponge cake cut and split in finger sized strips. Sprinkle generously with rum, and let soak for at least 1 hour.

Soak gelatin in cold water. Beat egg yolks until light in color; then gradually add sugar, beating constantly. Add a little of the yolk mixture slowly to the scalded milk; then add the milk to the yolks, stirring constantly. Add vanilla and almond extract. Rest a pottery bowl in a large pan of boiling water so that the bottom of the bowl is approximately 2 inches above the water. Cook, stirring constantly until the mixture is smooth, slightly thickened, and coats a wooden spoon. The mixture should have the consistency of thin to medium cream sauce and will thicken as it cools. Remove from heat and add softened gelatin, stirring until dissolved. Cool, stirring occasionally to prevent a thickened layer from forming on the top. Just before assembling the Tipsy Squire, fold in the whipped cream.

Spoon custard into the center of each compote and spike the surface with toasted almonds so the entire area is covered with nuts about 1 inch apart. Pile whipped cream in tall peaks about 1 inch apart around the outside rim of the compotes. Dust with freshly grated nutmeg and decorate each peak of cream with a candied violet or rose.

Carrot Tea Cake

¾ cup, plus 2 tablespoons corn oil
2 cups sugar
4 eggs, beaten
2 cups raw carrots, finely grated
2 cups flour

1 teaspoon salt
2 teaspoons baking soda
3 teaspoons cinnamon
1 teaspoon nutmeg
Sugar for sprinkling

Mix together oil, sugar, eggs, and carrots. Add flour, salt, baking soda, cinnamon, and nutmeg. Bake in a 9-inch springform pan at 350° for 1 hour. A Bundt pan may be used instead if greased well. Serve with a dusting of sugar and slice very thin.

Whiskey Apple Pie

And there they hung them for the flies
'til mother turned them into pies.

12 ounces dried apples
1 cup whiskey, or applejack (preferred)
1 cup cider
1 cup brown sugar

1 teaspoon cinnamon
1 teaspoon ginger
Generous grating of nutmeg
9-inch pieshell, unbaked
Butter for dotting

Soak dried apples in 1 cup whiskey, or applejack, and 1 cup cider for several hours, or overnight. If apples are still quite dry, add enough cider to barely cover and cook for 10 minutes over medium heat to soften. Add brown sugar, cinnamon, ginger, and nutmeg to apples and juice. Place mixture in the pastry shell and dot with butter. Bake in a preheated 400° oven for 20 to 25 minutes. Watch carefully and lace with extra cider if necessary. This pie has no top crust and will be flat in appearance.

Tansy Pie

PASTRY JIG

Beloved tansy, first herb to greet the springtime, was used for spring tonics needed after long, hard winters. Here it is used not only for flavoring but also as the green coloring agent common in eighteenth-century cooking.

6 eggs, separated
2 cups heavy cream
½ cup sugar
½ cup white wine, or sherry
¼ pound Savoy or Naples biscuits (lady fingers), broken up

½ tablespoon nutmeg
3 sprigs of fresh or dried tansy (a few drops of green food coloring are optional)
10-inch pieshell, unbaked

Place egg yolks in a saucepan and beat slightly. Stir in cream, sugar, and sherry; then add biscuits and nutmeg. Cook, stirring until the mixture thickens. Add green coloring if desired, but give preference to tansy pressed in a stone mortar until it becomes pulpy and the juices are evident. Beat egg whites until they form stiff peaks and fold into the hot cream mixture. Pour into the pieshell. Bake at 450° for 10 minutes; then reduce to 350° and bake for 30 minutes more. The pie will be puffy and golden but may sink somewhat as it cools. Garnish with rounded mounds of whipped cream sprigged with fresh tansy and dusted with nutmeg. You may wish to take it to the table on a footed cake stand.

Original

"Beat seven eggs, yolks and whites separately; add a pint of cream, near the same spinach juice, and a little tansy juice gained by pounding in a stonemortar; a quarter of a pound of Naples biscuit, sugar to taste, a glass of white wine, and some nutmeg. Set all in a saucepan, just to thicken, over the fire; then put into a dish, line with paste to turn out and bake it."—Charles Carter, The Complete Practical Cook, 1730

Sweet Dishes and Confections

Candied Peel

Cut rind of 8 oranges into quarters. Cover with cold water. Bring slowly to the boiling point. Remove pan from fire. Drain well. Repeat this process, boiling the orange peel in a total of 5 waters. Drain well each time. With scissors, cut into strips or leaf designs. Make a syrup with ¼ cup water and ½ cup sugar. Add the peel and boil until all the syrup is absorbed. Cool briefly. Roll the peel in granulated sugar and spread to dry on waxed paper. When thoroughly dry, the peel may be dipped at one end in chocolate coating. Peel may also be rolled in freshly grated coconut, then sugared. Store in airtight tins, or freeze.

Chocolate Coating

In a shallow pan over warm water place 4 ounces semisweet chocolate, 2 tablespoons butter, and 1-inch square of paraffin. When melted and blended, add 5 drops of vanilla extract. Remove from heat and dip the end of the peel quickly into coating. Return to waxed paper to dry. Cool before storing or freezing.

SUGAR CUTTER

Whiskey Nut Balls

50 pecan halves	2 pounds confectioners sugar
100-proof Bourbon (enough to cover nutmeats)	5 squares or 5 ounces semisweet chocolate
¼ pound butter, softened	1-inch square of paraffin

Soak the pecans in a jar overnight covered with bourbon. Place 1 box of sugar and the butter in a bowl and mix. In another bowl mix bourbon drained from the nuts and the other box of sugar. Combine contents of the 2 bowls. Chill the mixture. Roll into balls with a nut in the center of each: then chill. Coat balls in chocolate that has been melted together with a 1-inch piece of paraffin. These special confections should be stored in a tin in a cool place. They will disappear if you turn your head. Makes 50.

LOWESTOFT BOWL

Drams and Punches

Empire Room Punch

Juice and rind of 10 lemons
1 bottle rum
1 bottle brandy
1 bottle port wine

1 bottle white wine (or strong tea)
½ pint Curaçao
3 cups sugar

Take the rind from the squeezed lemons and add it to stock containing all other ingredients. Stir well. Let stand for a couple of hours. Strain and bottle the stock in ordinary wine bottles. When punch is needed, take 8 bottles of club soda to 4 bottles of stock, with plenty of ice. Stir well and serve. Will serve 25 to 30 people. Serve in a punch bowl and float roses on the top.

New Jersey Stone Fence Punch

Potent Applejack, or "Jersey Lightning," was made in Cranetown stills. Two cups and a man can leap a stone fence.

1 quart applejack
1 quart fresh sweet cider
1 quart cold sparkling water

Lemon or orange slices
Cloves

Pour all at once over an ice ring or block of ice into a punch bowl and stir until well mingled. Garnish with lemon and orange slices studded with cloves. Serve in punch cups. This makes 30 servings. Allow 3 servings per person.

Supper Served in the Warming Kitchen

Visitors often enjoyed the simple elegance of Fanny Pierson Crane's hospitality at supper parties.

MOCK CLARY

SLICED TONGUE   BAKED ELIZABETHTOWN CRAB

MACED GREEN BEANS   CARROT PUDDING

MADEIRA MOLDED JELLY

HOT PUMPKIN BREAD   MOLDED BUTTER PRINTS

CRAB APPLE AND ROSEMARY JELLY

TOMATO-GINGER PRESERVES   ROSE GERANIUM JELLY

Sampling of Sweets

TANSY PIE

GLAZED ORANGE CAKE   COBBLESTONES

SOFT MOLASSES CAKES

MADEIRA   NUT MEATS   PORT

An Evening Collation

To entertain a sizable number of people, the dining-room table was covered with meats, pastries, cakes, confections, fools, flummeries, nuts, and dainties of all kinds, first to be admired and then to be sampled. To refresh the spirit, an exceeding good punch was always served.

HAM FROM THE SMOKEHOUSE   NATIVE STUFFED AND ROASTED TURKEY

CHEDDAR BISCUITS   MUSHROOM SAVORIES

FLOWERS AND FRUIT IN WHITE WINE JELLY

DESSERT PYRAMIDS

Kisses Ginger Cakes Savoy Biscuits Macaroons

GLAZED ORANGE CAKE   MAIDS OF HONOR   PRINTED SPICE CRINKLES

CARROT TEA CAKE

CHOCOLATE TRUFFLES   WHISKEY NUT BALLS   CANDIED PEEL

DATE AND ALMOND CAKE

TIPSY SQUIRE

NEW JERSEY STONE FENCE PUNCH   ROSE GERANIUM SPICED TEA PUNCH

Magdelena Hoch Keim
of Lobachsville, Pennsylvania

Keim Homestead

In 1752, at the age of twenty-two, Magdelena Hoch, daughter of the prosperous farmer Johann Hoch of the Oley Valley, married twenty-eight-year-old Jacob Keim, sixth and youngest child of Johannes Keim, formerly of Germany and the founder of the Keim family in Pennsylvania. In marrying, they continued the ancestral family line that was to remain in the same Germanic stone cabin and larger manor house near Lobachsville until the early years of the twentieth century.

Magdelena was a twin, and one of eleven children raised in the Hoch household; she and Jacob were neighbors. Not of the plain Amish or Mennonite sects, their families were members of the Reformed, or Lutheran, Church—the German settlers who kept ties with urban culture, and who were not completely involved in a religious life. Although Jacob was six years her senior, they often saw each other on special days when the families of the valley feasted, worshiped, or mourned together, or on the road to Philadelphia in the summer and fall when the great Conestoga wagons took the bountiful produce to market. She brought a sizeable dowry to Jacob, and with him she settled in the stone cabin to continue the diligent and happy farm life that she had always known. Within the first years of their marriage three children were born.

118

It is thought that Jacob was a weaver as well as a farmer, and on winter evenings the spinning wheels were brought in from an outer room, and Magdelena and her daughters, by the light of two fat lamps and candles, spun the flax and fleece of their own flocks that Jacob would weave into clothing, board-clothes, bedding, and coverlets. Through the generations the weaving continued, and when the last of the descendants were gone, chests were found that held ninety-seven homespun linen table covers, thirty-three homespun coverlets, twenty-eight of which were woolen, bearing names and dates, forty cases for featherbeds, and hundreds of yards of homespun linen.

Jacob also made their furniture, turning and fashioning the black walnut wood found outside their door; and they painted their chests and chairs in bright colors, adorning them with motifs that their parents remembered from Germany—angels and birds, tulips and pomegranates, stars and rosetrees, and the lily.

Magdelena's knowledge of traditional dishes from Germany, coupled with her ingenuity in utilizing what she found around her, gave her table a unique though distinctly Pennsylvania-German character. She spent her summer and fall days preserving foods for the long winter, drying the corn, *schnitz* (apples), peas, and beans; fermenting her sauerkraut, wines, and doughs; salting and smoking her fish and meat; and pickling her many more than "seven sweets and seven sours."

She used the beautiful clay slipware dishes, some simple with fluted edges, and some with designs of soldiers, flowers, and signatures for baking her pies, and the Turk's-head mold for her sponge cakes, or *loch kuka* ("hole cake"), and light wheat breads.

As the century progressed, Magdelena became less frugal and more bountiful. She combined cottage cheese and apple butter (*schmerkaas* and *lekvar*) for a bread-spread and used humble ingredients for new soups—*rivvel*, or "lump soup," pepperpot, and pretzel soup—for hearty eating. She utilized the entire hog as other colonists did, but she introduced scrapple, or *pawnhaus* to her family. With imported molasses she delighted her children with shoo-fly pie.

When Jacob Keim died in 1799 he left not only a beautifully tended estate of 124 acres but a fortune of almost 2,000 pounds of gold and silver, "Lawful Money of Pennsylvania." His son John inherited the entire estate, with a substantial amount of wealth designated for the use of the widow Magdelena. According to Jacob's will of 1789, Magdelena was to have the "bed and bedstead with curtains" (canopy bed) and also a "Cloth Dresser standing in the Dwelling room" (*kas* or linen press). She was also to have "rights and privileges to the Stove Room," which was the Great Room in the Keim Manor heated by the five-plate German stove.

Bless you, Magdelena Keim.

"A German farm may be distinguished from the farms of other citizens by the superior size of their barns, the plain but compact form of their houses, the height of their enclosures, the extent of their orchards, the fertility of their fields, the luxuriance of their meadows, and a general appearance of plenty and neatness in everything that belongs to them."
—*Benjamin Rush, Philadelphia*

The Keim Homestead

More than 275 years ago, Johannes Keim staked claim to more than 300 acres of land in a vast virgin forest of black walnut trees in the Oley Valley and thereby established the Keim family in America. It was in this remote but lovely countryside that the Keim stone cabin and manor house were built. From 1698 to 1911 the house would remain in the Keim family, untouched and in beautiful, original repair.

In 1698 Johannes Keim, answering William Penn's urgent plea to the Rhinelanders to form a utopian colony in the New World, had entered the port city of Philadelphia and travelled through Germantown, his Bible and few worldly effects in hand, along the Manatawny stream. He knew from experience in his agrarian hometown of Speier in Alsace that huge black walnut trees meant limestone underground— and a sweetness of soil unparalleled.

ROBERT WALCH

KEIM TEA CUP

He returned to Europe and married Bertha deTurck, a French Huguenot. Together they returned to the rich farmland the English had overlooked, to settle (with more than 280,000 German immigrants by 1763), the land we now call the fertile country of the Pennsylvania Dutch, or Germans. This was the beginning of a full-blooded German culture of farmers, cabinetmakers, ironmongers, gunsmiths, and potters whose German industriousness turned the native bounty of the new America to good use. They left their unique imprint on this nation, and especially on Pennsylvania for hundreds of years to come.

The heritage of the land and its holdings was to surround his sixth and youngest child, Jacob Keim, born in 1724, who at the age of twenty-two bought a fifty-acre tract for 150 pounds from his neighbor, Johann Hoch. He then courted the beautiful Magdelena Hoch,. and when they married, Jacob bought an additional fifty-acre tract from Herr Hoch for only fifty pounds, out of "love and affection for our son-in-law and his advancement into the world."

The enterprising Jacob then proceeded to build the larger manor house (with the help of masons from Philadelphia) immediately adjacent to the stone cabin. As the family prospered and grew larger, a wing was added to the north end, forming the complete manor house that we see today.

Architecturally, the house is typical of the simple and unpretentious German structures built of native field stone found throughout southeastern Pennsylvania. The red tile roof was made from clay dug in the area, and Oley Valley bricks form the arches above all the windows. The deep reveals of the windows point to the thickness of the outer walls, and the garden was enclosed with a "pale fence and gate."

Today, the Oley Valley still seems to have been saved from the mainstream of modernization. The major trade routes bypass the valley on all sides, connecting metropolitan areas around it; the agricultural economy seems to depend little on the outside world; and the Pennsylvania-German character remains strong in the people whose greatest joy is to preserve their bountiful land for generations to come.

"It is my habit to walk about each town where I stop and to wander through all of its streets, in the evening. It is at this time that practically all the inhabitants, whether returned home from the plow, from the workbench or from trade, sit on their porches in the company of their wives and children, breathing the cool evening air and having intimate and sweet conversation amongst themselves. There is no drunkenness, no loud shouting. Recreation and entertainment for these people is rest and quiet. All the conversation was in German. . . . The open doors of the houses showed to the passer-by the German's worldly goods, that is, a featherbed almost reaching to the ceiling, a cupboard with pewter utensils, burnished until they shone. The decorations on the wall—usually seven copper engravings made in Augsburg and representing the story of the prodigal son. From this story the fathers give to their sons all their moral instruction—Julian Niemcewicz, Under Their Vine and Fig Tree, 1797–99

Soups and Savories

Philadelphia Pepperpot

Traditionally thought to have been invented for George Washington and his troops during their winter at Valley Forge, this soup was later to be hawked, piping hot, on the streets of Philadelphia.

1 pound cleaned tripe, in ½-inch cubes
1 pound veal shank in 2 pieces
4 to 6 whole black peppercorns
1 teaspoon salt
4 tablespoons butter
1 cup onion, chopped

½ cup celery, chopped
½ cup green pepper, chopped
3 tablespoons flour
2 potatoes, in ¼-inch dice
Dried hot red pepper, crushed
Freshly ground black pepper

Cover the tripe and veal with at least 2 inches of water. Bring to a boil over high heat. Add peppercorns and salt, reduce heat, and simmer partially covered for 2 hours, or until the tripe is tender.

Transfer the tripe and veal to a cutting board. Remove the meat from the veal bone; cut veal and tripe into ½-inch pieces. Strain liquid and reserve 6 cups. In the same pot, sauté onions, celery, and green pepper in butter for 5 minutes, or until the vegetables are soft. Add flour and mix well. Return 6 cups of the liquid slowly until the soup thickens. Add potatoes, tripe, and veal and simmer for 1 hour. Correct seasonings. Add enough dried red pepper and ground black pepper to give it a unique peppery taste. Serves 8.

Sweet and Sour Raisin Soup

1 cup raisins	¼ cup flour
1 large onion, diced	½ cup milk
2 ribs celery, diced	½ cup sugar
3 tablespoons parsley, chopped	Juice of 1 large lemon
1 teaspoon caraway seeds	3 egg yolks
6 cups chicken broth	1 cup soured cream
½ teaspoon salt	

Soak the raisins in water to plump them. Add vegetables and caraway seeds to the broth and simmer for 20 minutes, or until cooked. Add salt. Drain raisins and add to the stock. Continue to simmer. Blend flour with milk and stir into stock until slightly thickened. Add sugar and lemon juice, stirring briskly. Remove from heat. Whip the egg yolks and beat in the soured cream. Whisk this into the soup and keep it warm until ready to serve. Take the soup to the table in a stoneware tureen. Garnish with fresh caraway and serve with slices of pumpernickel bread. Serves 8.

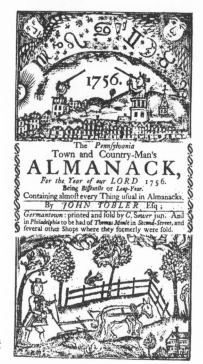

The Pennsylvania
Town and Country-Man's
ALMANACK,
For the Year of our LORD 1756.
Being Bissextile or Leap-Year.
Containing almost every Thing usual in Almanacks.
By JOHN TOBLER Esq;
Germantown : printed and sold by C. Sower jun. And
in Philadelphia to be had of Thomas Maule in Second-Street, and
several other Shops where they formerly were sold.

Fish, Meat, and Fowl

Hunter's Stew Baked with Sauerkraut

A frequent dish at elegant hunter's parties in the Rhineland, this stew pleases "feinschmeckers" of the Oley Valley, especially on Feast Days in the fall after krautmaking is over.

10 pounds fresh sauerkraut, or 6 cans best quality (29-ounce size)
1 pound slab bacon, diced
4 large onions, coarsely chopped
3 pounds beef, cubed
3 pounds pork loin, cubed
Salt and pepper to taste
4 cups water
2 pounds smoked garlic-flavored German sausage, sliced
5 bay leaves
2 small onions, quartered

Drain the sauerkraut and rinse with cold water. Fry the diced bacon and remove to a platter. Add onions to the bacon fat for 3 to 4 minutes. Season the beef and pork with salt and pepper and sauté with the onion until slightly browned, about 10 minutes. Place the sauerkraut in large kettle with the water and bring to a boil. Simmer for 10 minutes. Drain. In a large baking or roasting pan add the drained sauerkraut to all the meat, including bacon and meat juices from the skillet. Add 1 pound of sliced sausage to the kraut and meats. Add bay leaves and quartered onions. Mix all thoroughly and sprinkle the top with the remaining pound of sliced sausage. Bake for 2½ hours at 350° covered for the first hour. If very juicy, thicken with *beurre manié* (4 tablespoons flour rubbed into 1 tablespoon butter). Serve with boiled and buttered caraway potatoes, pumpernickel bread, and mugs of cold bock beer. Serves at least 20 hungry hunters.

Saffron Chicken Potpie (Hinkle Bott-Boi)

In Pennsylvania-German cooking Chicken Potpie bears no resemblance to the pastry-topped pies eaten in most parts of America. Here, with the flavor and golden color of saffron, the pie is in the pot.

6-pound chicken, cut up
1 stalk of celery, chunked
¼ teaspoon saffron threads, or
   ground saffron
2 large onions
1½ tablespoons salt

6 peppercorns
1 stalk of celery, chopped
3 potatoes, largely diced
2 tablespoons fresh parsley,
   chopped
Pepper to taste

Cover the chicken with hot water and add chunked celery, saffron, onions, salt, and peppercorns. Bring to a boil; then simmer covered until the chicken is done (test after 30 minutes). While chicken is cooking prepare potpie squares.

Strain, remove the chicken from the bones, cut into 1-inch pieces, and return 2 quarts of stock to the pot. Add chopped celery and potatoes to the broth, bring to boil, drop in potpie squares, and cook uncovered until the squares are tender. Stir in the chicken and parsley and cook until heated through. Correct seasonings. Add fresh pepper. The potpie can be served while the consistency is souplike, or allow it to reduce for a stewlike consistency by simmering 10 minutes longer. Serves 12.

Potpie Squares

3 tablespoons shortening
2 cups flour
½ teaspoon salt
½ teaspoon baking soda

¾ teaspoon cream of tartar
1 egg, beaten
⅓ cup water

Cut the shortening into the combined dry ingredients. Lightly stir in the egg and water. On a floured board, roll out the dough as thinly as possible. Cut into 2-inch squares with a pastry jig.

Baked Ham with Walnut and Mushroom Stuffing

12- to 14-pound ham, boned and
fully cooked
1 pound mushrooms, finely
chopped
½ cup onion, finely chopped
½ cup butter
2 cups fine bread crumbs
2 tablespoons fresh parsley,
chopped

Freshly ground pepper
½ pound liver pâté, or 2 4½-
ounce cans
1¾ cups walnuts, chopped
¼ cup Rhine wine
⅓ cup honey

Trim the rind off the ham, leaving some around shank end. Sauté
mushrooms and onion in butter until moisture is absorbed. Stir in
crumbs, parsley, and pepper. Remove from heat and work in pâté. Add
1 cup walnuts and wine, using more wine if mixture seems dry. Stuff
the cavity of the ham left by the removal of the bones. Skewer the
ham at the opening and lace with cord if necessary. Place the ham
on a shallow rack and bake for 2 hours at 325°. Remove from oven
and slash the top into a pattern. Spread half of the honey over the
fat area and sprinkle with ¾ cup chopped walnuts. Spoon the rest
of the honey over the nuts. Cook for approximately 1 hour, or until
ham is beautifully glazed. Cook the remaining stuffing in the buttered
top of a double boiler and add a spoonful to each serving of ham.
Serve with red cabbage and apples. Serves 16.

Schnitz und Kneppe

*Schnitz ("cut") has come to mean cut apples dried in the Pennsylvania-
German manner—in the open sun or on trays in a slack oven. They are
combined here with* kneppe *(fluffy dumplings), cooked with ham for a unique
and appetizing flavor.*

3-pound ham butt
2 cups dried sweet apples
(schnitz)
½ cup brown sugar
1 egg, beaten
1 cup flour

¾ teaspoon baking soda
1¼ teaspoons cream of tartar
¼ teaspoon salt
2 tablespoons butter
⅓ to ½ cup milk

Soak the apples in water overnight. Simmer the ham in water for
several hours. Add apples and brown sugar. While these are cooking,
prepare the *kneppe*. Drop *kneppe* batter from spoon into the bubbling

ham and apples. Cover tightly and steam for 15 minutes without un-covering. "You dassn't peek."

Kneppe

Mix beaten egg with sifted flour, soda, cream of tartar, and salt. Add butter and milk, mixing lightly.

Roots and Vegetables

Red Cabbage and Apples

2 medium onions, finely chopped
¼ cup butter
½ teaspoon nutmeg
2 teaspoons salt
Freshly ground pepper
2 cups water

2 tablespoons cider vinegar
2-pound head of red cabbage, quartered, cored, and shredded
4 firm apples, peeled, cored, and sliced
3 tablespoons fresh lemon juice

Sauté onions in butter with nutmeg, salt, and pepper and cook until golden. Add water and vinegar and stir in cabbage. Cover and cook for 30 minutes. Add the apples to the cabbage and continue cooking, covered, for about 30 minutes. Stir in lemon juice. Serves 8.

To Dry Corn

To each 8 pints of raw sweet corn (cut off and not blanched) add 6 tablespoons granulated sugar, 4 teaspoons coarse canning salt, and ½ cup of sweet cream. No substitutes! Boil the ingredients for 20 minutes in a heavy pan while stirring constantly so that mixture doesn't stick. Then, spread the cooked corn on shallow trays in an oven turned to its absolutely lowest possible temperature. Stir the grain often as it dries further. When the kernels are crispy, dump them into clean brown paper sacks. Tie the bags securely (to keep out insects) and hang them in your home's driest room. The corn will be completely dry when it rattles inside the sacks. At that point it can be stored indefinitely in glass jars sealed with airtight lids. Prepared this way, the corn does not need to be soaked before cooking. It is especially delicious simmered in cream and butter.

Hot Potato Salad

8 potatoes
1 stalk of celery, diced
2 hard-boiled eggs, sliced
1 onion, minced
1 tablespoon parsley, minced
4 slices bacon, diced
2 eggs, well beaten

1 cup sugar
½ teaspoon salt
¼ teaspoon pepper
½ cup vinegar, diluted with ½ cup cold water
2 tablespoons prepared mustard (or to taste)

Boil the potatoes in their jackets; then peel and dice them. Add the celery, hard-boiled eggs, onion, and parsley. Fry bacon in a skillet until crisp and brown. Beat the eggs; then add the sugar, salt, pepper, and vinegar and water. Mix well. Pour egg mixture into the hot bacon fat and stir until mixture thickens, about 10 minutes. Pour over the potato mixture and mix lightly. Add crisped bacon and serve to 10.

Pickles and Preserves

Apple Butter (Lattwerk)

"*We made in one season six barrels of cider into applebutter, three at a time. Two large copper kettles were hung under the beech-trees, down between the springhouse and smoke-house, and the cider was boiled down the evening before, great stumps of trees being in demand . . . the rest of the family gathered in the kitchen and labored diligently in preparing the cut apples, so that in the morning the "schnits" might be ready to go in.*"
—*Phebe E. Gibbons*, The Pennsylvania Dutch

3 quarts sweet cider
8 pounds ripe apples, peeled, cored, and quartered
2½ cups brown sugar, packed
2 teaspoons ground cloves

2 teaspoons cinnamon
1 teaspoon allspice
½ teaspoon salt
Sassafras bark (optional)

Cook the cider over high heat, uncovered, for 30 minutes, or until reduced by half. Add apples and cook over low heat until tender. Work through a food mill and return puree to the kettle. Stir in sugar, spices, and salt. Cook over low heat, stirring almost continuously until the apple butter thickens. Ladle into hot sterilized jars and sink a small piece of sassafras bark (optional) into each jar. Seal. Makes 6 pints.

Sassafras (Sossafross) added excellent taste to apple butter. It was Grandfather's duty to hunt, dig, and clean the root bark on the day of applebutter cooking. The root bark was sunk into the hot apple butter as it was put into crocks for future use.

Pear Honey

Place 4 cups of fresh pears peeled and finely chopped in a pan. Add ½ lemon finely cut up, 2 cups of sugar, 2 tablespoons cracked ginger, and 1 cup water. Bring to a boil, reduce the heat, and cook until thick, stirring frequently. When as thick as pear butter, add water to expand it to a honey consistency. Check seasoning and add additional freshly ground ginger if necessary. Continue to simmer until the flavors blend and the consistency is pulpy but looser than pear, peach, or apple butter. Strain to remove the lemon and cracked ginger and store in a crock in the springhouse, or in preserve glasses. Serve very cold for special hot or cold breakfast breads. The honey should be cool to the taste but gingery to swallow. Makes 6 half-pints.

Lemon Butter

| 2 lemons | 1½ cups sugar |
| 5 eggs | ½ cup butter |

Grate the lemon peel and squeeze the juice. Beat eggs and sugar in saucepan. Stir in the juice and peel and add butter. Cook for 15 minutes, or until mixture thickens. Refrigerate for 3 hours before using.

Dilled Pickled Beans

2 pounds fresh green beans
3 cups water
1 cup white vinegar
2 tablespoons pickling salt

2 tablespoons dried dill weed
¼ teaspoon cayenne
2 cloves garlic, minced

Trim the ends from the beans; then wash and drain. Cut to fit pint jars. In a pan cover beans with boiling water; cook, uncovered for 3 minutes. Drain. Pack lengthwise into canning jars. In a large kettle combine 3 cups water, vinegar, pickling salt, dill weed, cayenne, and garlic and bring to a boil. Cover beans with pickling liquid to within ½ inch of top. Adjust lids. Process in boiling water bath for 10 minutes. Makes 4 pints.

Pumpernickel Bread

1½ cups water
½ cup cornmeal
½ cup molasses
1 tablespoon each butter and salt
2 teaspoons sugar
1½ teaspoons caraway seeds, slightly pounded
½ square, or ½ ounce, semisweet chocolate

1 package dry yeast
¼ cup warm water (110°)
1 cup mashed potatoes
3 cups rye flour
1 cup whole-wheat flour
1 egg white
1 tablespoon cold water

Combine water and cornmeal in a saucepan and cook until thickened. Remove from heat. Add molasses, butter, salt, sugar, caraway seeds, and chocolate. Stir until blended. Pour into a bowl until cooled to luke warm. Dissolve yeast in water. Add yeast and mashed potato to mixture in the bowl. Stir in rye flour and whole-wheat flour.

Turn out dough on a floured surface. Knead for 10 to 12 minutes until the dough is elastic but stiff. Place dough in a greased bowl in a warm

BUTTER MOLD

place, cover with a towel, and let rise until doubled in bulk, about 1 hour. Punch down. Knead out the air bubbles and form into a round, smooth ball. Place on a baking sheet dusted with cornmeal. Cover and return to a warm place for a second rise until doubled in bulk, about 50 minutes.

Brush the loaf with egg white mixed with the cold water and bake in preheated 375° oven for 50 minutes, or until tapping yields a hollow sound.

Fastnachts

The Rhineland festival of Fastnacht, or Shrove Tuesday, was celebrated to usher in Lent. Yeast dough for these doughnuts was set to rise the night before. The last one at the table in the morning was a "lazy fastnacht" and got a doughnut shaped from the remains of the dough. This practice was followed in order to use up all the fats in the house before Ash Wednesday —and to use up all the dough so that a new starter could be made the next day.

3 potatoes, boiled and mashed	4 eggs beaten
1 yeast cake dissolved in ½ cup boiled potato water	½ cup melted butter
	1 cup sugar
½ teaspoon salt	½ teaspoon mace
6 cups sifted flour	Fat for deep frying
2 cups lukewarm milk	

Early in the evening mix the potatoes, yeast, salt, and 1 cup flour. Cover and let rise. Two hours later add 5 cups flour and 2 cups lukewarm milk. Cover and let rise overnight. Next morning add the eggs, butter, sugar, and mace. Knead until stiff enough to roll out, adding more flour if needed. Let rise until doubled in bulk. Roll out on a floured board, ¼ inch thick. Cut in shapes with a doughnut cutter and fry quickly in deep hot fat. Roll in sugar. Makes 60 doughnuts.

German Christmas Bread (Schnechen)

Bread	Filling
3 packages dry yeast	1½ cups light brown sugar
1 cup warm water	1½ cups currants
1 teaspoon salt	1½ cups pecans
½ cup sugar	2 teaspoons cinnamon
½ cup butter, softened	
7 egg yolks, or 3 eggs	*Caramel cream*
1 cup warm milk	
1 teaspoon vanilla extract	½ cup butter
½ teaspoon grated lemon rind	½ cup brown sugar
4 to 5 cups flour	1 tablespoon corn syrup

To prepare the bread, mix the first 4 ingredients and let stand. Beat the softened butter; add eggs, milk, vanilla, and lemon rind. Beat in the flour. Turn out on a floured board and knead for 10 minutes. Set, covered with a towel, in a warm place to rise, about 30 minutes. Roll out to ¼-inch thickness into 2 6″ x 24″ rectangles.

Sprinkle filling ingredients over each pastry rectangle and roll up jelly-roll fashion to make a 24-inch roll. Combine ingredients for caramel cream and butter the cups of three 12-cup muffin tins with this mixture. Slice each roll of dough crosswise into eighteen pieces and place each *schnechen* (snail) into a muffin cup. Let rise for thirty minutes, then bake in 350° oven for 20 minutes on middle or top shelf to prevent the caramel bottom from burning. Remove from oven and invert *schnechen* immediately on rack to allow the caramel to spread over the outside of the roll. Makes 36.

TULIP BUTTER MOLD

Uncommon Cakes and Pies

Printed Spice Crinkles

¾ cup soft butter or margarine
1 cup packed brown sugar
1 egg
¼ cup molasses
2¼ cups flour

2 teaspoons baking soda
2 teaspoons cinnamon
2 teaspoons ginger
¾ teaspoon ground cloves
¼ teaspoon salt

In a bowl mix butter, sugar, egg, and molasses. In another bowl stir together flour, soda, spices, and salt. Mix dry ingredients into shortening mixture. Chill dough for 2 hours, or overnight.

Roll dough into balls the size of large walnuts. Dip tops in sugar. Place little cakes sugared side up 3 inches apart on a baking sheet. Bake at 375° for 10 to 12 minutes until set but not hard. Firmly press each little cake with a butter print as soon as it comes from the oven. Makes 4 dozen.

Almond Wafers (Mandel Plaettchen)

1 cup butter
1 cup sugar
2 eggs
1 teaspoon grated lemon rind
⅛ teaspoon salt
½ teaspoon nutmeg

¼ cup sherry
3 cups flour, sifted
½ cup shredded almonds
1 egg yolk
2 tablespoons milk

Cream the butter and sugar together and beat 2 eggs in, one at a time. Add lemon rind, salt, nutmeg, and sherry. Beat in flour. Stir in almonds by hand and chill for 2 hours. Roll the dough very thin and cut into shapes using old tin cutters, if you have them. Brush tops with mixture of 1 egg yolk and 2 tablespoons milk. Bake on a greased tin at 350° for 10 minutes, or until golden. Makes 4 dozen.

Chocolate Sauerkraut Cake

½ cup butter
1½ cups sugar
3 eggs
1 teaspoon vanilla extract
2 cups sifted flour
1½ teaspoons baking soda

¾ teaspoon cream of tartar
¼ teaspoon salt
½ cup cocoa powder
1 cup water
2 cups, or 1 pound, sauerkraut,
    drained, rinsed, and chopped

Cream the butter and sugar until light. Beat the eggs in one at a time. Add vanilla. Sift together all dry ingredients and add to creamed mixture alternately with water. Make certain that sauerkraut has been drained, *rinsed*, and chopped. Stir into batter. Bake in a greased and floured 13" x 9" x 2" pan at 350° for 35 to 40 minutes. Cool and frost.

Frosting

6 squares, or 6 ounces, semisweet
    chocolate
4 tablespoons butter
½ cup soured cream

1 teaspoon vanilla extract
¼ teaspoon salt
2 cups confectioners sugar,
    sifted

In double boiler melt chocolate and butter over low heat. Remove from heat and blend in soured cream, vanilla and salt. Gradually add sifted confectioners sugar.

Hickory Nut Cake

Found in an Oley Valley receipt book belonging to Mrs. Annie Griesemer and now owned by her daughter Mrs. Alice Trout of Pleasantville.

1 cup butter
2 cups sugar
4 eggs
1 cup buttermilk
1 teaspoon baking soda

1 teaspoon cream of tartar
2 cups hickory nuts, chopped
3½ cups flour
1 teaspoon vanilla extract

Cream the butter and sugar. Add the beaten eggs. Sift the dry ingredients and add to the creamed mixture alternately with the buttermilk. Stir in the vanilla. Coat the nuts with flour and fold them into the batter. Bake in a greased and floured Bundt pan at 350° for 40 to 60 minutes.

Funnel Cake (Drechter Kucha)

An odd delight of Pennsylvania-German cooking, these fried cakes of spiraling batter topped with powdered sugar need a vital utensil—a large tin funnel.

1⅓ cups flour	2 tablespoons sugar
¼ teaspoon salt	1 egg
¾ teaspoon baking soda	1 cup milk
½ teaspoon cream of tartar	Fat, or cooking oil, for deep frying

Sift dry ingredients together in one bowl. In another bowl beat the egg and add the milk. Add dry mixture and beat until smooth.

Pour about 1 inch fat or cooking oil in a frying pan and heat to 375°. While pouring the batter into a large tin funnel hold your finger over the bottom opening. When oil is sufficiently hot, remove your finger from the hole and with a circular motion guide the batter into a cylindrical design as it drops into the pan. Fry until lightly brown; turn to the other side. When golden brown, remove and drain on paper towels. Sprinkle with powdered sugar and serve. Especially good for breakfast with country sausage, fried apples, and stewed rhubarb.

Wet-Bottom Shoofly Pie

When is a pie not a pie? When it doesn't have a crust on top, say the Pennsylvania Dutch who call any pie without a lid a cake. This specialty of the region is a brown sugar and molasses cake baked in a crust.

¾ cup flour	2 tablespoons shortening
½ cup brown sugar	1 egg yolk, beaten well
½ teaspoon cinnamon	½ cup barrel molasses
⅛ teaspoon each nutmeg, ginger, and ground cloves	¾ cup boiling water
	½ teaspoon baking soda
½ teaspoon salt	Piecrust dough for 9-inch pie

Combine flour, sugar, spices, and salt with the shortening. Work into crumbs with your hands. Add beaten egg yolk to molasses. Pour boiling water over soda until dissolved; then add to molasses mixture. Line a 9-inch pie plate with pastry and fill it with the molasses mixture. Top with the crumb mixture. Bake at 400° until the crust browns, about 10 minutes. Reduce to 325° and bake until firm.

Drams and Punches

Magdelena's May Wine (Maiwein)

The use of the German herb sweet woodruff, or Waldmeister, *is the main ingredient for this Maibowle. Indigenous to the Black Forest of Germany, where it grows wild, the beautiful white-flowered ground cover smells of new-mown hay, and was traditionally used in May Day festivals and for spring tonics, both in Germany and in Pennsylvania.*

12 sprigs or more sweet woodruff	1 cup granulated sugar
	1 gallon Rhine wine
1½ quarts fresh strawberries	2 cups brandy (optional)

Pick fresh woodruff and place half of it in the oven to bring out the coumarin. When dry let it stand in the wine for 3 to 7 days to steep.

Slice and mash ½ quart of the fresh strawberries with the granulated sugar. Place a block of ice in a large bowl. Drain the dried woodruff, ladle the steeped wine over it, and add brandy if you wish. Stir. Add the mashed strawberries and sugar to the wine mixture. Stir in the quart of strawberries and add remaining fresh woodruff, making certain that fresh white flowers of the herb are there for garnishing, to join the floating strawberries. Fresh diced pineapple is a lovely addition. Serves 20.

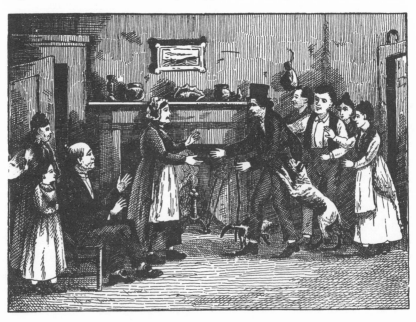

Freundschaft Gather to Dress the Loom

Dressing, or threading, Jacob's weaver's loom was just one more reason for the freundschaft, or family connections, to gather in the fall of the year to share their bountiful harvest table and to set about the task of threading the warp through the string heddles in either a simple "Cross and Table" pattern or a more complex "Sorrel Blossom," and then winding the warp on the warp beam. The sheep had been sheared in May, and the wool had been washed, carded, dyed, and spun. Magdelena and Jacob's fifteen sisters and brothers and their families found this a welcome time to gather together —the men working in the stone cabin where the loom was set up, and the women preparing the food for the long harvest table outdoors while exchanging Oley Valley news and pleasantries.

HUNTER'S STEW BAKED WITH SAUERKRAUT

BAKED HAM WITH WALNUT STUFFING

SCHNITZ UND KNEPPE

RED CABBAGE AND APPLES   LOBACHSVILLE POTATO FILLING

A SAMPLING OF SWEETS AND SOURS

Pear Honey   Apple Butter

Cottage Cheese

Cucumbers in Cream   Dilled Pickled Beans

PUMPERNICKEL BREAD   LEMON BUTTER

HICKORY NUT CAKE   CHOCOLATE SAUERKRAUT CAKE

WET-BOTTOM SHOOFLY PIE   FUNNEL CAKES FOR THE CHILDREN

COLD SWEET CIDER   MUGS OF BOCK BEER   SARSPARILLA

COFFEE

Mary Cowgill Corbit of Odessa, Delaware

Corbit-Sharp House

In 1767 William Corbit, a young tanner and farmer from Cantwell's Bridge (now Odessa), bought the following from David Wilson's store: cider, linen, three hides, some damaged calf skins, two more hides, rum, more hides, more rum, paper, some chocolate, and a comb. It was obvious that William Corbit was a bachelor. He was the marrying kind, however, for he took three wives (all of whom died at a young age), before marrying Mary Cowgill from Dover in April, 1791.

At the time of their marriage, when they moved into the fine brick "dweling house," William Corbit was already established in his tanyard with money invested in real estate. The post-Revolutionary period was a prosperous time for him. His tanyard was close to his home and he worked hard. The purchasing of cattle, horse, goat, dog, or buffalo skins, the liming to loosen the hair and soften the skins, and the tanning with oak bark from his land holdings required close attention. He sold his leather to local farmers and to the nearby Philadelphia market, where he often traveled by direct water route. Trade was constant between Odessa and Philadelphia; the rich yield of wheat, corn, and barley from Odessa's farms was shipped to Philadelphia and foreign ports from the town wharves on the Appoquinimink Creek.

Mary Cowgill Corbit's main responsibility was the rearing of William's other children, as well as six of her own. She was strong, forthright, strict, religious, a good manager, and a good cook, judging from the ledger of Corbit receipts. As Quakers, the Corbits kept no slaves in the household, but Mrs. Corbit, with Alice ("Alcy") Murry, the housekeeper who lived with the Corbits for over thirty years, supervised the servants in all of the cooking and household chores. They did not live as extravagantly as their nearby Maryland neighbors, but they enjoyed the same kinds of food from the land, river, and bay.

Mary Corbit was a hardworking woman who enjoyed good health and prosperity. Yet, the uncertainty of "this transitory life" is apparent in her story. William had sired thirteen children in all, but only two survived Mary when she died in 1845, twenty-eight years after William. But with all the sorrows, there were joys. The family was close, and John Higgins, a grandson, remembered that even after the children were grown, when family members met, "they literally fell on each other's necks in transport of joy and affection."

The Corbit–Sharp House

Using a Philadelphia townhouse as a model and English design books for the interior detail, William Corbit erected a fine home suitable for

COURTESY THE HENRY FRANCIS DU PONT WINTERTHUR MUSEUM

a wealthy Quaker. It was simple but most beautiful. It was not osten-
tatious, although in its setting in Odessa, Delaware, it was indeed grand,
and some Quaker relatives chided him by calling it Castle William, indicating that not everyone approved of its grandeur. The bricks were made
locally but the lumber, nails, hinges, glass, and paints were purchased
from Philadelphia firms and carried by boat down the Delaware River,
then up the Appoquinimink Creek to Cantwell's Bridge.

The house, begun in 1772 and completed two years later, has a center
hall with four rooms on the ground floor. Upstairs there are three bedrooms and a long room, perhaps a drawing room, across the front of
the house. When the Corbits ordered furniture, they requested the
"best sort but plain," expressing the Quakers' aesthetic principle of
beauty. The basement kitchen has a brick floor that was fireproof and
easy to clean. An oven to the rear of the large fireplace is unusual for
a Delaware house, where it is more common to have the kitchen in a
separate building. The walls were plastered and whitewashed. It was
well equipped with the implements necessary for Mrs. Corbit, the
housekeeper, and the servants. The room is built somewhat above
cellar-floor level to allow for full-sized windows to admit light. Whitewashed storerooms, large and ample, were used to keep apples, molasses,
lard, and even salted fish. Unusual doors with wooden slats in the cellar
provide for cross-ventilation.

Later, in 1790, when Mary and William Corbit's growing family required it, a new kitchen wing was built adjacent to the dining room with
a bed chamber above it.

Many detailed Corbit building accounts, saved for two centuries, have
proved to be a rare find for architectural historians. These and other
inventories, wills, accounts, and the ledger of Corbit receipts tell us
about the family who lived in this house.

The Ledger of Corbit Receipts

The Corbit family manuscript cookbook contains over fifty prized
family receipts passed down for several generations after Mary and
William Corbit lived in the big house in Cantwell's Bridge. Many have
been adapted and appear in this chapter. All the receipts are for typical
Delaware foods, carefully recorded by the Corbits and by Delaware
women in other early cookbooks and preserved for generations of Americans to prepare and savor.

Soups and Savories

Mary Corbit's Very Special Clam Soup

This is not like the northern chowder; it is very different in flavor, creamier in texture. The old Corbit receipt warns not to use too much of the clam juice. "We think it too strong, but do as you like about it." Serve as a very special first course to a holiday dinner.

½ to 1 cup fresh clam juice,
   or juice from canned clams
2 dozen large raw clams, or
   2 8-ounce cans minced clams
1 medium onion, grated
3 tablespoons butter
2 tablespoons flour
1 cup milk

2 cups light cream
1 egg
2 tablespoons Madeira
½ teaspoon thyme
1 teaspoon salt
Dash of cayenne
Grating of pepper
2 tablespoons parsley, chopped

Drain the clam juice through a linen napkin to remove the grit. Wash the clams and chop them coarsely. Sauté the onion in 1 tablespoon butter. Add the remaining butter and flour to make a roux and cook for about 1 minute. Stir in the milk and cream and cook until thickened. Slowly mix in the egg and the remaining ingredients and cook over a low fire, stirring until the soup is thick and creamy. Allow the soup to sit for a while to improve the flavor. Reheat and serve with a sprinkling of parsley. Serves 6.

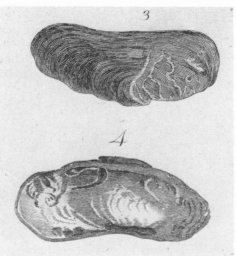

Alcy's Carrot Soup

2 tablespoons butter	1 cup heavy cream
½ cup onion, chopped	1 cup milk
4 medium-size potatoes	½ teaspoon Worcestershire sauce
8 to 10 carrots, peeled and sliced	½ teaspoon sugar
6 cups chicken broth	Salt and pepper to taste
Bay leaf	A few dashes of Tabasco sauce
2 sprigs of fresh thyme, or	
½ teaspoon dried thyme	

Sauté onion in butter. Add potatoes, carrots, broth, and herbs. Cook until tender, 30 to 40 minutes. Puree in a blender. Add cream, milk, and remaining seasonings and bring just to boiling point. Remove bay leaf. Let cool. This soup can be served hot or cold. "Chopped mint is nice for a garnish." Serves 10.

Cream Cheese

"Take a quart of thick soured cream; mix 1 level tablespoonful of salt; tie in a piece of muslin and hang in a cool place to drip for three days."
—Mrs. Grace Townsend

POTTERY COLLANDER

Scolloped Clams

Clams, oysters, crab, shad, and terrapin came to Cantwell's Bridge fresh from the Delaware waters. Both the Delaware Bay and the Delaware River were great fishing grounds for these staple foods.

24 raw clams	Dash of cayenne
1 onion, chopped	Pepper to taste
1 tablespoon butter	3 egg yolks, beaten
1 cup cream	Grated bread crumbs
½ teaspoon salt	Paprika
Grated nutmeg	Butter

Drain and mince the clams. Chop and sauté the onion in butter. Stir the clams into it and add cream, salt, nutmeg, cayenne, and black pepper. Bring the mixture to a boil and then cook over a *very* low fire for 10 minutes. Remove and stir in the beaten egg yolks. Put the mixture in an 8-inch pie plate. Cover with grated bread crumbs and sprinkle with paprika. Scatter lumps of butter over the top. Brown in a hot oven (400°) for 15 minutes. Serves 4.

Stuffed Rockfish

Rock, as it is commonly called—a native fish abundant in Chesapeake and Delaware waters—is known elsewhere as striped bass.

½ cup bread, crumbled	2 eggs
1 small onion, chopped	Cayenne, salt, and pepper
2 tablespoons parsley, chopped	1 tablespoon lemon juice
¼ cup celery, chopped	½ cup sherry
2 tablespoons green pepper, chopped	½ pound crabmeat
	1 large rockfish, 3 to 5 pounds
4 tablespoons butter	A few pieces of bacon

Sauté bread, onion, parsley, celery, and green pepper in butter. Mix all together with eggs, salt and pepper, lemon juice, sherry, and crabmeat and fill the rockfish. Keep the head and tail on if possible. Brush fish with butter and put several pieces of bacon on it. Bake uncovered at 350° for 45 minutes. Baste occasionally. "Send it in with sliced lemon and parsley for garnish." Serves 6.

Baked Boneless Shad with Roe Sauce

1 large shad, unboned   Brown paper bag
Melted butter   Melted bacon fat
Salt and pepper

Wipe shad inside and out with butter and season with salt and pepper. Grease a paper bag with fat and place fish inside. Fold and seal the end. Place in a covered roasting pan and bake at 250° for 6 hours. The bones dissolve with this slow cooking. Serve with sauce to 6.

Roe Sauce

1 pair shad roe   ½ cup cream
3 eggs, separated   2 tablespoons parsley, chopped
1 tablespoon butter   1 teaspoon lemon juice
½ cup sherry   Salt and pepper to taste

Parboil shad roe for 10 minutes. Remove the membrane and break up the roe. Beat the egg yolks and whites separately. Melt butter in a chafing dish, add roe, and stir briefly. Add beaten egg yolks and whites, sherry, lemon juice, cream, and parsley and cook very slowly, stirring constantly until sauce has thickened. Do not overcook or the sauce will harden.

   A *variation*: Broil filleted shad. Spoon sauce over fish; then return to broiler until sauce bubbles and browns.

(Adapted from the receipt of Frances Pitcher)

Ragoo of Lamb—A Made Dish

Mary Corbit's guests—men in particular—would have appreciated this "made dish" on her dining table. It was prepared on the hearth in a spider (frying pan), set over a bed of coals pulled from the fire, then allowed to simmer until the flavors blended and the mushrooms were done.

2 pounds uncooked lamb (shoulder or leg) cut into 1-inch pieces	½ can water
	Bay leaf
3 tablespoons butter	Salt, pepper, Kitchen Bouquet
¼ teaspoon nutmeg	(or browning agent)
1 pound mushrooms, sliced	1 can artichoke bottoms or hearts
3 tablespoons flour	4 teaspoons fresh orange juice
1½ cans beef bouillon	10 thin slivers of orange rind

Sauté lamb in butter until brown. Sprinkle with nutmeg. Remove to separate dish. In the same frying pan sauté mushrooms. Return meat to pan and add flour. Slowly add hot bouillon, water, and bay leaf and stir until a rich gravy forms. Correct seasoning with salt and pepper and color with Kitchen Bouquet. Simmer for 5 or 10 minutes to blend flavors and tenderize meat. Just before serving, put in artichoke pieces and squeeze orange juice into the sauce. Heat thoroughly. Garnish with slivers of orange rind. Serves 6.

(Adapted from Eliza Smith, *The Compleat Housewife*, 1729)

TALL SPIDER

Delaware Chicken Salad

A well-made chicken salad is as elegant a dish as can be made. Ladies from Delaware vied for the best receipt and then often kept it a guarded secret.

Take a boiled chicken; skin, bone, and cut it up in pieces (not too small). Cut up celery, about half the amount of chicken. Mix the chicken and celery together and put the dressing on it just before serving. "This dressing is enough for several hens."

Dressing

Beat all of the following ingredients together until smooth. (Today this can be done in the blender.) "If the seasoning does not seem sufficient add more, as it requires to be seasoned very high."

4 hard-boiled eggs
3 gills rich cream (1 gill
    equals ½ cup)
1½ gills salad oil, or oil
    from the chicken
1 gill good cider vinegar

2 teaspoons mustard
½ teaspoon cayenne
2 teaspoons sugar
4 egg yolks, well beaten
Salt and pepper to taste

(Adapted from the ledger of Corbit receipts and the Cowgill Cookbook)

Chicken and Oyster Pie

3-pound chicken
24 oysters
1 cup celery, chopped
¾ cup butter
6 tablespoons flour
1 cup chicken broth
1 cup oyster liquor
1 cup cream

Salt and pepper to taste
½ teaspoon nutmeg
Juice of 1 lemon
1 teaspoon lemon rind
Piecrust dough
1 egg, beaten, or cream, for
    brushing crust

Stew chicken until just tender. Cool. Drain oysters and save liquor. Sauté celery in the butter and stir in the flour. Add broth, oyster liquor, and cream and stir until thickened. Season with salt, pepper, nutmeg, lemon juice, and lemon rind. Take chicken from the bone in large-sized pieces and put in a 3-quart casserole with oysters. Pour sauce over all. Cover with a piecrust. Brush top with beaten egg or cream. Bake at 400° for 40 minutes, or until crust is browned. Serves 8.

Roots and Vegetables

To Dress Cauliflower

2 small cauliflowers
Milk and water for boiling
1 cup butter

2 spoonsful water
Flour
Salt and pepper to taste

"Boil the 2 till barely done in milk and water. Pull one to pieces. Leave the other whole. Melt butter and add water to fry pan. Dust cauliflower with flour and fry it in the butter until it becomes a light brown. Season with pepper and salt. Lay the whole one in the middle of the dish and put the rest 'round it."

Make 1 cup of cream sauce and add ¼ cup Parmesan cheese. Spoon over the top of the cauliflower. Dust with additional cheese and bread crumbs. Brown briefly in a hot oven. Serves 8.

(Adapted from an old New Castle cookbook belonging to the W. T. Read family)

Garden Peas and Lettuce

4 cups fresh peas or 2 packages
    frozen peas
1 small lettuce head, shredded
6 spring onions, tops and bottoms,
    chopped
2 sprigs of parsley, chopped

1 teaspoon salt
2 teaspoons sugar
2 sprigs of mint, chopped
¼ cup light cream
2 tablespoons butter

Cook peas, lettuce, onions, parsley, and seasonings in very little water until just tender. Do not overcook. Drain most of the liquid and stir in cream and butter. Taste to correct seasoning. Additional chopped parsley, mint, and onion may be used to garnish. Serves 8.

Fried Tomatoes

½ cup cornmeal
½ cup flour
2 tablespoons sugar
1 teaspoon salt

¼ teaspoon pepper
Firm tomato slices
Shortening

Mix all ingredients except tomatoes. Coat both sides of tomato slices with cornmeal mixture. Fry in melted shortening until brown on both sides. Serve hot. Green or partly ripe tomatoes may be preferred.

Pickles and Preserves

Unrivaled Ripe Tomato Catsup

½ bushel tomatoes
6 cups vinegar
½ pound salt
¼ pound pepper
1 tablespoon cayenne

2 tablespoons ground cloves
4 tablespoons allspice
2 pounds brown sugar
2 tablespoons celery seed
(optional)

Boil the tomatoes for 3 hours. Strain the skins and seeds and add the rest of the ingredients to the tomato pulp. Boil for 1 hour. Seal in sterile jars. "Cannot be excelled."

To Pickle a Ham

Every family from New Hampshire to Georgia had a receipt for curing hams. Virginia hogs, fed on peanuts, became famous, but Delaware farms produced good-tasting, home-grown, cured hams as well.

"*1 gallon Rain Water, 1 pint molasses, 1¾ pounds salt, 1 teaspoonful Saleratus [baking soda], a little salt petre. Let lay six weeks and smoke.*"
—ledger of Corbit receipts

Peach Preserves

4 cups peaches, peeled and cut up
2 cups crushed pineapple, drained
1 cup cantaloupe, diced, or 1 cup
  fresh red plums, pitted and
  skinned

Juice of 1 orange
6 cups sugar
1 lemon, seeded and finely sliced

Put all ingredients together in a heavy pan and cook slowly for 2 hours, stirring occasionally. Pour in sterile jelly jars and seal with paraffin.

Grandmother's Potato Rolls

Potatoes were used to make moist and tender rolls and bread. The Corbits and other Delawareans seem to have been especially fond of these bread-stuffs, judging from their frequent appearance in early cookbooks.

When young James Corbit was at boarding school, thoughts of good food reminded him of his grandmother's house, and he wrote to his Uncle Daniel in 1827: "Indeed if I was home I should think it paradise eating Grand-mother's bread & butter. O Dear me if I had only the least piece of her nice bread & butter, I would eat it as greedy as a hog."—Antony Higgins, The Corbits of Appoquinimink.

2 cups warm mashed potatoes,
  riced
½ cup sugar
1 tablespoon salt
¾ butter or margarine

1 cup milk
1 envelope dry yeast
2 eggs beaten
5 cups flour

Stir together potatoes, sugar, and salt. Heat butter or margarine in milk until it melts and allow to cool to lukewarm. Dissolve yeast in this mixture. Add to potato mixture. Add the eggs and stir in 3 cups of the flour. Add remaining flour and knead into a medium-stiff dough. Cover and let rise in a warm place until light. When doubled in bulk, punch down; then make into rolls. Place them in a greased 24-muffin tin. Let rise again. (You may fill 2 small loaf pans 8″ x 5″ x 3½″ to make crusty loaves if desired.) Bake loaves at 375° for about 1 hour. Rolls take less time, about 20 minutes. "Buttering the tops of rolls before you bake them makes them nice."

(Adapted from the ledger of Corbit receipts)

HEATING A BEEHIVE OVEN

Keep a steady fire of hardwood blazing in the oven for at least two hours, longer if necessary. Remove the coals to the hearth with an iron peel. Sweep oven with a dampened broom and then close the oven door tightly. Put your bare arm in the oven. If you can count to 20, your oven is moderate. If to 10, it is hot; to 40, it is slack.

No specific baking time or temperature was ever given in early receipts, which makes it difficult for the modern cook to convert from oven to stove. And it stands to reason that the heat in beehive ovens varied depending on the wood used, the size and duration of the fire, the weather, wind, and the size of the oven. Each housewife had to become acquainted with her own oven, which was not exactly like any other. Mrs. Corbit's kitchen chimney is said to have smoked. Perhaps it was abandoned when the new kitchen wing was built in 1790.

Uncommon Cakes and Pies

Coconut Jumbles with a Honey Glaze

Almost all Delaware cooks, including Mrs. Corbit, record Jumbles in their treasury of favored receipts. They are as varied as the families themselves, and these little cakes, except for the name, bear almost no resemblance one to another. Perhaps that is what the name means—a jumble of ingredients arranged to please the family that eats them. Methods of baking include "drop, roll thin, cut with a scalloped edged jumble cutter, or roll into a rope and twist or tie end."

1 cup sugar	1 tablespoon grated lemon rind
½ cup butter or margarine	1 tablespoon grated orange rind
2 eggs, beaten	¼ teaspoon nutmeg
¼ teaspoon baking soda	3 cups flour
¼ cup sour cream	1 cup grated coconut
Pinch of salt	Honey and 1 cup grated coconut
1 tablespoon orange juice	for glazing
1 teaspoon lemon juice	

Cream sugar and butter together. Add beaten eggs. Combine baking soda and sour cream and add salt, juices, grated rinds, and nutmeg to mixture; then add flour and 1 cup of coconut. Chill a short time for easier handling. Take about a level teaspoonful of the dough. On a lightly floured surface, roll with your hand into a coil of dough about 4 inches long. Shape into rings ("the size of a hen's egg," said one old receipt). Bake at 350° for 8 minutes, until barely done.

To Glaze Jumbles: Paint the top of the Jumble with honey and press it into loose coconut. Run under the broiler (set at 350°) until the coconut toasts and the honey glazes. Colored sugar, or grated semisweet chocolate, may also be used with honey.

Lady Cake with Chocolate Dressing

1 cup butter	4 cups flour
2 cups sugar	2 teaspoons cream of tartar
8 egg whites	1 cup milk
2 teaspoons almond extract, (or bitter almond)	1 teaspoon baking soda

Cream butter and sugar. Beat egg whites until stiff and fold in whites and almond extract. Add flour and cream of tartar, and the milk and baking soda last. Bake in a greased and floured angel-food-cake pan at 375° for 50 minutes. Cool upside down. Top with chocolate dressing. Serves 12 or more.

Chocolate Dressing

1 square, or 1 ounce, unsweetened chocolate, grated	1 cup milk
1 cup sugar	2 teaspoons vanilla extract

Cook chocolate, sugar, and milk in a double boiler until mixture thickens, about 10 minutes. Flavor with vanilla. Allow cake to cool and spread with warm icing. Brown-sugared almond crumbs may be sprinkled on the top before adding the dressing.

(Adapted from ledger of Corbit receipts)

Molly Corbit's Peach Tart

½ cup butter or margarine
2 cups stale cake crumbs, or
   macaroon crumbs, or graham
   cracker crumbs
Light brown sugar (about 1 cup)

Cinnamon
12 peach halves, fresh or canned
2 egg yolks
1 cup heavy cream, or sour
   cream

Melt butter on the bottom of a large pie plate. Pat on crumbs. Sprinkle liberally with cinnamon and about ½ cup sugar. Place peaches on top and sprinkle with more sugar and cinnamon. Whip egg yolks and cream together and spread on top. Bake in a hot oven (400°) for 30 minutes. Remove. Sprinkle light brown sugar on top and run under the broiler to glaze. Serves 8-10.

Shrewsbury Cakes—An English Legacy

⅓ cup dried currants
5 tablespoons brandy
1 cup butter
1½ cups sugar

2 eggs
½ nutmeg, grated
2 cups flour

Soak the currants in brandy overnight. Cream butter and sugar. Add eggs, nutmeg, flour, currants, and brandy. Drop the mixture by spoonsful onto a greased cookie sheet and bake at 350° until the edges brown, about 10 minutes.

PEWTER MUG

Family Dinner at Three O'Clock

When the tall-case clock in the dining room struck three, dinner was served to William and Mary Corbit, their brood, and visiting relatives from Dover.

CARROT SOUP

SCOLLOPED CLAMS   BONELESS SHAD WITH ROE SAUCE

RAGOO OF LAMB   SMOKED COUNTRY HAM

DRESSED CAULIFLOWER   GARDEN PEAS AND LETTUCE

FRIED TOMATOES

POTATO ROLLS   PEACH PRESERVES

DATE PUDDING   LADY CAKE WITH CHOCOLATE DRESSING

PEACH TART   APPLE FLOAT

CIDER   COFFEE   TEA   CHOCOLATE

Sweet Dishes and Confections

Date Pudding

1 cup dates, chopped
1 cup almonds, chopped
¾ cup sugar
3 eggs, beaten
½ teaspoon baking soda

1 teaspoon cream of tartar
2 tablespoons flour
Pinch of salt
½ pint heavy cream, whipped

Mix together all ingredients and pour into a shallow 8″ x 8″ greased pan. Bake until set, about 30 minutes at 350°. Cool, cut in squares, and serve with whipped cream. Rich and satisfying to the palate. Serves 6 to 8.

NUTMEG AND MACE

Minced Pies

"To one tongue add the same weight of apples. 1 lb of raisins, 1 lb currants, 1 nutmeg, a small quanity of cinnimon, orange peel, mace, and allspice, ¼ lb. Suet, ½ pint wine, ditto Brandy, cider to make it moist as you like and sugar to your taste."—manuscript cookbook of Mrs. Charles Henry Black, courtesy Historical Society of Delaware

Court Dessert

So named because chocolate was expensive, and if used lavishly was indeed worthy of a king. A very old receipt, brought up to date and easily made. Records show that the storekeeper David Wilson sold chocolate to the Corbits.

1½ cups coarse macaroon crumbs, or 8 large macaroons, coarsely broken up
½ cup sherry or Madeira
1 small package chocolate pudding
2¼ cups milk
1 square, or 1 ounce, unsweetened chocolate, grated
1¼ teaspoons vanilla extract, or almond extract
½ cup, plus ⅛ cup slivered almonds
1 cup cream, whipped

Choose a glass or crystal bowl and line it with macaroon crumbs. Douse with sherry or Madeira. Cook pudding slowly following package instructions adding an extra ¼ cup milk and grated chocolate. Stir in vanilla and ½ cup nuts. Decorate the top with the remaining nuts, sticking them in vertically. Cover the bowl to prevent a skin from forming. Mound 6 peaks of whipped cream on top before serving. Serves 6 elegantly.

(Adapted from Charles Carter, *The Complete Practical Cook*, 1730)

"In the variety of female acquirements, though domestic occupations stand not so high in esteem as they formerly did, yet when neglected they produce much human misery. There was a time when ladies knew nothing beyond their own family concerns; but in the present day there are many who know nothing about them. Each of these extremes should be avoided."—A New System of Domestic Cookery, 1808

Simples

Isolated from the city, Mary Corbit had to learn receipts for medicines such as these. Her large family relied on her to cure them of simple complaints. The doctor was called only in time of crisis. Made primarily of herbs in combination, some remedies were effective. Most were not. The following receipts are from the cookbook of Jane Wilson, 1828.

Whooping Cough Medicine

"1 Teaspoonful fresh sweet oil. Grate nutmeg on it to cover the oil. Morning and night. Affords relief for 4 or 5 days."

Receipt for a Cough—Wild Cherry Syrup

"Wild cherry bark: 2 large handfuls. ½ gallon of water. Boil it down to get 1 quart. Add ½ pound of rock candy and ½ ounce of paragoric. The dose is 1 wine glass full."

Odor for the Sickroom

"A few drops of the oil of sandalwood when dropped on a hot shovel will diffuse agreeable balsamic perfume in a sick room."

Margaret Tilghman Carroll
of Baltimore, Maryland

Mount Clare

Margaret Tilghman came from a prominent Maryland family and married Charles Carroll, Barrister, a man of substance and property. The Carrolls were large landowners. Wheat, tobacco, and iron ore were the commodities that allowed the Carrolls to maintain a townhouse in Annapolis, the mansion house Mount Clare, to breed race horses, to experiment with horticulture—in short, to live a comfortable and prosperous life similar to their English counterparts.

Charles Carroll, called "the Barrister" to distinguish him from Charles Carroll of Carrollton, is less well known but is credited with framing the state's constitution and Declaration of Rights. He was a member of Maryland's state senate and a delegate to the Continental Congress. Apparently he was also a man who could afford to indulge his wife's fine taste. Through his letterbooks, which contain orders to and invoices from agents in England, we can see how magnificently they lived.

Margaret Tilghman Carroll moved to her new home after her marriage in 1763, and began to order many luxuries and costly necessities. Their letterbooks show long lists of goods—tea, spices, tables, chairs, china, silver, pewter, curtains, damask tablecloths, playing cards, books, a microscope, a distiller for rosewater, even a set of fine French furniture for the wing drawing room.

Mrs. Carroll developed a scholar's interest in horticulture. She grew

MARGARET TILGHMAN CARROLL

and experimented with tropical fruits—including pineapples, lemons, and oranges—in her greenhouse and orangery, and fruit trees, grass seeds, roses, and even broccoli in her garden. And she had an English gardener to help her. Her husband ordered seeds for her from "Hales Compleat Body of Husbandry," and he always requested that they be put in the captain's cabin to protect them "from the damp."

Her expertise was well known; even George Washington requested advice on plants to grow in his greenhouse. A view of her gardens prompted John Adams to write in his diary that "there is a most beautiful walk from the house down to the water, there is a descent not far from the house, you have a fine garden, then you descend a few steps and have another fine garden, you go down a few more and have another."

It is a pity that none of Mrs. Carroll's records on gardening or horticulture exist, and her receipt book offers no clue to her garden's bounty except for its lavish use of lemons. We *can* assume from her intense interest in the land and her surroundings, which impressed at least two

American presidents, that Mrs. Carroll was intelligent, interesting company and a gracious hostess. She created a hospitable atmosphere for the many guests and travelers who passed through Mount Clare.

Mount Clare

Mount Clare, the mansion house of Margaret and Charles Carroll, Barrister, once stood on 848 acres looking down to the Patapsco River a mile away; it is, today, in the heart of Baltimore. It was built in the Georgian style with fine pink brick, and was begun in 1754 by the father, Dr. Charles Carroll, and completed in 1763 by his son. Charles Carroll's letterbooks to his English agent disclose that many building materials were imported, including 150 gray flagstones, stone columns from Bath, and marble tiles. It was to this splendid country seat that Charles Carroll, at the age of forty, took his twenty-one-year-old bride.

Her domain was great; she supervised as many as thirty-six servants, and was fortunate to have the services of an English housekeeper. Margaret Carroll tended to many of the details of kitchen, field, dairy, and

M. E. WARREN

orchard as well as to those of her greenhouse. Her greenhouse was her particular joy, it was so important to her, in fact, that she bequeathed the plants and tropical fruit trees in the greenhouse to James, her husband's nephew, who inherited Mount Clare.

Originally Mount Clare had two large wings and many outbuildings. In addition to the greenhouse, there was a washhouse, smokehouse, milkhouse, shed, and two necessaries. The last of the Carrolls left the mansion in 1840. Photographs taken at the time of the Civil War show all the outbuildings gone; the house was used as a barracks

for Northern officers. Fortunately, it has been fully restored in the high English style of the eighteenth century and many original Carroll pieces have been returned to their former home.

Mrs. Carroll's Receipts

Mrs. Carroll's receipt book, written in her own hand, includes receipts for rusk, rice pudding, companion pudding, rice waffles, Portugal cake, Shrewsbury cakes, almond pudding, muffin bread, calf's foot jelly, peach cordial, blanc mange, macaroons and, of course, gingerbread. Breadstuffs, cakes, and confections predominate as in most manuscript cookbooks of the day, perhaps because housewives and servants were expected to know how to cook main-course dishes. There is no mention of vanilla or chocolate. Instead the sweets are flavored with lemons or oranges, rosewater, almonds, wine, and spices. Eggs and butter are used abundantly, and Mrs. Carroll, unlike many ladies, gives directions in addition to ingredients. But what seems most remarkable is that there is not one receipt for crabs, oysters, fried chicken, or terrapin. The methods for their preparation must have been so well known to mistress and servants that it was not necessary to record them.

Soups and Savories

Garden Soup for Supper

2 or 3 big bones (or 1 each beef, veal, and mutton)
"As many chicken or turkey feet as you have"
1 or 2 stalks of celery
1 carrot
2 bay leaves
1 sprig of parsley

2 or 3 onions
Several pieces asparagus, cabbage, broccoli, or lettuce
1½ cups chicken broth
2 cloves garlic
Salt, pepper, and dash of cayenne
Juice of 1 orange

Fill a large pot ¾ full with water, add all ingredients except salt, pepper, and orange juice and simmer for 2 hours. Add more water if necessary. Strain stock by mashing all vegetables through a sieve. Return meat to the stock. Discard vegetable pulp and bones.

Vegetables for soup

1 celery stalk, chopped
1 onion, chopped
2 cups fresh or frozen mixed vegetables
1 can tomatoes
1 can creamed corn

½ cup cabbage, chopped
½ cup okra, cut
½ cup barley (optional)
1 potato, diced
2 small apples, chopped
2 medium turnips, diced

Add vegetables to stock and cook for another 30 minutes. Taste and season with salt, pepper, and cayenne. "When ready to serve add the strained juice of 1 sweet orange to this quantity. The soup may require a touch of sugar. If you have any oyster juice, add it to the soup."

A meal in itself, this soup satisfied the heartiest appetite of any gentleman.

(Adapted from a receipt of Frances Pitcher)

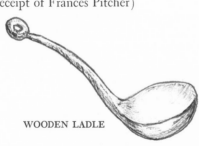

WOODEN LADLE

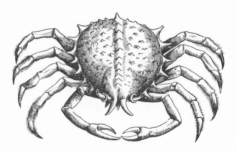

Fish, Meat, and Fowl

Carroll Crab Imperial

The crown of Maryland cookery, receipts for this dish vary with each house-hold; but for her sauce Mrs. Carroll would have been certain to use fresh heavy cream from her dairy.

4 tablespoons butter	1 cup heavy cream
½ cup green pepper, chopped	½ teaspoon salt
1 teaspoon dry mustard	Several dashes of cayenne
1 tablespoon Worcestershire sauce	1 pound crabmeat
¼ cup sherry	½ jar pimento, chopped
1 tablespoon lemon juice	Paprika
2 tablespoons flour	

Melt butter and cook peppers for several minutes. They should stay firm. Add mustard, Worcestershire sauce, sherry, and lemon juice and cook briefly to blend flavors. Add flour, then cream, salt and cayenne, and stir until thick. Add crabmeat and pimento and swirl until all blends well. This may be served in a chafing dish or in ramekins. If in ramekins, sprinkle with paprika and bake for 10 minutes at 350° until hot and bubbly. Serves 4.

To Dress a Crab

"Having taken out the meat, and cleansed it from the skin, put it into a stew-pan, with half a pint of white wine, a little nutmeg, pepper, and salt, over a slow fire. Throw in a few crumbs of bread, beat up one yolk of an egg with one spoonful of vinegar, throw it in, then shake the sauce pan round a minute, and serve it on a plate."—Mrs. Hannah Glasse, The Art of Cookery Made Plain and Easy, 1812

Soft Shell Crab

Buy fresh in season from the fishmonger and be sure he has removed the "sandbag," "dead men," and "apron." Rinse, pat dry, and roll crabs lightly in flour, salt, and pepper. Melt some lard and butter, approximately half and half, in an iron skillet about ¼ inch deep. Fry crabs until golden brown, about 5 minutes on each side. Allow 2 per person and eat everything, claws and all! This delicacy is beautiful to behold, simple to prepare, and delicious to taste. It is so sweet and succulent it needs no sauce.

Fried Oysters

24 oysters, drained	¼ teaspoon pepper
3 eggs, beaten	⅛ teaspoon cayenne
1 cup bread crumbs or cracker meal, finely pounded	Crisco, or other fat, for deep frying
1 teaspoon salt	

Dip oysters into the beaten eggs. Remove them and roll in the bread crumbs or cracker meal, which have been highly seasoned with the salt, pepper, and cayenne. Pat meal or crumbs onto oysters with your hands to coat well. Fry oysters in hot fat in a deep skillet until brown. Serve 4 to each person as an appetizer or 8 for a main dish. Serve garnished with parsley and lemons.

Maryland Fried Chicken

Approximately 1 cup flour
Salt and pepper to taste
3- to 3½-pound frying chicken, cut
   in pieces

½ cup fresh bacon fat and 1½
   cups Crisco, or all Crisco (about
   2 cups for an 11-inch frying pan)

Put flour seasoned with the salt and pepper into a paper bag. Add chicken pieces and shake to coat thoroughly. Put fat and shortening, or shortening, in a large iron skillet and heat to the point where it will brown a piece of bread a deep golden color. The fat should be deep enough to cover at least half the chicken. Put chicken in the hot fat and turn when it is a deep brown, about 10 to 15 minutes. Cover the pan for part of the remaining cooking time. When done, drain the chicken on absorbent paper. Do not refrigerate. If you wish, a delicious cream gravy can be made by skimming some of the fat from the pan drippings and adding milk and chopped, cooked giblets. Cook until thickened, stirring constantly.

Boned Turkey Breast with Mushroom and Oyster Forcemeat and Oyster Sauce

1 turkey breast
2 onions, finely chopped
½ cup celery, finely chopped
½ pound mushrooms, sliced
3 tablespoons butter
3 cups dried bread crumbs,
   crumbled
6 oysters, chopped

Several gratings of nutmeg
¼ cup sherry
¼ cup oyster liquid (or more)
½ cup parsley, snipped
Salt and pepper to taste
2 eggs
Butter for basting

Parboil the turkey in water until bone can be removed from the meat with ease, about 30 minutes. Make a stuffing by briefly sautéing onions, celery, and mushrooms in butter. Add bread crumbs and oysters. Mix in nutmeg, sherry, oyster liquor, and parsley. Season with salt and pepper. Place the forcemeat stuffing in the boned cavity of the turkey breast. Wrap or roll the skin underneath and tie the breast so that the ridge line is centered at top.

Mix 2 eggs with the leftover forcemeat and form into balls. (Forcemeat balls were very common in early cookery.) Surround the stuffed turkey with the balls. Generously butter the turkey and add several tablespoons of butter to the bottom of the roasting pan. Bake at 375° for about 45 minutes. Keep the turkey covered part of the time, but remove the cover long enough for the turkey to brown. Serve with oyster sauce to 8 diners.

Oyster Sauce

12 oysters and their liquor	2 tablespoons cognac
2 tablespoons butter	Salt to taste
1 tablespoon flour	½ cup sherry
⅔ cup cream	

Heat oysters in their liquor just until the edges curl. Chop oysters in large pieces. Make a roux of the butter and flour. Add cream, cognac, sherry, and salt and simmer to thicken. Put oysters in last. Thin the sauce with oyster liquor if necessary.

(Adapted from Mrs. B. C. Howard, *Fifty Years in a Maryland Kitchen*)

Roots and Vegetables

To Make a Salamagundy

"Mince 2 chickens, boiled or roasted, or veal if you please. Mince yolks of hard eggs very small. Mince whites separately. Shred pulp of 2 or 3 lemons very small. Then in your dish add a layer of each of the following: the minced chicken or veal, egg yolks, egg whites, anchovies, shredded lemon pulp, pickles, sorrel, spinach, lettuce, and shallots. When dish is filled, garnish with horseradish scraped and sliced lemon.

Beat up some oil with the juice of lemon, salt, and mustard, thick, and serve it up for a second course, side dish, or middle dish, for supper."—Mrs. Hannah Glasse, The Art of Cookery Made Plain and Easy, 1812

Fresh Corn Pudding

3 eggs, separated
1 cup milk
Cornkernels scraped from 9 large
  ears, uncooked

Salt and pepper to taste
1 tablespoon sugar

Beat egg yolks, add milk, and beat again. Add corn and seasonings. Fold in stiffened egg whites. Put in a greased casserole and bake at 350° for about 40 minutes. Serves 6.

Carrot Pudding

3 eggs, separated
4 tablespoons sugar
1½ tablespoons cornstarch
1 cup milk
3 cups, or 2 pounds, mashed carrots

1 cup fine bread crumbs
3 tablespoons butter
1 teaspoon salt
1 cup light cream
¼ cup cream sherry
¾ teaspoon freshly grated nutmeg

Beat the egg yolks and sugar until light. Mix the cornstarch with a small amount of milk until dissolved. Heat remaining milk, add cornstarch, and stir until smooth and slightly thickened. Blend a small amount of the hot thickened mixture into the egg yolks and sugar. Mix well and return to the remaining hot milk and cornstarch mixture, cooking over medium heat and stirring until smooth and thick. Add carrots, bread crumbs, butter, and salt and blend evenly. Stir in cream; add sherry and nutmeg. Mix well. Beat egg whites until firmly peaked and fold into carrot mixture. Pour into a greased 2-quart pudding pan. Place pudding pan in hot water and bake at 300° for 30 minutes; then increase to 350° and bake an additional 50 minutes.

SILVER GRAVYBOAT

Pickles and Preserves

Green Tomato Pickle

1 peck (8 quarts) green tomatoes
8 cups onions
6 sweet red peppers
6 green peppers
About ½ cup salt

2 pounds brown sugar
1 teaspoon turmeric
2 ounces celery seed
1 tablespoon red pepper
2 quarts vinegar

Slice tomatoes, onions, and peppers thin. Sprinkle with salt. Soak overnight. In the morning squeeze out and pour off juice. Then add all seasoning. Boil for at least 2 hours. It is not necessary to peel tomatoes.

At Mrs. Carroll's request, her husband wrote that, "we are in need of a sober, orderly woman of good character that understands Cooking, Pickling, Preserving and the other Requisites for a Housekeeper. If elderly we shall Like her the Better. She must not be of the flirting kind or one that will give herself airs. If above the ordinary rank of servants, my wife will Like her Better as she will meet with all kind treatment."—Letterbooks of Dr. Charles Carroll, Ms. 208, Maryland Historical Society.

Spicy Plum Molded Jelly

1½ cups fresh ripe plums, pitted
and chopped
1 cup red wine
1 teaspoon grated lemon rind
1½ envelopes unflavored gelatin
½ teaspoon cinnamon

⅛ teaspoon ground cloves
1 cup currant syrup (available in
specialty food stores)
1 cup boiling water
Juice of ½ lemon

Mix plums, wine, and lemon rind and let stand for several hours. Combine gelatin, cinnamon, cloves, and currant syrup. Add boiling water and stir until gelatin is dissolved. Strain the plums. Stir wine and lemon juice into the gelatin mixture. Pour into a mold. When partly set, stir in plums. Unmold on a footed stand and serve with main-course meats.

Breadstuffs

Jamie's Corn Meal Waffles

2 cups finely ground cornmeal,
   white or yellow
2 heaping tablespoons white flour
1 teaspoon salt
2 teaspoons cream of tartar

1 teaspoon baking soda
2 eggs
1½ cups milk
2 tablespoons corn oil

Sift dry ingredients. Add eggs and milk. Beat quickly. Add the oil last. Bake as usual in your waffle iron. They are best when crisp and well browned. Serve with sausage and syrup.

Uncommon Cakes and Pies

WAFFLE IRON

Little Sugar Cakes

1 cup butter
2 cups sugar
3 eggs
1 cup sour cream
1 teaspoon baking soda in sour
   cream

3½ cups flour
1 teaspoon lemon extract
Raisins

Cream butter and sugar. Beat in eggs. Add sour cream, baking soda, and then flour. Drop by teaspoonsful onto a greased cookie sheet. Place a fat raisin in the center of each cake before you turn them into the oven. Bake at 350° until brown around edges but still light on top, about 8 to 10 minutes.

(Receipt of Elizabeth Ritchie)

Sand Tarts

1 cup butter, creamed
2 cups sugar
6 eggs, separated
½ teaspoon baking soda

2 tablespoons milk
4 cups flour
Cinnamon and sugar for dusting
Blanched almonds

Mix butter and sugar. To this add the beaten egg yolks, and mix well. Add baking soda to the milk and pour into mixture. Add 4 cups flour, or a sufficient amount to allow for rolling. Cut with a round cutter. Brush with beaten egg whites. Dust lightly with cinnamon and sugar and place blanched almonds on each. Bake at 400° until done, about 8 minutes.

Maryland Rocks

½ cup sugar
½ cup brown sugar
⅔ cup butter
2 eggs
1½ cups flour
1 teaspoon baking soda in a little hot water

1 teaspoon cinnamon
1 teaspoon ground cloves
¼ teaspoon allspice
2 cups nuts, chopped (black walnuts, English walnuts, or pecans)
1 pound raisins

Cream the sugars and butter. Add eggs. Blend in flour, baking soda, and spices. Fold in nuts and raisins. Drop by tablespoonsful onto a greased cookie sheet. Bake for 10 minutes at 350°. This receipt doubles well and the rocks will keep for a month.

Macaroons

3 cups almonds, blanched	4 egg whites
1 tablespoon rosewater	2 cups sugar

Place almonds and rosewater in a blender and blend until the nuts are very fine. (The original receipt says to pound in a mortar, but the result in the blender is similar.) Beat egg whites until frothy. Gradually add sugar and beat until stiff. Fold in finely blended nuts. Drop them with a spoon in little round cakes on buttered paper. Put the paper on a cookie sheet and set in a gentle oven (300°) for 25 to 30 minutes. Makes approximately 8 dozen macaroons.

(Adapted from Mrs. Carroll's receipt book.)

Light Cake

"4 lbs. of flour—a lb. and ¼ of sugar—a lb. of butter, 8 eggs, leaving out 4 whites, a gill of wine—a pint of new milk, a pint of yeast—one nutmeg, a dessert spoonfull of mace—and a large one of cinnamon."— Receipt of Mrs. Carroll

SILVER CAKE BASKET

Applesauce Fruit Cake

At Mount Clare, as on most large plantations and small farms, apples were common and used abundantly. Spices and nourishing fruit make this early receipt a good choice for fall lunch baskets.

1 cup butter or shortening	1 teaspoon salt
2 cups brown sugar	1 cup nuts
2 cups applesauce	1 cup raisins
2 teaspoons baking soda	1 cup currants
4 cups flour	1 cup figs, dates, or citron, or a
1 teaspoon each ground cloves, cinnamon, and nutmeg	combination

Cream butter and sugar. Add applesauce and baking soda. Put flour and seasonings together and stir into mixture. Nuts and fruit, 4 cups in all, go in last. Bake in a moderate oven (350°) for 1½ hours. Makes one large cake. To store, top may be doused with sherry and put in covered cake tin.

(Receipt of Elizabeth Ritchie)

Date and Almond Cake

1 cup heavy cream	1½ cups sifted flour
2 eggs	1 teaspoon vanilla extract
1 cup sugar	

In a large bowl beat cream until stiff. In another bowl beat eggs until frothy. Add eggs to cream, beating at medium speed; then mix in sugar, flour, and vanilla. Bake in 2 buttered and floured 8-inch-round cake pans at 350° for 20 to 25 minutes, or until tests done. The cakes will seem flat.

Date Topping

1 pound dates, pitted and halved	A few drops of lemon juice
Honey	Whole almonds, blanched

Place dates, honey, and lemon juice in pan and gently warm on low heat until honey is melted. The dates should retain their shape. Cool slightly. Arrange date halves and almonds on top of each cake in a circular pattern, alternating dates and nuts. Pour small amount of honey over the top of each cake and allow to stand for a few minutes. Repeat once more after honey has been absorbed by cake.

Sweet Dishes and Confections

WATERFORD
GLASS COMPOTE

Orange Pudding

"To Come in Pudding Time" meant to English colonists like Mrs. Carroll to come at the beginning of a meal, not at the end. Puddings took the edge off the appetite. Hearty puddings of rice, bread, Indian grain, suet, oatmeal, curd, or sweet potato, some boiled in a bag, others baked, accompanied the

joints of meat offered in the first course, or in simple homes might constitute a whole supper. Near the end of the eighteenth century, lighter puddings made with more eggs, butter, and cream came into favor. Today, of course, Americans prefer sweet puddings only as desserts.

1½ envelopes unflavored gelatin	1 cup fresh orange juice
½ cup cold water	1 tablespoon grated orange rind
3 egg yolks, beaten	Juice of 1 lemon
2 cups milk	Rind of 1 lemon, grated
1 cup sugar	½ cup heavy cream, whipped

Soften the gelatin in cold water. Beat the egg yolks. Combine milk and sugar in a saucepan and heat until "milk scalds." Dissolve the gelatin in the hot mixture. Very slowly beat the egg yolks into the hot mixture, stirring briskly with a whisk until they are thoroughly combined. Next, stir in the fruit juices and rinds. Chill the mixture. When it has jelled slightly (check after about 30 minutes), whip the cream and fold it into the pudding. Pour the pudding into a silver or glass serving bowl and chill until firm. Spread a thin layer of whipped cream over the top. Accompany the pudding with delicate little cakes. Meringues or macaroons could be made with the leftover egg whites. Serves 8.

Snow Pudding

This dessert is both delicious and settling to those who have eaten heartily of the main course. An elegant finish to a fine dinner.

1 tablespoon unflavored gelatin	¼ cup, plus 1 tablespoon lemon juice
¼ cup cold water	
1 cup boiling water	1 tablespoon grated lemon rind
1 cup sugar	3 egg whites, stiffly beaten

Soak gelatin in cold water. Dissolve in boiling water. Add sugar, lemon juice, and lemon rind. Set aside in the refrigerator, or in the freezer if you are hurried, until it becomes soft jelly. Beat the gelatin mixture until smooth; then fold in the stiffly beaten egg whites. Continue beating the mixture until thick and smooth. Pour into your best serving bowl and chill until served. Prepare custard sauce. Serves 8. This receipt can be doubled and tripled with success. Snow pudding should be ornamented on top with fresh strawberries and served with custard sauce poured from a silver or crystal pitcher. Pass a rich pound cake to your guests.

Custard Sauce

3 egg yolks
2 cups milk
⅛ teaspoon salt

½ cup sugar
1 teaspoon vanilla extract

Beat the egg yolks. Add milk, salt, and sugar and cook slowly over low heat until thick, stirring constantly. Add vanilla. Cool and store in the refrigerator.

Tilghman's Huckleberry Pudding

¼ cup butter
1 cup sugar
2 eggs, beaten
½ cup sour cream, or yogurt

½ teaspoon baking soda
2 cups flour
½ teaspoon cream of tartar
1 pint huckleberries

Cream the butter and sugar. Add the beaten eggs. Then, add sour cream, or yogurt, to which the baking soda has been added. Stir in 1 cup of flour and the cream of tartar. Lastly, add the berries well dusted with the other cup of flour. Bake in a greased mold at 350° for about 1 hour. Serve with brandied hard sauce. Commercial blueberries may be used and yogurt works well in place of sour cream. Serves 8.

BELL METAL SKILLET

Frozen Peaches

"2 quarts of peach juice (rub the peaches through a collander), 1 pint of water, 2 lbs. of sugar. When frozen it is very nice."—Coale Collection, Ms. 248, Maryland Historical Society

Apricot Fool

"My wife takes much Pleasure in gardening and sends you a List of Peaches each of which she would be glad if you would send some of the stones of those of them that can be met with, Tied up in Different Parcels and the names of each wrote on the Parcel and Likewise Some of the Stones of your best Apricots and Nectarines."—Charles Carroll, Letterbooks, July 20, 1767

3 cups mashed apricots, or 2 29-ounce cans drained and pureed.	1 cup heavy cream, whipped
	1 tablespoon sugar
¼ cup orange brandy	Rind of 1 lemon, grated

Drain apricots. Mash to fill 3 cups; then puree in a blender. Stir in liqueur, whipped cream sweetened with the sugar, and lemon rind. Pour into dessert dishes. Top with preserved ginger or large flakes of semi-sweet chocolate. Serves 8.

Fresh Brandied Nectarines

9 medium nectarines	½ cup brandy
1 cup sugar	½ cup heavy cream
1 cup water	2 tablespoons confectioners sugar
2 tablespoons rosewater	2 tablespoons brandy

Blanch first and then peel the nectarines. Bring fruit, sugar, and water to a boil and simmer for 1 minute. Add rosewater and ½ cup brandy. Let stand until cool, then refrigerate. Mix together the cream, confectioners sugar, and 2 tablespoons brandy. Put drained nectarines in a compote and spoon the cream over them. Garnish with several fresh raspberries bedded in a small mint leaf or two.

Drams and Punches

Mrs. Carroll's Iced Sangaree

When Martha Washington passed through Baltimore on her way to New York for the first inauguration, she stopped at Mount Clare. Mrs. Carroll entertained the new First Lady's entourage with refreshments. "We found a large bowl of salubrious iced punch, with fruits &c which had been plucked from the trees in a green house, lying on the tables in great abundance; these, after riding 25 or 30 miles without eating or drinking, was no unwelcome luxury; however, Mrs. C could not complain that we had not done her punch honor, for in the course of 1 quarter of an hour (the time we tarried) this bowl, which held upwards of two gallons was entirely consumed to the no little satisfaction of us all."—from Robert Lewis's journal in Douglas Southall Freeman, George Washington

2 peach stones
¼ cup sugar
1 cup brandy
2 ripe peaches, sliced
2 slices fresh pineapple, cubed or crushed
2 ripe nectarines, sliced

1 orange, sliced and seeded
1 lemon, sliced and seeded
10 strawberries
2 nectarine stones
1 bottle claret wine
2 cups club soda

Crack peach stones and take out the kernels. Add sugar and brandy to the fruit, nectarine stones, and peach kernels and let stand for several hours in the bottom of a punch bowl. When ready to serve, remove nectarine stones and peach kernels and pour claret and club soda into the bowl. Add an ice ring made with fresh peach leaves or sprigs of fresh mint. Add a portion of fruit to each cup.

Mount Clare Peach Cordial

1 dozen ripe peaches	½ gallon brandy, or apple brandy
2 cups sugar	1 handful peach kernels
2 quarts boiling water	1 teaspoon allspice

Scald peaches in boiling water for 1 minute; then cool quickly in ice water. Peel and halve. Crack peach stones and take out the kernels. Put peaches into a large stone jar with sugar and pour the boiling water over them. Add brandy or apple brandy, one handful of peach kernels, and allspice. Shake them frequently. Let stand for 4 to 6 months. "They will be fit to use on New Year's Day," Mrs. Carroll wrote on her receipt.

(Adapted from Mrs. Carroll's receipt book)

---

*New Year's Day Collation
at Mount Clare*

CRAB IMPERIAL   OYSTER LOAVES
BONED TURKEY BREAST WITH FORCEMEAT AND OYSTER SAUCE
FRIED CHICKEN   MARYLAND HAM
FRUITS IN WHITE WINE JELLY
BEATEN BISCUITS   SALLY LUNN

APRICOT FOOL   MINCED PIES
POUND CAKE   LIGHT FRUIT CAKE
MARYLAND ROCKS   LITTLE SUGAR CAKES
COCONUT JUMBLES
PEACH CORDIAL   SYLLABUB   EGG NOG
SANGAREE

Dinner for Governor Eden
Before His Departure for England

Charles Carroll, the Barrister, was chairman of the committee that relieved Governor Eden of his office in 1776. The night before Maryland's last colonial governor sailed for England, Mr. Carroll entertained him at dinner. This was the epitome of gracious manners and civility; Marylanders did not hate the governor himself, they just abhorred his politics. It was probably an affair for gentlemen only, in Annapolis, but Mrs. Carroll would have planned the menu to suit their hearty appetites.

DRESSED CRAB

STUFFED ROCKFISH   FRIED OYSTERS

BROILED GAME BIRDS

MARYLAND HAM   CHICKEN AND OYSTER PIE

MOLDED SPICED PLUM JELLY

CARROT PUDDING   BROCCOLI

SPOON BREAD   APRICOT NUTBREAD

BRANDIED NECTARINES   PINEAPPLE CHUTNEY

ORANGE PUDDING   APPLESAUCE FRUIT CAKE

MACAROONS   LEMON CHEESECAKES

PUNCH   MADEIRA   PORT

ALMONDS   RAISINS

FRESH FRUIT

"Pray let the [London tradesmen] know that we have, tho' out of the Sound of Bow Bells, a Distinguishing faculty in our Tastes and for the future Let us have his best.—Charles Carroll, Letterbooks, 1765

Betty Washington Lewis
of Fredericksburg, Virginia

Kenmore

Betty Washington and her husband, Fielding Lewis, lived in the center of a self-sufficient world. Kenmore, their home, was an elegant brick Georgian structure. The interior was designed with infinite care: Large windows and high ceilings gave an air of spaciousness and light to the well-proportioned rooms, and the sculptured plaster and finely-carved woodwork made each room a masterpiece of form and design. Accompanying the house were separate dependencies—the kitchen and laundry, slaves' quarters, stables, schoolhouse, smokehouse, and cowhouse. A flower garden, kitchen garden, and fields of hay, corn, and tobacco stretched to the river.

This mistress of such a household had to be able to attend to a multitude of tasks in an orderly and competent manner. For this role, Betty was well prepared. Born on June 20, 1733, she grew up in a houseful of boys (including her brother George, who would one day be President) and learned independent ways early.

Just before her eighteenth birthday, in May of 1750, Betty married Fielding Lewis, a Fredericksburg merchant and a widower. Like so many gentlemen of his day, Fielding Lewis was a man of many interests; he farmed, bought and sold land and farm products, and was active in local politics.

About this same time, the Lewis family moved into their new home, Kenmore. Fortunately, the house was large, for it was to accommodate

178

an ever-increasing household. Eleven children were born to the Lewises (although only five reached maturity), and Fielding's son and daughter by another wife also lived with them.

Nine of Betty's eleven children were sons. As the young boys grew to manhood, the spirit of revolution grew within the country. They saw their father training and equipping the Frederick County militia. As their Uncle George traveled from his home at Mount Vernon to the General Assembly in Williamsburg, he stopped overnight at Kenmore. Late into the evening, Fielding, Betty, George, and other Fredericksburg neighbors lingered round the dining table discussing the repressive activities of the Colonial Governor and the reactions of the Virginia patriots.

When war finally came, George Washington had a special task for his brother-in-law. The Continental Army needed guns and ammunition, so Fielding Lewis and Charles Dick established a factory to provide the arms. But in so doing, Lewis's health declined and he died in 1781.

A widow at the age of forty-nine, Betty Lewis was left with three teenage boys still at home. Most of the family's financial assets were tied up in the munitions factory, which lost its value once the war ended. Betty still owned the plantation, but she had meager funds with which to maintain it. For the next fourteen years Betty superintended the plantation, selling off small pieces of the land as financial necessity dictated. She opened a small school in her home, employing a

BETTY WASHINGTON LEWIS

COLONY STUDIOS

tutor and enrolling neighborhood children in order to provide education for her sons. She cared for her mother, Mary Washington, until her death in 1789. At George's request, she opened her home to her orphaned niece, Harriet, who apparently needed some motherly supervision. "Harriet has sense enough," wrote George, "but no disposition to industry, nor to be careful with her clothes. Your example and admonition, with proper restraints may overcome the last two." Betty instructed Harriet in housewifely skills and introduced her to Fredericksburg society. Once Harriet was married, Betty felt free to leave Kenmore. She moved to Mill Brook but was there only briefly, for while visiting her daughter Elizabeth Carter at Western View, she died in March of 1797.

Kenmore

The Lewis home is one of the most beautiful American adaptations of Georgian architecture. A wide walk of bricks set in a herringbone pattern leads to the house, which was designed by John Ariss, who was probably also the architect for the renovations at Mount Vernon. While the brick exterior of the building is stern and stark in its simple Georgian lines, the interior, furnished in Chippendale and Queen Anne, is warm and welcoming. Most striking is the elaborate plaster relief decoration—an overmantle in the drawing room depicts Aesop's fable of

the Fox and the Crow and an elaborate festoon of fruit and flowers enhances the library fireplace. The ceilings of the three principal rooms are also intricately sculptured in plaster designs, perfectly scaled to the size and the shape of the rooms.

The Kenmore kitchen is located in a separate dependency linked to the dining room by a brick path across a small courtyard. This brick building is divided in half with one side housing the laundry and candlemaking facilities, the other the kitchen. Dominating the kitchen is a wide, open fireplace, where five large pots could sit easily within the raised hearth or be suspended above the flames on one of the two large cranes. To the left of the fireplace opening is a beehive oven. Herbs from the garden just outside the door hang from a long wooden drying rack across the chimney. One can imagine the brick-floored kitchen as it was in Betty Lewis's day with various tables for cleaning and chopping vegetables, bins of flour and cornmeal, and kegs of cider and ale. Light from windows on three sides of the room make the kitchen a cheerful and pleasant room in which to perform the many tasks necessary for a large Virginia household.

The only cookbook mentioned in the household inventory of Betty and Fielding Lewis was *The Compleat Housewife* by Eliza Smith. One of the most widely distributed cookbooks in colonial America, it was first published in London in 1727. In 1742 a Williamsburg printer, William Parks, reprinted Mrs. Smith's book, making it the first known cookbook printed in British America. Since it is very possible that Betty Lewis owned the Williamsburg edition of *The Compleat Housewife*, many of the following receipts are adapted from that edition of Mrs. Smith's book.

Soups and Savories

Fresh Sorrel Soup

Sorrel—a pot-herb known as sour-grass—"sharpens the appetite, assuages heat, cools the liver and strengthens the heart." It is best eaten in the early spring when young and tender.

4 tablespoons butter
1 medium onion, chopped
4 tablespoons flour
1 pint fresh sorrel leaves, chopped
3 large lettuce leaves, chopped
3 tablespoons fresh chervil, or 1½ tablespoons dried

5 cups strong, fresh chicken broth
1 cup soured cream
1 tablespoon fresh basil, finely chopped
4 egg yolks
Salt and pepper to taste

In a large pan melt the butter, add the chopped onion, and cook for 2 minutes without browning. Sprinkle with flour, stir well, and add the chopped sorrel and lettuce (there should be 2 cups of greens). Continue to stir. Add basil and chervil chopped fine. Add the chicken broth. Cook until the greens are tender, about 10 minutes. Place the soup over boiling water until ready to serve. Remove from the fire and gradually stir in 1 cup soured cream that has been beaten together with the egg yolks. Season with salt and coarsely ground pepper and serve at once. The basic soup can be made and frozen in the spring or summer for winter use: Defrost the soup, heat it, and add the cream and eggs.

Anchovy Toasts

"Cut some slices of bread tolerably thick, and toast them slightly; bone some anchovies, lay half of one on each toast, cover it well with grated cheese and chopped parsley mixed; pour a little melted butter on, and brown it with a salamander; it must be done on the dish you send it to the table in."—Mrs. Mary Randolph, The Virginia Housewife, *1846*

Today's cook might like to serve anchovy toast as an appetizer, using melba toast, chopped anchovies, and grated Swiss or cheddar cheese. Keep warm in a 300° oven, or pass quickly under a preheated broiler.

Fish, Meat, and Fowl

Oyster Loaves

Oysters in abundance supplied inventive cooks with ingredients for elegant dishes such as this, which can be made rather simply by using scallop shells.

"Take a quart of oysters, stew them a little while in their own liquor, then strain the liquor and take care that there is no shells amongst the oysters. Then put your oysters and liquor in a sauce pot with a bitt of butter, a little pepper, a blade of mace. Stew them all together a little while. Then have a little parsley shred small and put it in. Toss it all together, then take four french rolls and cutt a round hole in the top and shape out all the crumbs and fill up with oysters and liquor. Then put the pieces of crust on again. To fry the rolls in a very good butter, there must be butter enough in the pan to fry up to the top of the holes, but not over them. So serve them up hott. Oysters in scallop shells are done the same way, only when they are stewed as foresaid, you must lay them handsomely in scallop shells with little lumps of butter. Strew them over with crumbs of white bread. So broil them on a gridiron a little while and just before you send them up, take a red hott iron fire shovell and hold over them to brown to crisp the crumbs. So serve them up."—The American Domestic Cookery, 1808

Baked Ham from the Smokehouse

With a ham in the smokehouse and a good frock in the press, a lady can face any occasion.

Soak one Virginia country ham overnight in cold water. Scrub with a stiff wire brush to remove the mold. Place the ham in a large container with a lid and barely cover with water. Bring to a boil and boil vigorously for 30 minutes; then reduce heat and simmer for 5 hours, turning after 2 hours.

Remove outer skin from the ham, leaving a layer of fat. Combine equal amounts of dry bread crumbs and brown sugar with just enough cider vinegar to moisten slightly. Pat this mixture on the top and sides of the ham. Dot with cloves. Bake at 375° for 30 minutes. Serve thinly sliced on a platter. For greater elegance place the ham on a ham rack and garnish with glacéed fruits.

To Make a Country Ham

"To each ham put one ounce saltpeter, one pint bay salt, one pint molasses, shake together 6 or 8 weeks, or when a large quantity is together baste them with the liquor every day; when taken out to dry, smoke three weeks with cobbs or malt fumes."—The Economical Housekeeper, 1730

Shoulder of Mutton Roasted with Garlic and Rosemary

This receipt is adapted from one found in the manuscript cookbook written by Frances Parke Custis, mother of Martha Washington's first husband. When Betty Lewis's son Lawrence married Nelly Custis, her Grandmamma Martha Washington presented this book of treasured family receipts to the new bride.

4-pound shoulder of mutton	1 teaspoon freshly ground pepper
2 cloves garlic	1 tablespoon flour
1 tablespoon salt	1 cup claret wine
1 teaspoon rosemary, crushed	

Have the butcher bone and roll the shoulder. Cut the garlic into small slivers; pierce the outside of the roast in several places and insert garlic. Mix together salt, rosemary, pepper, and flour. Rub this mixture on the outside of the roast. Roast on a spit before the fire, basting every 10 minutes with claret. Or, preheat oven to 450°, add meat, and cook for 10 minutes; then reduce heat to 350° and cook until done, about 1½ hours, basting often. Make a gravy with the wine and pan juices, thickening it with 1 tablespoon flour dissolved in ¼ cup water. Serve on a platter garnished with mint or parsley accompanied by oven-browned potatoes and minted green peas. Serves 6.

BETTY LEWIS' SILVER MEAT COVER

Christmas Morning at Kenmore

Now Christmas comes, 'tis fit that we
Should feast and sing, and merry be
Keep open House, let Fiddlers play
A Fig for Cold, sing Care away
And may they who thereat repine
On brown Bread and on small Beer dine.
—Virginia Almanack, 1766

For Christmas, 1769, George and Martha Washington and Mother Washington joined the family at Kenmore (or Millbank, as it was called then). The house was full and the families were happy to share the Christmas festivities with each other.

Christmas brunch was an extremely festive meal. The stately dining room was bedecked with silver, candles, and greens. Central to the feast was a Virginia ham. It was provided, perhaps, by George and Martha, whose hogs fed upon the mash from a distillery on the Mount Vernon property, producing a flavorful, succulent ham. Fried Virginia apples were (and are still today) a must for any brunch. Fresh fish and oysters from the Rappahannock River were plentiful and certain to have been a part of the Christmas menu, as was corn from Fielding Lewis's own fields. For dessert there were mince and chess pies, honey flummery, and filbert pudding.

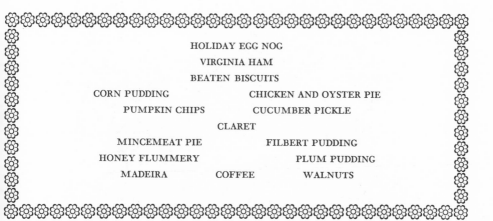

HOLIDAY EGG NOG

VIRGINIA HAM

BEATEN BISCUITS

CORN PUDDING   CHICKEN AND OYSTER PIE

PUMPKIN CHIPS   CUCUMBER PICKLE

CLARET

MINCEMEAT PIE   FILBERT PUDDING

HONEY FLUMMERY   PLUM PUDDING

MADEIRA   COFFEE   WALNUTS

Venison Steak with Wine Sauce

6 venison steaks, cut ¾ inch thick
6 slices bacon
2 tablespoons flour
1 teaspoon sage
1 teaspoon celery salt

½ teaspoon thyme
⅛ teaspoon cayenne
2 tablespoons butter
1 cup burgundy wine

Remove all fat and gristle from the steaks. Wrap bacon around the outside of each steak and secure with a toothpick. Mix together flour and spices. Dust this mixture over both sides of the steaks, and fry in butter over a hot flame for 3 minutes on one side, 5 minutes on the other side. Remove from the frying pan to a heated platter. Add burgundy to the frying pan, stirring to dissolve all pan juices. Simmer until sauce is slightly thickened; then pour over meat. Serve with wild rice, spinach, and orange-and-onion salad.

Wild rice was familiar to some eighteenth-century colonists. Julian Niemcewicz, a Polish visitor to America, describing a dinner in Philadelphia with Thomas Jefferson and Dr. Scandella, stated, "The Dr. showed us a bag of Wild Rize and wild oats, Zizania Aquatica, grains which grow wild in marshy places in all of America up to the Hudson Bay. Cattle are extremely fond of it. It even provides good nourishment for people."—Julian Niemcewicz, Under Their Vine and Fig Tree, *1797–99*

Sweetbread and Oyster Pie

"This is the most delicate pie that can be made," wrote Mrs. Mary Randolph in her collection of Virginia receipts.

1 pair sweetbreads
9-inch pie shell, unbaked, and dough for a top crust
2 tablespoons butter
2 tablespoons flour
1 cup light cream
1 teaspoon salt
¼ teaspoon pepper
1 dozen oysters
Milk for brushing

Soak sweetbreads in cold salted water until they become white, about 30 minutes. Rinse; then simmer gently in fresh water for 30 minutes. Remove from heat and drain. Prepare a rich pastry shell. Make a white sauce by melting butter, stirring in flour, and then slowly stirring cream into the mixture. Stir until thick. Add salt and pepper. Layer the oysters and sweetbreads in a pie shell. Cover with white sauce; then cover with piecrust. Brush the top with milk. Bake at 350° for 40 minutes. Serves 6.

(Adapted from Mrs. Mary Randolph, *The Virginia Housewife*, 1846)

Jellied Chicken

1 envelope unflavored gelatin
2 cups chicken stock
1 teaspoon lemon juice
1 teaspoon wine vinegar
1 tablespoon Madeira, or dry sherry
½ teaspoon salt
2 cups chicken, cut in bite-size pieces
1 cup celery, sliced
2 hard-boiled eggs, sliced
¼ cup stuffed olives, sliced, or 1 4-ounce jar artichoke hearts

Dissolve gelatin in 1 tablespoon of the cold chicken stock. Bring remaining stock to a boil and stir into the gelatin mixture. Add lemon juice, vinegar, and Madeira or sherry. Add the remaining ingredients and pour into an oiled 5-cup mold. Chill. Serve with homemade mayonnaise to which a dash of curry powder has been added. Serves 6 to 8.

(Adapted from Mrs. Mary Randolph, *The Virginia Housewife*, 1846)

Broccoli in Sallad

Vegetables appear infrequently in eighteenth-century cookbooks, and when they do appear they are generally too overcooked and underspiced for twentieth-century palates. An exception to this is the following receipt for broccoli, which is excellent served cold on lettuce.

"Trim about eighteen heads of broccoli; wash them, boil them green as you can, and lay them in a dish; mix the yolk of a hard egg with a cruet of oil, a little vinegar, a spoonful of mustard, a little salt and pour over them."—Richard Briggs, The New Art of Cookery, 1798

Squash and Peanut Pie

3 pounds tender yellow squash
1 medium onion, finely chopped
¼ cup butter
½ cup heavy cream
1 teaspoon salt
½ teaspoon grated nutmeg

⅛ teaspoon cayenne
½ cup salted peanuts, finely chopped
½ cup dry bread crumbs
2 tablespoons melted butter

Slice the squash but do not peel it. Cover with water and boil until tender, about 5 minutes. Drain thoroughly, shaking colander often to be sure all liquid is gone. Mash the squash; add onion, butter, cream, salt, nutmeg, cayenne, and ¼ cup of the peanuts (or whiz all ingredients together in a blender.) Pour into a buttered pie plate or a shallow baking dish. Combine remaining ¼ cup of peanuts, bread crumbs, and melted butter. Sprinkle over the squash mixture. Bake at 375° for 30 minutes until the top is lightly browned. Serves 8.

Mess of Pease

"To have them in perfection, they must be quite young, gather early in the morning, kept in a cool place, not shelled until they are to be dressed; put salt in the water and when it boils, put in the pease; boil them quick according to their age; just before they are taken up add a little mint, chopped very fine; drain all the water from the pease, put in a bit of butter and serve them up quite hot."—Mrs. Mary Randolph, The Virginia Housewife, 1846

Fried Cucumbers

"You must brown some Butter in a Pan and cut the Cucumbers in thin Slices; drain them from the Water, then fling them into the Pan, and when they are fried brown, put in a little Pepper and Salt, a Bit of an Onion and Gravy, and let them stew together, and squeeze in some Juice of Lemon; shake them well, and put them under your Mutton."—Eliza Smith, The Compleat Housewife, 1742

Pickles and Preserves

Pickled Green Beans

As the string beans were harvested at Kenmore, Betty Lewis had to preserve some of the crop for the family's winter table. This green-bean pickle is an especially delicious way to store the summer's bounty.

4 pounds fresh green beans
2 cups water
3 cups cider vinegar
2 cups sugar
2 teaspoons mustard seeds

2 teaspoons peppercorns
2 teaspoons salt
2 cinnamon sticks
4 cloves garlic

Wash the beans. Snap off the ends, but leave the beans long. Cover with cold water, bring to a boil, and boil until they are done but still quite crisp, about 15 minutes. Drain, reserving 2 cups of the water. Combine water, vinegar, sugar, and spices. Bring to a boil and stir until the sugar dissolves. Add the beans and bring to a boil again. Pour into hot sterilized jars. Add 1 clove garlic to each jar. Seal. Chill before serving. Makes 6 pints.

Breadstuffs

Virginia Spoonbread

2 cups milk	1 teaspoon salt
1 cup white cornmeal	3 eggs, separated
1 teaspoon sugar	½ cup butter

Heat milk to the boiling point; stir in cornmeal, sugar, and salt and cook until thick, stirring constantly. Remove from heat and cool slightly; then add lightly beaten egg yolks and butter. Fold in stiffly beaten egg whites and pour into a heated, buttered 2-quart casserole. Bake at 350° for 50 minutes. Spoon the hot bread onto a plate and top with a thick pat of butter. Serves 6.

OVAL DUTCH OVEN

Cracklin' Bread

4 strips of bacon	
1½ cups white cornmeal	1 teaspoon salt
1 teaspoon baking soda	1 cup buttermilk

Fry the bacon until crisp and brown. Reserve the bacon grease. Stir cornmeal, baking soda, and salt into the buttermilk. Add cooled bacon grease and crumbled bacon. Pour into a well-greased 8-inch-square pan and bake in a hot oven (400°) for 25 minutes, or until well browned. Serve with sorghum molasses. Serves 8.

Sally Lunn

Hawked on the streets of London as Soleil-Lune—the sun and the moon— this lovely yeast bread is baked in a Turk's-head mold and now known as Sally Lunn.

1 cup milk	⅓ cup sugar
¼ cup water	2 teaspoons salt
½ cup shortening	2 packages dry yeast
4 cups sifted flour	3 eggs

Heat the milk, water, and shortening until very warm (about 120°). Blend about ⅓ of the flour, sugar, salt, and dry yeast in a large mixing bowl. Blend warmed liquids into flour mixture, beating with an electric mixer at medium speed for 2 minutes. Gradually add another ⅓ of the flour, then the eggs, and beat at high speed for 2 minutes. Add the remaining flour and mix well. Cover with a towel and let rise in a warm place until doubled in bulk; then beat down well with a wooden spoon. Pour into a well-greased iron or earthen Turk's-head mold and let rise again until almost doubled in bulk. Bake in a moderate oven (350°) for approximately 40 minutes. Turn out on a pressed glass cake stand, if you wish, and serve at tea time with rose geranium jelly. Unsurpassed when served piping hot with butter and marmalade.

Uncommon Cakes and Pies

Lemon Tea Cakes

Paste

1 cup flour, sifted
⅓ cup confectioners sugar
½ cup butter, softened

KENMORE TEAPOT

Sift flour and sugar together; cut butter into this mixture until it becomes crumbly. Pat this mixture into the bottom of an 8-inch-square pan. Bake at 350° for 12 minutes, or until slightly brown.

Filling

3 eggs
¼ cup lemon juice
Rind of 1 lemon, grated

3 tablespoons flour
1½ cups sugar

Lightly beat the eggs; add lemon juice and grated lemon rind. Mix flour with sugar and add to the lemon mixture. Blend well. Pour it over the baked paste. Return to oven. Bake for 25 minutes at 350° (or until custard is set, if you use a beehive oven). Remove from oven. While still warm, cut into 1-inch squares and sprinkle the top with sifted confectioners sugar. When cool, remove from the pan. Makes 36 1-inch square cakes.

(Adapted from Eliza Smith, *The Compleat Housewife*, 1742)

Raspberry Tart

½ cup currant jelly
4 tablespoons dark rum
1 quart raspberries

8-inch pie shell, baked and cooled
2 cups heavy cream
¼ cup sugar

Heat currant jelly and 2 tablespoons of rum and beat until smooth. Put the berries in the pie shell and pour jelly over them. Cool. Whip the cream with the sugar and the remaining rum until stiff and mound in peaks over the surface of the tart. Be sure to make as many mounds as there are pieces to be served.

Sweet Dishes and Confections

Honey Flummery

"When I had last the Pleasure of seeing you I observ'd your fondness for Honey; I have got a large Pot of very fine in comb, which I shall send by the first opportunity."—Betty Lewis To George Washington, July 24, 1789

2 egg yolks
2 cups milk
1 envelope unflavored gelatin
½ cup honey

¼ cup candied ginger, finely
chopped
1 tablespoon sherry
1 cup heavy cream, whipped

In a saucepan lightly beat the egg yolks and add milk. Sprinkle the gelatin over the milk mixture to soften; then stir in the honey. Cook over low heat until creamy and slightly thickened, stirring constantly. (Do not worry if the mixture curdles slightly.) Remove from heat; add finely chopped ginger and sherry. Cool in a bowl of ice water, stirring occasionally until the mixture mounds. Fold in the whipped cream. Pour into a 4-cup mold and chill until firm. Serve on a platter surrounded by fresh peach slices that have been tossed with ¼ cup honey and 1 tablespoon lemon juice. Serves 8.

Vanilla Ice Cream

Ice cream was not a common eighteenth-century dessert; few Americans had ever tasted it. It was served in France, and perhaps Lafayette or some of the other French officers introduced George Washington to this delicacy. At any rate, he bought the first recorded ice-cream freezer in America; his ledger for May, 1784, shows an expenditure of almost two pounds for "a cream machine for ice." Thomas Jefferson, too, enjoyed ice cream and left several receipts for the dessert. He had tasted vanilla ice cream in France and was most disappointed when he returned to America to find the vanilla bean was virtually unheard of. In 1791 he requested William Short, the American chargé at Paris, to send him fifty pods of vanilla so that he could introduce this new flavor to his friends. The following receipts are adapted from those used at Monticello.

4 cups light cream	6 egg yolks
1 2-inch piece of vanilla bean, or 2 teaspoons vanilla extract	1 cup sugar

Put the vanilla bean in the cream and scald the cream. Remove the bean and reserve. Lightly beat the egg yolks and add sugar. Slowly add hot cream to this mixture, stirring constantly. Add vanilla seeds from the bean. Cook in the top of a double boiler over barely simmering water until the custard coats the spoon, about 10 minutes. (At this point, add vanilla extract if vanilla beans are unavailable.) Pour the mixture into an ice-cream freezer and turn until frozen. Remove paddle from ice cream, replace top, and let the ice cream sit in the ice covered with a canvas or heavy towel until ready to serve, 30 to 60 minutes.

To serve according to Thomas Jefferson's instructions, remove paddle, "put it in moulds, jostling it well down on the knee, then put the mould into the same bucket of ice, leave it there to the moment of serving it. To withdraw it, immerse the mould in warm water, tossing it well until it will come out & turn it into a plate." Makes 2 quarts of ice cream.

Strawberry, Raspberry, or Peach Ice Cream

1 quart strawberries, raspberries, or peaches	Sugar to taste
	4 cups heavy cream

Select ripe fruit. Mash it and add sugar to your taste (½ to 1 cup). Pour into an ice-cream freezer and turn until firm. Makes 2 quarts.

Greengage Plum Ice Cream

1 pint greengage plum preserves
Juice of 2 lemons
2 cups sugar

6 cups milk
4 cups heavy cream
Pinch of salt

Mix together all ingredients. Pour into an ice-cream freezer and turn until firm. Makes 4 quarts.

Filbert Pudding with Apricot Sauce

Native to Virginia, the filbert, or hazelnut, tree was prized by Indians and white settlers alike for its edible nuts. When Betty Lewis wanted to send a gift to George Washington to celebrate his return to Mount Vernon after the Revolution, she chose some filbert sprouts that he could plant near his beloved home.

1 envelope unflavored gelatin
2 cups milk
½ cup sugar
2 egg yolks

½ cup filberts, ground
2 tablespoons brandy
1 cup heavy cream, whipped

Soak the gelatin in ¼ cup milk. Scald the remaining milk and then add the gelatin mixture to the heated milk. In the top of a double boiler beat the sugar and egg yolks together. Stir the warm milk into this mixture slowly; then cook the custard over simmering water until it thickens. Remove from heat and cool. Stir nuts and 2 tablespoons of the brandy into the cooled custard. Fold in the whipped cream. Pour into a fluted 1-quart mold and chill until set. Unmold the pudding on a platter and pass the heated sauce to each guest. Serves 6.

Apricot Sauce

4 ounces dried apricots
1 tablespoon butter
1 tablespoon brandy

Cover dried apricots with water and simmer until soft, about 30 minutes. Drain the apricots; then push them through a sieve or puree in a blender. Heat the puree with 1 tablespoon butter just to the boiling point and stir in brandy.

Chocolate Truffles

When Thomas Jefferson moved into the White House in 1801, he brought with him a fondness for French cookery and customs, acquired when he was American Minister to France. His influence was felt throughout the states, and none more than in the Lewis household, where the French Chocolate truffles found their place on the collation table.

8 squares, or 8 ounces, semisweet chocolate
¼ cup confectioners sugar, sifted
3 tablespoons butter
3 egg yolks, slightly beaten
1 tablespoon brandy
2 squares, or 2 ounces, semisweet chocolate, grated
½ teaspoon cinnamon

In the top of a double boiler over hot but not boiling water, melt 6 squares of chocolate with sugar and butter. Remove from heat. Slowly stir a small amount of hot mixture into slightly beaten egg yolks; return to hot mixture, stirring well. Blend in brandy. Chill, without stirring, for 1 to 2 hours. Shape into 1-inch balls. Mix grated semisweet chocolate and cinnamon. Roll the balls in the grated mixture. Store in the refrigerator.

Thomas Anburey, an English soldier who published a series of letters in 1789 entitled Travels Through the Interior Parts of America, *described the life of a Virginia planter. "In the summertime," Anburey wrote, "the average planter rises in the morning about six o'clock; he then drinks a julep made of rum, water and sugar, but very strong. . . . He rides around his plantation, views all his stock and all his crops, and breakfasts about ten o'clock on cold turkey, fried hominy, toast and cyder; the rest of the day he spends in trying to keep cool."—U. P. Hedrick,* A History of Horticulture in America to 1860

Drams and Punches

Fielding Lewis's Egg Nog

2 dozen eggs, separated
1½ pounds sugar
2 quarts whiskey
4 ounces rum

4 ounces brandy
8 cups light cream
4 cups heavy cream, whipped
Nutmeg for sprinkling

In a large bowl beat the egg yolks until fluffy. Add sugar slowly; then add whiskey, rum, brandy, and light cream. Beat egg whites until stiff and mix in thoroughly. Chill. Just before serving, whip heavy cream and pour the egg nog into a punch bowl. Top with whipped cream. Sprinkle with grated nutmeg. Serves 25.

Cider Posset

4 cups heavy cream
2 cups sweet cider
10 egg yolks

4 egg whites
1 cup Madeira
Grated nutmeg

Mix heavy cream and sweet cider. Beat the egg yolks until smooth. Beat the egg whites. Mix these with the cider-cream mixture. Mix in Madeira and grate a whole nutmeg over the mixture. Set over low heat and simmer until the mixture becomes thick. Remove before it reaches the boiling point. Serve hot or cold. Correct taste, adding more cider or Madeira. Grate additional nutmeg over the posset as it goes to the table. Serves 20.

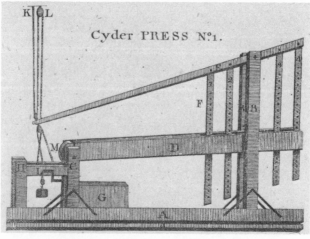

Henrietta Miksch (of the Miksch Tobacco Shop) of Salem, North Carolina

Miksch Tobacco Shop

Maria Christina Henrietta Petermann came to Bethlehem, Pennsylvania, from Germany when she was eighteen years old. Ten years later she married Johann Matthaeus Miksch, who had been called by the Moravian Brethren to their far-off settlement in the wilderness of North Carolina. He became the proprietor of the first tobacco shop and owner of the first private home in the colonial Moravian town of Salem, North Carolina.

This pioneering venture must have been taxing for a young girl far from her native land; however, Henrietta and her husband eventually became established members of the small community. On April 18, 1771, "Matthew Miksch and his family moved this day into their new house." The house, made of logs to which clapboards were latter added, cost two hundred and fifty dollars. It was a simple three-room dwelling with an unusual corner-kitchen fireplace that fed into the best room five-plate stove.* At first there was only the kitchen and shop; later a bedroom and an upstairs bedroom were added.

---

* A five-plate, or jamb, stove, made in Pennsylvania, was shipped to North Carolina. The heat from the kitchen fireplace was channeled through the wall into the adjoining room's stove, providing heat.

197

Henrietta helped with the many chores required to run her husband's shop—curing tobacco, making candles and soap, baking gingerbread in an outside oven, and making pickled cucumbers. The town council stated, "careful consideration was given to the question of how to help Brother Miksch secure a livelihood, but his circumstances make it difficult. We agreed that, if he is industrious, he could make his living by making candles, snuff, shaving, and first-cut tobacco, selling oil and whale oil, growing young fruit trees, selling garden seeds, cabbage, pickled cucumbers, turnips, dried fruit and the like. He will have a hard time in the beginning."

The Moravian diaries tell us that the family were faced with a continual financial struggle: "Brother and Sister Miksch would rather sell their own gingerbread than white bread from the baker." It appears that the Mikschs went around the town in the morning selling bread, cake, and zwieback, thus eliminating the need for the single sisters to secure bread from the single brothers' house—a practice deemed unhealthy by the town council.

For many years Brother and Sister Miksch were *Saal-Dieners,* or servers, at the lovefeast celebrations in the church services. This ceremonial task highlighted the otherwise simple, industrious life they led, obeying the laws of the church and the town council. The people of this western colonial settlement were far removed from the elegance of Charleston, Eastern North Carolina and Virginia.

One can visit the restored Miksch Tobacco Shop in Old Salem and see the tiny kitchen with its corner fireplace filled with implements such as a peach pitter, a coconut dipper, and a roaster with grease drip. In the best room is the five-plate stove with the inscription, *"las dich nicht gelgsstend deines neststen gut,"* ("thou shalt not covet they neighbors goods"). Tobacco pigtails, pipes, snuff boxes, jars of sugared nuts, and other salable items line the walls. In the back is the tobacco curing hut, and an outside oven would probably also have been there.

Although we have no original receipts from Henrietta Miksch, we can reconstruct some of the foods known to have been typical of this early town. Moravians are known for their moist sugar cakes made with potatoes, paper-thin, spicy Christmas cookies, citron tarts, and other sweet delicacies. Today, a delicious gingerbread, or an entire meal, can be sampled at the Old Salem Tavern.

The receipts in this chapter are lasting reminders of this small band of faithful men and women who brought their European heritage to America in the eighteenth century.

The Moravian Lovefeasts

In the fifteenth century John Hus, the Bohemian scholar and priest, was burned at the stake for opposing the Roman Church by preaching sermons in the language of the people. This was one hundred years before Martin Luther's *Ninety-five Theses* were written and the advent of the Protestant Reformation. The followers of John Hus, or the *Unitas Fratum* (Unity of Brethren), were forced to hide and they survived only because of their own courage and the generosity of Nicholas Lewis, Count of Zenzendorf, who gave the Brethren (or Moravians, as they were called) land on his estate in the town of Herrnhut in Saxony. From Herrnhut, small groups of men and women seeking religious freedom (and in a missionary effort to the Indians) set out across the Atlantic, where they settled first in Georgia and then in Bethlehem, Pennsylvania, in 1740. They finally purchased 100,000 acres in Piedmont, North Carolina, from Lord Granville of England, who was impressed by the success of the Moravians as colonists. The tract of land cost the church about thirty-five cents an acre. The first settlement was called Bethabara, meaning "the house of passage." Salem, near Bethabara, later became the center of the Moravian settlement.

One cannot speak of the Moravians without mentioning their traditional lovefeasts. Lovefeasts were originally celebrated by the early Christians, who met and broke bread together to signify their union and equality. The first Moravian lovefeasts in North America were held in Savannah, Georgia, from 1735 to 1740. In Salem, the first lovefeast was

held on the evening of the colonists' arrival, November 17, 1753, at Bethabara. Here, a small group of settlers shared stewed pumpkin, cornmeal mush, turnips, and journey cakes.

Today, this apostolic custom takes the forms of a musical service, during which simple, unconsecrated food—traditionally coffee and buns —is passed among the congregation.

Soups and Savories

Pumpkin Soup

3 tablespoons butter
½ cup onions, chopped
2 cups pumpkin puree, fresh
    or canned
1 teaspoon salt

Dash of sugar
Dash of nutmeg
Dash of pepper
3 cups chicken broth
½ cup light cream

In a saucepan heat the butter. Add onions and gently sauté for 10 minutes. Add pumpkin puree, salt, sugar, nutmeg, and pepper. Slowly add chicken broth and heat thoroughly. Stir in cream. Serve with toasted croutons. Serves 6.

200

Fish, Meat, and Fowl

"Meat has been scarce, and we have had only four deer and two small bears —the bears generally are smaller than in Pennsylvania. Hunting has not proved profitable, and we give little time to it. . . . We have been trying to build up a herd of cattle, and now have twelve cows, twelve calves, one bull, and one steer. The cattle in North Carolina are generally very wild, for it is usual to feed them little and let them run in the woods, so that the settlers get little good from them. The Brethren have been trying to tame our cattle, at night tying the cows to the feed troughs and it is gradually coming to pass that at the right time in the evening the cows come home."—Adelaide L. Fries, The Road to Salem

Moravian Beef with Gravy and Dumplings
(Hairhutter Rinsflaish Mit Doonkes)

1 teaspoon sage, or poultry seasoning	3 tablespoons lemon juice
½ teaspoon thyme	4-pound pot roast
½ teaspoon pepper	2 tablespoons butter, or fat
2 teaspoons whole cloves	1 carrot, chopped
2 teaspoons allspice	1 onion, chopped
2 bay leaves, crumbled	2 tablespoons flour
2 cans beef bouillon	2 tablespoons butter
2 tablespoons grated lemon rind	1 cup soured cream

Combine seasonings, bouillon, lemon rind, and lemon juice. Heat but do not boil. When this has cooled, pour it over the meat and put it in the refrigerator overnight to marinate, turning several times. Remove meat from the marinade and dry, saving the marinade. Melt 2 tablespoons butter or fat in a Dutch oven or a heavy pan. Add meat and brown on all sides. Add vegetables and marinade and cover, simmering until meat is tender, about 2 to 3 hours. Remove the meat and strain the gravy. Make a paste with 2 tablespoons butter and the flour and gradually add to the gravy, stirring until smooth. Add soured cream. Place the meat back in the pot and drop the dumplings in the hot gravy. Cover and simmer until the dumplings have risen and are cooked through. Serve the meat sliced with the dumplings and gravy. As an accompaniment, mustard and horseradish are excellent. Serves 6.

DUTCH OVEN

Moravian Dumplings

2 cups flour
1 teaspoon salt
1 teaspoon baking soda
2 teaspoons cream of tartar

¾ cup milk
2 tablespoons melted butter
1 egg, well beaten

Sift the dry ingredients and add the milk, butter, and egg. Mix thoroughly and add more milk if necessary to make a stiff batter. Drop by spoonsful into the simmering stew.

A Deep-Dish Pie Made with Chicken and Country Ham

3 cups flour
1 teaspoon salt
1 cup shortening
Ice water for mixing dough
8 to 12 chicken breasts,
   or 2 broilers, cut up
1 tablespoon salt
Freshly ground pepper to taste

1 teaspoon thyme
1 teaspoon sage
A few pieces of country ham
   (optional)
2 tablespoons flour
2 tablespoons butter
Butter for dotting

Mix first 4 ingredients and roll out half of the dough into a 2-quart casserole dish. Set aside and reserve the remaining dough.

Cook the chicken in water to cover and add salt, pepper, thyme, and sage. Drain the chicken, reserving the broth. Take the chicken from the bone and cut into bite-size pieces. Place the chicken in the dish lined with the dough. Thicken the broth with *beurre manié* (2 tablespoons butter mixed in 2 tablespoons flour) and pour it over the chicken. Add ham if desired. Dot with butter. Cover with the remaining pastry. Prick the top of the pastry. Cook 1½ hours in a slow oven (300°). Serves 10.

Roast Pork Stuffed with Dried Apples

Apples—peeled and sliced and placed in specially made fruit-drying baskets—were dried in the sun to be used in desserts, or in stuffing such as this.

1 cup dried apples, or dried mixed fruit	Salt and freshly ground pepper
4 to 5 pound pork roast, boned	1 onion, chopped
Powdered ginger and cinnamon (optional)	1 tablespoon bacon drippings
	1 cup bread crumbs
	1 cup apple cider

Soak dried fruit in water overnight. Sprinkle the roast (including the inside pocket) with ginger, cinnamon, salt, and pepper. Make a stuffing by sautéing the onions in bacon drippings and adding the drained fruit, bread crumbs, salt, and pepper. Stuff the roast and tie with string. Roast in a slow oven (300°), or on a spit, basting with the apple cider until done. Serves 6.

The town craftsmen were clever enough to fashion a variety of cooking implements, such as the grill with a drip spout, a rotisserie controlled by weights, and deep-well cookers. They even made a "washing machine," and created one of the earliest water systems in America by piping in water from springs using hollow pipes and the law of gravity.

Dried Apples

Pare, quarter, and slice apples and spread on a white cloth on a table outside in the sunshine. Protect from insects by covering with white fly netting. Take the apples in at sunset and repeat for a week of sunshine, or until the apple pieces are brown and leathery. Tie them in clean paper bags and hang in a dry place.

A Picnic in Salem
Following the Harvesting of Tobacco

"Idleness is the sepulchre of the living man."—John Amos Comenius, Moravian Bishop, seventeenth century

Many hands joined in the harvesting of tobacco. The stalks of the tobacco plants were slit and hung on a stick in the air to cure. The leaf was then processed in the log cabin behind the Miksch House in preparation for sale as tobacco pigtails or snuff tobacco in Matthew's shop. After the chores were completed, a picnic may have brought the villagers together for a respite from the day's work.

PUMPKIN SOUP

SMOKED COUNTRY HAM   MORAVIAN CABBAGE SALAD

SWEET POTATO BISCUITS

CUCUMBER PICKLE

TANGLEBRITCHES

SWEET POTATO PIE   OLD SALEM GINGERBREAD

LARGE TUBS OF LEMONADE

Roots and Vegetables

Country Green Beans

1 hambone	2 pounds green beans
1 large onion, chopped	1 tablespoon sugar
1 red pepper pod	Salt to taste
1 teaspoon peppercorns	

Cover the hambone with water; add onion, pepper pod, and peppercorns. Simmer, uncovered, over hot coals in the fireplace or on the stove for 2 hours. Remove the hambone and strain the liquor. Return the liquor to the kettle, add the beans and sugar, cover, and simmer for 1 hour. Remove the cover for the last 10 minutes so that most of the liquid can evaporate. Add salt to taste. Serve with sliced ham, hominy grits, fried apples, and beaten biscuits. Serves 8.

Yams and Chestnuts Baked with Pippins

Boil 6 medium-sized yams in their jackets until almost tender (test after 20 minutes). Peel and slice them for layering. Boil ½ pound chestnuts until tender; skin them and crumble; set aside. Peel, core, and slice 4 large tart apples. Butter a pudding dish and place alternate slices of apples and yams in layers. Crumble chestnuts over each layer. Sprinkle with ½ cup or more dark brown sugar, sprinkle with mace, and dot with butter. Pour ½ cup apple cider over them and bake at 350° until sizzling and tender, about 40 minutes. A lovely accompaniment to roast duck, game, or ham. Serves 6-8.

Moravian Cabbage Salad

1 head of cabbage, finely shredded	1 tablespoon green pepper,
1 tablespoon onion or scallion,	minced
minced	

Dressing

3 eggs	½ teaspoon salt
6 tablespoons vinegar	¼ teaspoon pepper
¼ teaspoon dry mustard	1½ teaspoons sugar
2 tablespoons butter	½ cup heavy cream, whipped

Beat the eggs until light. Add the vinegar, mustard, butter, salt, pepper, and sugar and stir constantly over boiling water until mixture begins to thicken. Cool, add cream, and mix with the cabbage, onions or scallions, and green pepper. Serves 8.

Pickles and Preserves

Cucumber Pickle

*Turmeric, the ground root of an Asiatic herb of the ginger family, found
its way early into American cookery. The Moravian diaries indicate that
Henrietta Miksch sold her turmeric cucumber pickles from the tobacco shop.*

8 pounds freshly picked cucumbers, about 5 inches long	3 pounds sugar
1 cup salt	1 tablespoon turmeric
9 cups water	1 teaspoon whole peppercorns
1 pound onions	1 teaspoon celery seed
6 cups cider vinegar	1 teaspoon mustard seed

Slice the cucumbers (unpeeled) and onions very thin. Dissolve the salt
in the water. Soak the cucumbers and onions in this mixture for 3 hours.
Drain off the brine and rinse the cucumbers *very well* to remove all
traces of the salt. Drain thoroughly. Combine vinegar, sugar, and
spices in a large kettle. Bring to a boil. When the sugar is dissolved,
add the cucumbers and onions and bring the mixture to the boiling
point again. Ladle into hot sterilized jars and seal. Let pickles stand for
at least 1 month before using. Chill before serving. Makes 6 pints.

Fig Conserve

*Early settlers planted a variety of imported fruit trees. Today, there is a
beautiful fig tree behind the Miksch House in Old Salem.*

3 pounds figs, peeled or unpeeled, chopped	1 lemon, thinly cut and seeded
2 pounds sugar	1 orange, thinly cut and seeded
	1 cup walnuts or pecans

Cook all ingredients together, except the nuts, until clear and transparent, about 25 to 30 minutes. Stir to prevent sticking. Add the nuts
about 15 minutes before the mixture is ready. Pour into sterilized jars
and seal. This conserve can be used for desserts, with meats, or as a cake
filling.

Breadstuffs

Strumbendles or Tanglebritches

1 cup butter
1½ cups sugar
4 eggs
1¼ teaspoons cream of tartar
¾ teaspoon baking soda
Flour to make a workable dough
  (5 to 8 cups)

1 cup milk
1 teaspoon nutmeg
Confectioners sugar for sprinkling
Fat for deep frying

Cream butter and sugar. Add the eggs and beat well. Sift the cream of tartar, baking soda, and 5 cups flour and add alternately to the first mixture with the milk. Add nutmeg. Add more flour until the dough can be easily rolled into a large ball. The dough can be handled more easily if allowed to rest in the refrigerator for several hours, or overnight. Roll out the dough on a floured board and cut in strips. Tie the strips into knots, or cut a slit in the middle and put one end through the slit. Fry in deep fat, drain, and sprinkle with confectioners sugar. Makes 4 dozen.

(Adapted from Elizabeth Hedgecock Sparks, *North Carolina and Old Salem Cookery*)

Lovefeast Buns

4 eggs, beaten
1 cup butter and lard, melted
1 cup warm mashed potatoes
4 cups sugar

2 tablespoons salt
3 packages dry yeast, softened
  in ½ cup warm water
10 to 12 cups flour

Mix eggs, butter and lard, potatoes, sugar, and salt and add to the yeast mixture. Add flour until the dough can be easily rolled into a ball. If necessary, add extra water. Place the dough in a clean, greased bowl, cover it with a cloth, and let rise in a warm place until "light" and doubled in bulk. Rework dough, shaping it into buns about 3 inches in diameter. Place on a greased baking sheet so they do not touch and let them rise. Bake until golden at 350°. Makes 45 buns. Halve the receipt for a smaller quantity. The buns can also be made into smaller rolls for a family dinner.

(Courtesy of the Home Moravian Church, Winston-Salem)

Old Salem Gingerbread

½ cup butter
½ cup dark brown sugar
1 cup molasses
2 tablespoons ginger
½ teaspoon coriander
½ teaspoon cinnamon
½ teaspoon nutmeg
3 eggs

3 cups flour
½ teaspoon cream of tartar
½ cup orange juice
1 tablespoon grated orange rind
1 teaspoon baking soda
1 tablespoon warm water
1 cup raisins (optional)

Cream the butter and sugar together. Add molasses and spices. Beat the eggs until light and thick. Sift the flour with the cream of tartar. Add the flour alternately with the eggs to the batter. Mix in the orange juice and orange rind. Dissolve the baking soda in the warm water and stir into the batter. Beat until very light. Add raisins if desired. Pour into a loaf, square, or oblong pan. Bake at 375° for 1¼ hours, or until a cake tester comes out clean.

(Courtesy of Old Salem Restoration, Old Salem, North Carolina)

Uncommon Cakes and Pies

Moravian Christmas Cakes

These delicacies are specially made at Christmastime in Moravian homes. They require some practice but are well worth the trouble of rolling very thin, and they keep well in a covered tin.

1 teaspoon baking soda
½ cup warm water
1 cup lard, or Crisco
1 cup brown sugar
1 cup molasses
1 heaping tablespoon ginger

1 heaping tablespoon cinnamon
1 heaping tablespoon ground
   cloves
½ teaspoon salt
About 4 cups flour

Dissolve baking soda in warm water. Mix together all ingredients except the flour. Then, add enough flour to allow for rolling a very thin dough. Allow the dough to cool. Roll on a floured board and cut with a simple, round tin cutter. Bake at 350° for about 9 minutes.

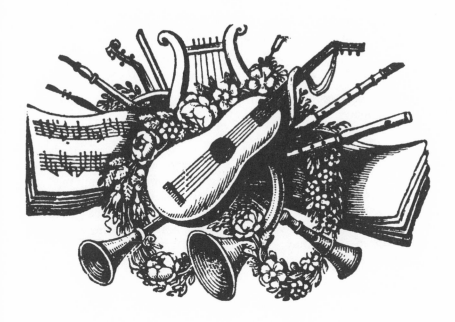

Moravian Sugar Cake

Christmas or Easter in Salem would be incomplete without this moist sugar cake made with mashed potatoes.

¾ cup butter and lard, mixed
Scant cup sugar
2 eggs
1 cup mashed potatoes
1 cup water in which the potatoes were cooked
1 teaspoon salt
1 yeast cake, or 1 package dry yeast

¼ cup warm water
Flour to make a soft dough (6 to 8 cups)
3 tablespoons butter
3 tablespoons brown sugar
3 teaspoons cinnamon
½ cup heavy cream

Cream together mixed butter and lard and sugar. Beat in eggs. Add mashed potatoes, potato water, salt, and yeast softened in the warm water. Add flour to make a soft dough. Place the dough in a clean, greased bowl and let rise in a warm place for 2 to 3 hours. Grease 2 square cake pans and pat out the dough in them. Let the dough rise again. Punch holes in the cake with a knife and fill with bits of butter and sprinklings of brown sugar, and cinnamon. Drip the cream over the top. Bake at 400° for 20 minutes, or until browned. Serve warm for special breakfasts during holidays with mugs of coffee or tea.

Zwieback Cake

Zwieback is another item that Henrietta and Matthew Miksch baked and sold in their shop, according to the Moravian diaries. A simple dessert can be made with zwieback that is especially appealing to children. Zwieback means "twice-baked" in German.

3 cups zwieback crumbs (about 1½ commercial boxes)
1 cup melted butter

1 heaping teaspoon cinnamon
¾ cup sugar
2 cups applesauce

Mix zwieback crumbs and melted butter with a fork. Mix cinnamon and sugar. Take a spring form pan and put a layer of the crumb mixture on the bottom. Sprinkle with the sugar mixture; then add a layer of applesauce. Alternate layers until the ingredients are used. Bake at 350° for 1 hour. When cool, invert onto a serving plate and serve with whipped cream. Serves 6-8.

Citron Tarts

The diaries of the Moravians note that men from the community made trips to Charleston to bring back such luxuries as lemons, which would have been dried for use during the year.

Butter "the size of an egg" (¼ cup)
6 egg yolks
1 cup light brown sugar

Lemon extract to taste
Piecrust dough to fill 12 small or 6 medium-size tart tins

The trick of preparing the filling is to chop (not stir) the mixture with a fork. Cut the butter into the egg yolks and chop in the sugar and lemon extract. Fill tart tins with piecrust dough and then fill these shells ¾ full with the custard. Bake until the filling sets and the crust is touched with brown.

Salem Lemon Pie

Juice of 2 lemons
1 tablespoon grated lemon rind
1¼ cups sugar
⅓ cup flour
4 egg yolks, plus 1 egg, beaten
Scant cup water
Pinch of salt

2 tablespoons butter
8-inch pie shell, partially baked (15 to 20 minutes at 350°)
2 egg whites
Pinch of baking soda
2 tablespoons sugar

Mix lemon juice, grated rind, sugar, and flour. Mix the beaten egg yolks and 1 egg with the water. Combine all these ingredients and add salt. Cook in the top of a double boiler until thick, stirring constantly. Add the butter and mix. Allow to cool before pouring into a partially baked pie shell. Beat the 2 egg whites with the baking soda and sugar until stiff to make a meringue. Spread the meringue on the pie, making sure that it covers the filling. Bake in a slow oven (300°) until golden brown. Serves 6.

Sweet Potato Pie

2 cups mashed sweet potatoes	½ teaspoon nutmeg
3 tablespoons butter	½ teaspoon cinnamon
½ cup sugar	½ teaspoon salt
1 cup brown sugar	1 teaspoon lemon extract
4 eggs	1 cup milk

Mix all these ingredients well and pour into a pastry-lined pie plate. (The mixture is supposed to be a little runny.) Bake at 450° for 10 minutes, then at 350° for 25 to 30 minutes, or until a knife inserted comes out clean.

A Good Pie Crust

1½ cups flour	3 tablespoons water
½ teaspoon salt	½ cup butter, or Crisco

Sift the flour and salt into a bowl. Make a paste with ¼ cup of the flour mixture and the water. Cut the butter or Crisco into the remaining flour and salt and mix until the mixture crumbles into the size of peas. Combine the two mixtures and blend well until the dough can be shaped into a ball. Roll out the dough. Makes 1 9-inch pie shell.

For a receipt that calls for a double crust use 2 cups flour, 1 teaspoon salt, ¼ cup water, and ⅔ cup butter or Crisco. Make the paste with ⅓ cup flour and ¼ cup water. Divide the dough and roll it out.

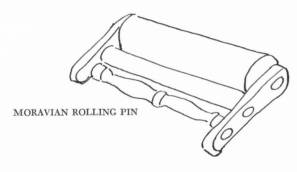

MORAVIAN ROLLING PIN

Persimmon Pudding

Persimmon trees are indigenous to North Carolina. Some think their abundance in the fall of the year is the sign of a hard winter. The early settlers probably helped themselves to this burnished fruit for puddings such as this, which is still made today by those fortunate enough to have a supply. Persimmons should not be eaten until after the first frost; otherwise, they will be bitter.

3 eggs, lightly beaten
2½ cups flour, sifted
1 cup milk
1 cup sugar
1 cup brown sugar
½ cup butter

1 quart persimmons, pureed, or
   put through a sieve
½ teaspoon salt
⅛ teaspoon baking soda
1 teaspoon cinnamon

Fold the eggs into the remaining ingredients and beat until smooth. Put into a greased baking dish and bake for about 1 to 1½ hours at 325°, or until set. Serve warm with brandy-flavored whipped cream. Nuts or raisins can be added to the batter if desired. Serves 6.

Candied Nuts

Displayed in the best room of the Miksch House are lovely old glass jars filled with candied nuts.

1 egg white
½ cup sugar
1 teaspoon salt

½ pound pecans or walnuts
⅓ pound butter

Beat the egg white until very stiff. Add sugar and salt. Fold in the nuts. Melt the butter in a casserole or pie plate. Add nut mixture and bake for 30 minutes at 300°, stirring several times. Remove the nuts from the oven and spread them to dry on heavy brown paper. Store in an airtight container.

Drams and Punches

Lovefeast Coffee

7 gallons water
3 pounds coffee
3 pounds sugar

2 quarts milk
1 quart light cream

Perk the coffee and water in a percolator, or boil with coffee tied in a cloth bag. The sugar, milk, and cream are added within the last few minutes, before the coffee is drawn for serving. Care must be taken that the coffee does not boil after the cream has been added. Serves 100 mugs.

(Courtesy of the Home Moravian Church, Winston-Salem)

Hot Mulled Wine

Spirits were used sparingly by the Moravians, as was tobacco, and such a brew would have been enjoyed only on special occasions. The aroma of spice fills the air when cloved oranges are roasting by the fire. Try this simple receipt at Christmastime.

1 orange studded with cloves
1 quart port wine

Roast the orange in front of the fireplace. Cut it into quarters and pour a quart of warmed port wine over it. Let this brew simmer for 30 minutes, then pour into punch glasses and garnish with a cinnamon stick.

A Moravian Christmas Gathering

At Christmastime Salem bustled with preparations for the season. Single sisters and brothers (as the unmarried were called), husbands, wives, and children participated in the festivities. Music resounded throughout the village with instruments such as the violin, organ, and French horn. Beeswax candles with paper frills at the base, which originated with the Christmas Eve lovefeast in Wetteravia in 1747, were lighted and passed around. Herb wreaths and fresh forest greenery adorned the simple houses, and sweet smells of cakes and other delicacies filled the air.

A menu such as this collection of sweets and punches would have been a lavish display for the simple communal society; but on an occasion as special as Christmas, memories of the German homeland prompted a flurry of excited activity and baking.

CHRISTMAS PORT

SPICED HOT CIDER

PAPER-THIN MORAVIAN CHRISTMAS CAKES

MORAVIAN SUGAR CAKE

CITRON TARTS

CANDIED NUTS

Elizabeth Matthews Heyward
of Charleston, South Carolina

Heyward-Washington House

In 1773 Elizabeth Matthews, daughter of the Honorable John Matthews, married Thomas Heyward. The life of Elizabeth Matthews was divided between the elegant townhouse on Church Street in Charleston and a plantation, "Whitehall," outside the city. While she no doubt had numerous slaves and servants to help maintain the two residences, her position as overseer must have been taxing. Their marriage produced one son and several children who died in infancy.

Elizabeth Heyward accompanied her husband to Philadelphia during the Continental Congress and was honored at a ball given there for the Dauphin of France, where George Washington crowned her "Queen of Love and Beauty."

She no doubt also possessed great strength, for while Thomas Heyward was a political prisoner in St. Augustine after Charleston was taken by the British in 1780, Elizabeth Heyward endured many hardships. She lived in the townhouse with her sister, Mrs. George Abbott Hall, after her plantation had been plundered and the slaves carried off. When the Charleston citizens were told by the British to illuminate their homes in celebration of a British military victory in 1781, she disobeyed and kept her house in darkness. On the anniversary of the fall of Charleston, when the order to illuminate was again given, she again defied the order and consequently her house was attacked by a mob of loyalists. During the attack, her sister died. The following year Elizabeth Heyward sacrificed her life, as well as that of her fifth child, in her effort to meet her husband upon his release from prison in St. Augustine.

The Heyward–Washington House

The Heyward-Washington House was built in 1770 by Daniel Heyward, a member of a great plantation family. He left the house to his son, Thomas Heyward, Jr., a delegate to the Continental Congress of 1776 and a signer of the Declaration of Independence.

During his visit to Charleston in 1791, George Washington was given this house for his stay. The president noted in his diary that "the lodgings provided for me in this place were very good, being the furnished house of a gentleman at present in the country, but occupied by a person placed there on purpose to accommodate me." He was surprised by a visit from some ladies of Charleston and remarked, "was visited about 2 o'clock by a great number of the most respectable ladies of Charleston—the first honor of the kind I had ever experienced, and it was as flattering as it was singular." The house has been called the Heyward-Washington House since his visit and has been owned and restored by the Charleston Museum since 1929. The entire restoration, including the formal garden and dependencies behind the house, has been carried out according to the date of President Washington's visit.

A square house with a bisecting hall entered from the street, it has four rooms on each floor. This is called a Charleston "double house." The paneled second-floor drawing room extends across the upstairs hallway and has good circulation for cool summer breezes in this semitropical city.

PETER MANIGAULT AND HIS FRIENDS

Behind the house is an enclosed courtyard with several buildings and the garden. There is one building that contains the kitchen and the wash kitchen, above which are servants rooms. Also in the courtyard are a carriage house, wood and toolsheds, and a necessary. The formal, symmetrical beds of the garden are planted with the flowers, herbs, and shrubs typical of eighteenth-century Charleston.

Entertaining was done lavishly in private homes in eighteenth-century Charleston. Included in a description of a ball given by Mrs. Thomas Radcliff for General James Wilkinson was this account by Mrs. Gabriel Manigault:

"General Wilkinson's band charmed us with some well-executed military pieces—during which we paced up and down the spacious corridor which was brilliantly illuminated, & into her handsome bedroom, which was likewise lighted. A variety of cakes, and wine, and fruit, and jellies, and all the nice things that could be collected were handed about. Everybody was in high spirits. They danced, and the band played during the intervals of dining—at eleven o'clock some delicious little oyster patties were brought up with other things of the same kind—after which the gentlemen were invited to partake of a supper of beefstakes and cold turkies—some of which was brought to the ladies—we retired at eleven but the party did not break up until two o'clock."—George C. Rogers, Jr., Charleston in the Age of the Pinckneys

SHRIMP PASTE   SODA BISCUITS

OYSTER PATTIES   CLAM FRITTERS

COLD SMOKED TURKEY   BEEFSTEAKS

RUM JELLY

PORT   EXCELLENT WINES   MADEIRA

BENNE SEED WAFERS   KISSES FOR A SLACK OVEN

ALMONDS   RAISINS   ORANGES

Soups and Savories

She-Crab Soup

This soup is so named because of the eggs which the she-crab contains. It can be made with any crabmeat, however. South Carolina's coastal waters are abundant with crab, and this soup is as famous in the Charleston area today as it was in colonial times.

1 tablespoon flour	1½ pounds crabmeat
4 tablespoons butter	She-crab eggs (if available)
2 hard-boiled eggs, mashed	Salt and pepper to taste
Grated rind of 1 lemon	Dash of cayenne pepper
4 cups milk, or light cream	½ cup dry sherry
4 blades of mace	

Blend flour and butter in a double boiler. Add hard-boiled eggs and lemon rind. Gradually add the milk or cream and mace and stir until mixture begins to thicken. Add crabmeat, crab eggs (optional), salt, and pepper. Stir in sherry at the last moment before serving. Serve in a soup tureen and accompany with soda biscuits. Serves 6.

*There were two important meals of the day in eighteenth-century Charleston
—breakfast and three o'clock dinner. Breakfast always included hominy with
butter, eggs, bacon, leftover cold meat or shrimp, and sliced tomatoes. Three
o'clock dinner fit into the plantation's daily schedule and the semitropical
climate and gave time for a long morning of preparation and work.*

Shrimp Paste

*This was served in Charleston for breakfast with hominy, but it is equally
delicious served with crackers as an appetizer.*

2 pounds shrimp, boiled, peeled,
    and deveined
½ cup butter

Dash of ground mace
½ teaspoon mustard, or to taste
1 tablespoon sherry

Pound the shrimp, or grind in a meat grinder or blender. Mix shrimp
with butter and add the rest of the ingredients. Chill well and place
in a crock. Before serving, let stand at room temperature until the paste
is of spreading consistency. Serve with crackers or toast.

Fish, Meat, and Fowl

Oyster Patties

2 tablespoons flour
3 tablespoons melted butter
1½ cups light cream
½ cup oyster liquor
1 tablespoon lemon juice
1 tablespoon Worcestershire
    sauce

1 cup oysters
Small pastry shells, baked (12
    small shells, or 6 larger shells)
Salt and freshly ground pepper
Dash of mace or nutmeg
Dash of cayenne
Grated lemon rind

In a saucepan stir the flour into the melted butter. Add cream and
oyster liquor and stir until boiling. Add lemon juice and Worcestershire sauce and simmer for a few minutes. Add oysters, being careful
to exclude any shells. Simmer until oysters curl. Season to taste. Fill
the pastry shells and serve very hot. Taste for seasoning. Sprinkle with
freshly ground pepper, mace or nutmeg, cayenne, and grated lemon
rind. The creamed oysters can also be served in scalloped shells, which
have been browned quickly in the oven. Serves 4.

Shrimp Pie

Elizabeth Heyward may have had several different receipts for shrimp pie. The following dish would have been appropriate for three o'clock dinner at the Heyward Plantation.

3 cups fresh bread crumbs
3 cups milk, scalded
2 tablespoons melted butter
1 tablespoon sherry
1 tablespoon onion, grated
2 tablespoons tomato catsup
Dash of hot pepper sauce

Dash of cayenne
½ teaspoon dry mustard
2 teaspoons Worcestershire sauce
5 eggs, well beaten
1 pound shrimp, boiled, peeled, and deveined
Salt to taste

Soak bread crumbs in milk. Add all other ingredients and mix thoroughly. Pour mixture into a greased baking dish. Sprinkle with bread crumbs, dot with butter, and bake at 350° until the custard is firm, about 30 minutes. Serves 6 to 8.

Two Sauces for Fish

Cucumber Curry Sauce

1 cup homemade mayonnaise
3 tablespoons lemon juice
Dash of hot sauce

¼ teaspoon curry powder
½ cup cucumbers, finely chopped

Blend all ingredients, except cucumber. Drain the cucumber and combine with the mayonnaise mixture. Chill for several hours before serving with cold, poached striped bass.

CANDLE STAND

Dill and Mustard Sauce

2½ tablespoons dry mustard
5 tablespoons sugar
½ teaspoon salt
2 tablespoons salad oil
1 tablespoon vinegar
½ cup soured cream
2 tablespoons fresh dill, chopped

Blend together mustard, sugar, and salt. Add the oil and vinegar alternately. Stir slowly until blended; then beat hard. Fold in the soured cream and dill. Serve with cold crab claws or other cold shellfish.

Probably the best-known book of receipts written in Charleston was *The Carolina Housewife*, by Sarah Rutledge, daughter of a signer of the Declaration of Independence. Sarah was born in 1782 and was taken to England in 1792. She brought back many French, English, and Spanish recipes, such as "potage à la julienne," "sauce piquante," and "omelette soufflée." She also included many plain cooked dishes, such as oyster soup, shrimp pie, and several different rice breads.

Here is a fanciful, unusually time-consuming example that will challenge today's housewife:

A Christmas Pie

"Make the walls of a thick standing crust, to any size you like, and ornamented as fancey directs. Lay at the bottom of the pie a beef-steak. Bone a turkey, goose, fowl, duck, partridge, and place one within the other, so that when cut the white and brown meat may appear alternately. Put a large tongue by its side, and fill the vacancies with forcemeat balls and hard eggs; then add savoury jelly—this last is better for being kept in a mould, and only taken out as required. Bacon chopped is a nice addition."

Wild Duck with Apples and Raisins

The South Carolina coastal plantations supplied the colonists with such delicacies as wild duck, doves, and marsh hens.

2 oven-ready wild ducks, or
  1 Long Island duckling
Salt and peper to taste
2 stalks of celery, chopped
2 apples, quartered
½ cup raisins

1 onion
1 stalk of celery
2 cups water
1 cup lemon juice
½ cup butter

Salt and pepper the inside and outside of the ducks. Reserve the giblets and necks. Combine chopped celery, apples, and raisins and stuff the cavities. Put the ducks in a roasting pan and roast at 350° for 1½ hours. Wild ducks have little fat, but if you use a Long Island duckling, skim off fat as the duck cooks.*

While the fowls are cooking, prepare a stock by simmering giblets and necks, onion, stalk of celery, and water.

Mix the lemon juice and butter and pour over the ducks during the last 15 minutes of cooking. Baste with lemon mixture. Remove the duck to a warm platter. Degrease the pan juices. Strain the stock; chop the giblets and discard the necks and vegetables. Add 1 tablespoon flour to the roasting pan. Stir and slowly add the stock and giblets to the pan juices. Serve the duck garnished with thinly sliced lemon and oranges and pass the sauce separately. Serves 6.

* Duck fat is considered a delicate fat to use in pâtés and for cooking.

Potted Doves

6 doves, cleaned and plucked
6 slices bacon
1 onion, sliced
1 tablespoon butter

Salt and pepper to taste
½ cup red wine
½ cup chicken broth
1 tablespoon flour

Cover the doves with water. Bring to a boil and pour off the water. Cover again with water and simmer for about 30 minutes. Place in a Dutch oven and put bacon, onion, butter, salt, pepper, wine, and broth over the birds. Sprinkle with flour. Bake at 325° for 1 hour. Serves 6.

This letter written by a woman of Charleston to a Northern relative describes a variety of local foods.

"Eliza eats hominy, rice and milk, eggs and oysters cooked in various ways, vegetables too, which we find in great perfection here; fruit is plenty of almost every description. The oranges raised here are not sweet, but are very large. Their olives, grapes and figs are excellent. Their meats and fish are not so good as ours. Their poultry is fine; a great plenty of venison, wild ducks, and small sea-fowl; so that, beside the change of climate, we have many of the luxuries of a Northern Summer."—Letters of Elizabeth Southgate, 1803

Roots and Vegetables

Eggplant Pie

2 eggs
2 cups boiled eggplant,
  peeled and mashed
½ cup bread crumbs
2 tablespoons butter
1 teaspoon fresh thyme, chopped

1 tablespoon parsley, chopped
1 tablespoon onion, sautéed
Salt and pepper to taste
½ cup cracker crumbs
2 tablespoons sharp cheese, grated
1 tablespoon butter

Beat the eggs and add to the eggplant, together with the bread crumbs, butter, thyme, parsley, onion, salt, and pepper. Pour into a greased ovenproof dish, sprinkle with cracker crumbs, and grated cheese, and dot with butter. Bake at 350° until brown and bubbly. Serves 6.

A Nice Way to Cook Okra

"Take a pint of young tender okra, chop it up fine, add to it half as much skinned, ripe tomato, and onion cut up in slices, a tablespoon butter, a little salt and pepper, and a spoonful of water. Stew all together till tender and serve with meat or poultry."—Charleston Museum collection of early cookbooks

Hoppin' John

Hoppin' John is traditionally served on New Year's Day in the South, a custom that started in colonial days. The name is derived from the time when children hopped around the table before being served this dish.

2 cups fresh cow peas
   (black-eyed peas)
8 cups water
1¼ cups rice
3 tablespoons bacon
   drippings

Salt and pepper to taste
3 slices bacon, cooked and
   crumbled

Soak peas overnight. Boil peas in the water until tender. Add the rice. When the rice begins to swell, add the bacon drippings and cook, covered, for 1 hour over low heat. Flavor with salt and pepper and stir with a fork. Serve with bacon crumbled over the rice and peas, and garnish with a sprig of mint.

(Adapted from Sarah Rutledge, *The Carolina Housewife*, 1847)

Red Rice

1 cup onions, chopped
½ cup green pepper,
   chopped
5 tablespoons bacon
   drippings
1 tablespoon salt
2 cups tomatoes, peeled and
   chopped

1 teaspoon sugar
Dash of cayenne
1 cup rice
1 cup shrimp, boiled, peeled,
   and deveined (optional)

Sauté onions and green pepper in bacon drippings until limp. Mix together all other ingredients but the shrimp (if desired) and let stand for a few minutes. Add the tomato-rice mixture to the onions and peppers and simmer for 30 minutes. Check the rice and finish cooking, covered, until done. Serves 6 to 8. An excellent accompaniment to fish or fowl. Fresh shrimp can be added at the last minute to make this into a hearty supper or luncheon made dish.

Hominy Soufflé

Hominy, a staple of American Indian origin, is often called "grist" in Charleston, meaning corn that has been ground. Hominy is corn that has been hulled and ground coarsely, in preparation for cooking with water and salt. Hominy "grist" appears on many South Carolina breakfast tables, and is mixed with butter, then eaten with eggs, bacon, and fish. The dish may appear again on the supper table, left over from breakfast, then fried or baked and served with shrimp, crab, or meat. This custom has endured since colonial days.

3 cups boiling water
2 teaspoons salt
¾ cup fine hominy
¼ cup butter
1 tablespoon sugar

1¾ cups milk
3 large eggs, beaten
½ cup sharp cheddar cheese,
   grated (optional)

Add salt to the boiling water and pour in hominy. Stir hominy and cook in a double boiler for 1 hour. (Fast-cooking hominy can also be used.) Remove from the fire and add butter, sugar, milk, and beaten eggs. Salt to taste. Beat well. Pour into a greased baking dish and bake at 325° for 1 hour. For additional flavor, add ½ cup grated sharp cheddar. Serves 6.

Spiced Persian Melon

Charleston, a major port of the colonies, provided such fruits from the West Indies as melons, lemons, and pineapple.

1 Persian melon, cantaloupe,
  or honeydew melon
¼ cup sugar

3 drops oil of clove
¼ cup water

Peel and slice the melon and cut into 2-inch cubes. Pack into a sterilized quart jar and pour the sugar, clove oil, and water, which have been boiled together, over the melon. Pack the jar into a warm-water bath and boil for 15 minutes. Seal with a sterilized lid.

Jerusalem Artichoke Pickle

The Jerusalem artichoke is the root of a sunflower plant known as the "sunflower artichoke." Its tubers, which are edible, are planted like potatoes, except that they can be set out in the early spring or even in the fall. Traditionally, they are grown in South Carolina and are either creamed, used in soups, or pickled, as in the following receipt.

½ peck artichokes, washed and
  scraped
6 large onions, sliced
1 gallon water
1 cup salt
2 pounds sugar

1 gallon cider vinegar
1 teaspoon celery seed
1 teaspoon mustard seed
1 tablespoon dry mustard
1 teaspoon turmeric
5 hot peppers (optional)

Soak artichokes (either whole or sliced) and sliced onions overnight in salted water. Next morning, drain and rinse well to remove salt. Boil onions, sugar, vinegar, and spices for 15 minutes. Add artichokes and simmer for 10 minutes. Put in sterilized jars. Add one hot pepper to each jar if desired. Makes 5 pints.

Breadstuffs

Soda Biscuits

2 cups light cream
½ cup butter
1 teaspoon salt
4 eggs

1 teaspoon baking soda
"As much flour as will
    make a dough to roll out"

Mix the cream, butter, salt, eggs, and baking soda. Add flour until the dough can be rolled easily. Roll dough and cut into squares or strips. Prick biscuits with a fork and bake at 350° until light brown. This makes a large quantity of dough, part of which can be saved for later use. The biscuits are delicious with soups or cheeses and can be kept in a tightly closed tin.

Cottage Cheese Biscuits

1 cup flour
1 teaspoon baking soda
1 teaspoon salt

1 cup cottage cheese
½ cup butter
1 egg yolk, beaten

Sift together the flour, baking soda, and salt. Combine with cottage cheese and butter. Blend well and shape into a ball. Knead on a floured board. Roll the dough to about a ½ inch thickness. With a cookie cutter (or the top of a glass), cut the dough into rounds. Place on a greased cookie sheet and brush the tops with beaten egg yolk. Bake in a hot oven (375°) for 12 to 15 minutes. Makes 2 dozen small biscuits.

Uncommon Cakes and Pies

Benne Seed Wafers

½ cup sesame seeds
¾ cup butter or margarine
1 cup light brown sugar, firmly
   packed
1 egg

1 teaspoon vanilla extract
1 cup flour
⅛ teaspoon salt
½ teaspoon baking soda

Put benne (sesame) seeds in a heavy skillet over medium heat, stirring constantly until they are golden brown. In a large bowl combine butter, brown sugar, egg, and vanilla and beat until smooth. Add the flour, which has been sifted with salt and baking soda; then add toasted seeds, stirring until well blended. Freeze, covered, for 2 hours, or refrigerate overnight.

Preheat oven to 375°. Drop dough from a slightly rounded teaspoon 2 inches apart onto an ungreased cookie sheet. Bake for 10 minutes until lightly browned around the edges. Let stand for 1 minute; then remove and allow to cool. Makes 5 dozen.

Kisses for a Slack Oven

3 egg whites
1 teaspoon vanilla extract
¼ teaspoon cream of tartar
Dash of salt
1 cup sugar
Red and green food coloring

In a mixing bowl combine egg whites, vanilla, cream of tartar, and salt. Beat until soft peaks form. Very gradually add sugar, beating until very stiff peaks form. The meringue should be glossy. Divide the meringue. Add cochineal (red food coloring) to one part and spinach juice (green food coloring) to the other. Drop from a tablespoon onto an ungreased cookie sheet about 1½ inches apart and bake in a slack oven (275°) for 30 minutes or more. Immediately remove from the cookie sheet and cool.

White Fruit Cake

This fruit cake should be made at least a month in advance so it can ripen with extra sprinklings of brandy. It keeps well for months if properly wrapped. The cake may be iced with almond paste before serving. Almonds were a delicacy in Charleston because they were not natively grown and had to be imported.

1 cup butter	¾ pound almonds, chopped
1 cup sugar	¾ pound walnuts, chopped
6 eggs	4 cups sifted flour
1 pound citron, thinly sliced	1 teaspoon each cinnamon,
1 candied orange, thinly sliced	nutmeg, mace, and almond extract
1 candied lemon, thinly sliced	½ cup sherry
¼ pound candied cherries, sliced	½ cup brandy
1 package golden raisins	1 tablespoon rose water
1 cup grated unsweetened coconut	A few extra candied cherries, halved almonds and walnuts
	Brandy for sprinkling

Cream together butter and sugar. Add the eggs one at a time. Dredge the fruits, coconuts, and nuts with the flour and spices. Add to the creamed mixture alternately with the liquors and rose water and stir until well blended. Bake in a large greased, paper-lined cake pan such as a Bundt pan in a slow oven (300°) for about 1½ to 2 hours. Place a dish of water in the bottom of the oven while baking. The cake may be steamed if desired. It is important that the cake bake slowly. Remove the cake from the oven and glaze the top with a sugar syrup (1 cup sugar and ½ cup water boiled down to a syrupy consistency, or you may use a prepared corn syrup); then decorate with the extra cherries and nuts. Allow the cake to cool and douse with brandy. Wrap in cheesecloth and store in a cool place. Unwrap every week and sprinkle with brandy. If desired, ice the cake before serving.

Almond Paste

1 pound confectioners sugar	1 tablespoon orange-flower water (optional)
2 egg whites	1 pound almonds, ground
2 teaspoons almond extract	

Combine egg whites and sugar. Add the flavoring and cream together well. Add almonds and mix well. If the icing is used, the cherries and nuts can be used to garnish the cake after the icing is applied.

Lemon Pound Cake

1 cup butter
½ cup vegetable shortening
3 cups sugar
5 large, or 6 medium, eggs
2 teaspoons lemon extract
¼ teaspoon salt

3 cups, plus 5 tablespoons
  sifted flour
1 cup milk
½ teaspoon baking soda
1 teaspoon cream of tartar

Cream butter, shortening, and sugar together well. Add eggs one at a time, blending just enough to mix. Add lemon extract and salt. Add flour and milk alternately, ending with the flour. Sprinkle baking soda and cream of tartar sifted together on top of the batter and fold in gently. Pour into a large, greased and floured tube pan and bake at 315° for 1 hour and 15 minutes. Do not open the oven until the cake is done. Sprinkle with powdered sugar, or glaze with a favorite icing.

Huguenot Torte

The French Huguenots came to Charleston in the late seventeenth century.

1 cup sugar
2 eggs, well beaten
¼ cup flour
1½ teaspoons baking soda
2 teaspoons cream of tartar
½ teaspoon salt

1 cup apples, peeled, cored, and
  chopped
1 cup pecans, chopped
1 teaspoon lemon juice
1 teaspoon vanilla extract

Beat the sugar into the eggs until the mixture is thick. Beat in the flour sifted together with the baking soda, cream of tartar, and salt. Stir in the apples, pecans, lemon juice, and vanilla extract. Pour the batter into a well-buttered 8″ x 10″ baking dish and bake in a preheated moderate oven (325°) for 45 minutes, or until browned. The torte will have a firm, crunchy top layer and a softer layer beneath. Serve with heavy whipped cream and a sprinkling of nuts. Serves 6.

Sweet Dishes and Confections

Pineapple Pudding

"One grated pine-apple, half a pound of butter, half a pound of sugar, six eggs, and three ounces of grated bread; rub the butter and sugar to a cream; beat the eggs, whites and yolks separately, and add them; then the fruit and bread, and bake them either with or without a crust."
—Sarah Rutledge, The Carolina Housewife, 1847

To Preserve Cream

To be poured over desserts or fresh berries.

"Take ½ pound white sugar, dissolve it in the smallest possible quantity of water. When melted boil it two minutes in an earthenware vessel, then pour into it half a pint of new cream while the sugar is still quite hot, and when cold pour it into bottles and cork tight."—Harriott Horry's receipt book, Hampton Plantation, 1770

Drams and Punches

The St. Cecelia Society, the pre-Revolutionary music society founded in 1735, still thrives in Charleston. Here is a receipt for a potent punch enjoyed at their annual gala at Hibernian Hall.

St. Cecilia Punch

6 lemons, sliced and seeded
1 quart brandy
1 pineapple, sliced
Sugar syrup (made with 1½ pounds sugar moistened with water)

1 quart tea
1 pint rum
1 quart peach or apricot brandy
4 quarts champagne
2 quarts club soda

Cover the lemons with brandy and allow to steep for 24 hours. Slice the pineapple into a large punch bowl. Add the lemon and brandy mixture, sugar, syrup, tea, rum, peach or apricot brandy. When ready to serve, add a large ice mold and pour over it the champagne and club soda. Serves 80 to 90 punch cups.

Hot Spiced Tea

A fancy tea party in Charleston would probably include this aromatic tea served either in tea cups or in punch cups. The lemons and oranges were imported from Spain and the spices from the Caribbean islands.

4 quarts freshly brewed tea
6 oranges, peeled, seeded and
  squeezed
4 lemons, peeled, seeded and
  squeezed

4 cups pineapple juice
3 sticks cinnamon
2 teaspoons whole cloves
2 quarts water
1½ cups sugar, or to taste

Combine tea and fruit juices. Simmer rinds of fruit, cinnamon, and cloves in 2 quarts water for 15 minutes. Strain and add to the punch. Sweeten to taste. Serve hot. Serves 25.

Orange Flower Ratifye

Eliza Lucas Pinckney was the first woman planter of South Carolina. She was largely responsible for the successful cultivation and exportation of indigo. The devastation to the land as a result of the Revolution caused the loss of this source of wealth; however, Mrs. Pinckney remained a famous figure and her handwritten receipt book has been preserved.

"One pound of orange flowers fresh pluck'd, one ounce cinnamon pounded, two ounces peach kernels, one pound sugar and one quart of boil'd water, cold, put all these ingredients into a Gallon of French brandy in a jugg to ferment for a month, taking care to shake it once or twice a day."—Eliza Lucas Pinckney's receipt book, 1756

Sarah Gibbons Telfair of Savannah, Georgia

The Telfair Mansion

Few women were as intimately caught up in the turbulence of the American Revolution as was Sarah Gibbons Telfair. Among her closest friends were those patriots who led the protest against British rule and established the first state government of Georgia. Wartime turmoil reached deeply into the heart of this new bride.

Born in 1758, Sarah Gibbons grew up in a large family of English ancestry that had moved to Georgia from the Bahamas before her birth. In 1774 Sarah married Edward Telfair, an established Savannah merchant twenty-three years her senior, who had immigrated from Scotland ten years earlier. Applying a shrewd business sense and an intelligent policy of land investment, Telfair became one of the wealthiest businessmen of early Savannah.

The spring of 1774 was an inauspicious time to marry since armed conflict with England threatened to erupt momentarily. Just two months after their wedding, Sarah's husband flaunted British authority by drafting resolutions in support of the beleaguered citizens of Boston. The next year he and her cousin William Gibbons joined other Savannah patriots in raiding the royal powder magazine of Savannah. At the same time, Sarah's cousin Thomas Gibbons, and her brother-in-law William Telfair supported British rule; similar to countless other colonial American families, the Gibbons and Telfair familes found themselves divided by conflicting allegiances.

233

SARAH GIBBONS TELFAIR

Edward Telfair was chosen by the Assembly to represent Georgia
in the Continental Congress in 1778. Whether Sarah accompanied
him to Philadelphia for his first term is not known; she may have been
reluctant to make the wartime journey. However, when Edward returned to Philadelphia in 1780, Sarah did join him, bringing with her
their new-born son Edward. For three years they remained in Philadelphia where another son, William, was born.

After the war, the Telfairs returned to an active life in Savannah.
After serving as a commissioner to negotiate peace with the Cherokee
Indian nation, Edward was elected to the Georgia legislature. In 1786
he was elected Governor. Sarah was busy with a rapidly growing family;
seven more children were born to the Telfairs in the years after the war.

After being elected governor, Edward took his family to live at The
Grove, a plantation just outside the state capital of Augusta.

The gracious hospitality for which the South is justly famous was
part of Sarah Telfair's way of life. A receipt book, written in her own
hand, has been preserved by the Georgia Historical Society. Tucked in
among the receipts, many of which are presented here, are lists of
nostrums suitable for fashionable entertainments, decorative hints, and
useful remedies for many common illnesses. Obviously Sarah took
her homemaking chores seriously.

One more thing must be said about this remarkable woman. Anyone who visits Savannah today will find the Telfair presence inescapable. The Telfair Academy of Arts and Sciences was bequeathed to the city by Mary Telfair, Sarah's daughter. Hodgson Hall, which houses the Georgia Historical Society Library, was the gift of Mary and another daughter, Margaret, in honor of Margaret's husband William B. Hodgson. The Telfair Hospital and the Telfair Widows' Home have provided for Savannah's sick and elderly citizens. The strong sense of community responsibility displayed by her progeny points to Sarah's effectiveness as a mother. She instilled in her children an unusual concern for the welfare of others and a dedication to expressing that concern; and by doing this, Sarah left ample testimony to her own strength of purpose.

The Telfair Mansion

Sarah Telfair's home in Savannah was probably destroyed either by the disastrous fire that burned two-thirds of Savannah in 1796 or by the hurricane that struck the rebuilding city eight years later. No record of her home remains. After the hurricane, however, Sarah's son Alexander built an elegant Regency townhouse designed by the English architect William Jay. The house was bequeathed to the Georgia Historical Society in 1875 to be used as a museum. Visitors to the museum can view the original kitchen, which has been restored and is open to the public at the Telfair Academy of Arts and Sciences.

As in most eighteenth-century Savannah homes, the Telfair kitchen is located beneath the dining room, lower than ground level but high enough so that windows in the walls could provide light. The room is large with white stucco walls and a floor of rectangular stone slabs. A wide stone fireplace stretches across most of one wall with its hearth raised a foot above the floor in order to lessen slightly the degree of bending required of the busy cook. Reaching across the width of the fireplace is a swinging iron crane that could hold several pots above the blazing fire. Pegs driven into the wooden mantlepiece keep the most essential kitchen utensils within easy reach.

An interesting feature of the Telfair kitchen is the location of the beehive oven. It is set into the wall at an angle diagonal to the fireplace so that the cook might stand in one place to shovel the hot coals from the fireplace into the oven—an early American step-saving innovation.

Convenience is also evident in the use of wall space. The long-handled utensils necessary for open-hearth cookery hang from pegs in boards set high upon the walls. Built-in shelves along one side of the room provide storage space for the iron pots and kettles; a large wooden hutch holds pewter and chinaware. In the center of the room stands a sturdy trestle table, its scarred top providing visual evidence of the many meals prepared on its working surface.

SAVANNAH, 1741

GEORGIA HISTORICAL SOCIETY

Oyster Bisque

3 tablespoons butter	1 teaspoon salt
3 tablespoons flour	½ teaspoon pepper
4 cups milk	1 quart oysters
½ cup celery, chopped	1 tablespoon Worcestershire
1 green pepper, chopped	sauce

In a large saucepan melt the butter, stir in flour, and slowly add 3 cups milk. Blend remaining cup of milk with celery and green pepper in an electric blender; add this mixture to the soup, stirring constantly. Add salt and pepper. Place oysters and their liquor in the blender and whisk quickly. Add to hot soup mixture slowly. Keep heated but do not allow bisque to boil or it may curdle. Add Worcestershire sauce just before serving. Serves 8.

Shrimp bisque may be made with the same receipt. Use one pound freshly cooked shrimp and blend the shrimp with the milk, celery, and green pepper.

Savannah Gumbo

Gumbo is the familiar name for okra, a plant of African origin that was probably brought to America by African slaves. Naturalist William Bartram observed large patches of the plant growing along the Georgia coast during his visit in 1773. Georgia colonists learned early to appreciate the distinctive taste of this unusual vegetable.

3-pound stewing chicken	4 quarts water
2 tablespoons butter or oil	20 oysters (1 quart)
1 medium onion, finely chopped	1 cup okra, chopped
2 teaspoons salt	1 teaspoon thyme
½ teaspoon pepper	2 teaspoons curry powder

Brown chicken in hot fat. Add onions, salt, and pepper and cover with 4 quarts of water. Simmer over hot coals for 2 hours. Remove chicken, discard skin and bones, and return chicken meat cut in bite-size pieces to the broth. Then add oysters, okra, and thyme and cook for 20 minutes. Add curry powder just before serving. Serves 12 as a main course or 20 as an appetizer.

(Adapted from Mary H. Freeman, *Colonial Receipts*)

A Scottish Rabbit

Scottish Highlanders, who originally came to Georgia in 1740 to defend the colony's southern border, added their distinctive cookery to the culinary heritage of Georgia.

"Toast a bit of bread on both sides then lay it on a plate before the fire. Pour a glass of red wine over it, and let it soak the wine up, then cut some cheese very thin and lay it very thick over the bread and put it in a tin oven before the fire and it will be toasted and browned presently. . . . You may stir in a little mustard."—Scottish manuscript cookbook of Moffatt family.

Fish, Meat, and Fowl

Ogeechee Shad with Roe

3 potatoes, pared and diced	¼ cup butter
3 pounds shad with roe	Salt and pepper to taste
1 small onion, chopped	½ cup water
1 tablespoon parsley, chopped	1 bay leaf

Boil potatoes until almost done. Drain. Scald roe for 2 minutes. Drain, split, and scrape out roe. Combine potatoes, onion, parsley, roe, 2 tablespoons melted butter, salt, and pepper. Stuff shad with this mixture. Put shad in a pan with the remaining 2 tablespoons butter, water, and bay leaf. Bake at 350°, basting frequently, until done, about 30 minutes. Garnish with lemon wedges and parsley.

Stuffed Fish with Creole Sauce the West Indian Way

Creole Sauce

4 cups canned or fresh tomatoes, skinned and chopped	1 teaspoon salt
½ teaspoon thyme	Dash of cayenne
1 bay leaf, crumbled	½ cup green pepper, chopped
1 tablespoon brown sugar	½ cup onion, chopped
1 clove garlic, chopped	2 tablespoons butter
	1 tablespoon flour

In a saucepan combine chopped tomatoes, thyme, bay leaf, brown sugar, garlic, salt, and pepper. Simmer until the mixture has been reduced to about half. In a separate pan, sauté onion and green pepper in butter until soft; stir in flour and then tomato mixture.

Fish

1 cup cooked crabmeat
1 cup cooked shrimp, chopped
½ cup dry bread crumbs
¼ cup parsley, chopped
1 tablespoon melted butter
½ teaspoon salt

Pinch of thyme, rosemary, and
  marjoram
1 teaspoon Worcestershire sauce
8 large fish fillets
Melted butter for brushing
Salt and pepper to taste

Combine all ingredients except fillets. Make a mound of this filling on each fillet, roll up ends, and secure with a toothpick. Place in shallow baking pan, brush with melted butter, and sprinkle with salt and pepper. Bake at 350° for 15 minutes; then ladle Creole sauce over the fish, reduce heat to 350°, and bake for 30 minutes more. Serves 8.

Beef à la Mode

¼ pound sausage
1 small onion, chopped
4 slices bread, cut into small
  pieces
½ teaspoon salt
½ teaspoon nutmeg
¼ teaspoon ground cloves
¼ teaspoon mace
Pinch of sweet herbs—summer
  savory, basil, marjoram, parsley,
  thyme

2-pound round steak cut ½-inch
  thick
Flour for coating
2 tablespoons butter
½ cup claret wine
1 tablespoon flour
1½ cups water

In a Dutch oven, brown sausage and onion. Stir in pieces of bread, salt, spices, and herbs. Pound steak flat, cover with the stuffing mixture, roll, and tie with a heavy string in several places. Flour rolled steak and brown in hot butter; then add claret, cover tightly, and simmer slowly on top of the stove or in a 325° oven for 1 to 1½ hours. Remove steak from pan and serve in slices with gravy made by thickening pan juices with 1 tablespoon flour dissolved in 1½ cups water. Serves 6.

(Adapted from the Telfair manuscript cookbook)

Scottish Veal Collops

"Cut some stakes out of the thick of a thigh. Thin and bate [beat] them with a rolling pin. Take the yolk of two or three eggs and put some on the stake with your fingers. Then take half an ounce of white pepper and the grate of a lemon minced with salt and put on some above the eggs. Then take the crumbs of a penny brick [bread crumbs] grated and some minched parsley and lay the stake on the bread on both sides but do not put much. Take a frying pan and put nigh a quarter a pound of butter in it. Always turn it to your right hand. When it all melted and like froth put in as many collops as it will hold. Do them a light brown."—Scottish manuscript cookbook of Moffatt family.

Roasted Spring Lamb

"Lay down to a clear good fire that will not want stirring or altering, baste with butter, dust on flour, baste with the dripping, and before you take it up, add more butter and sprinkle on a little salt and parsly shred fine; send to table with a nice sallad, green peas, fresh beans, or a colliflower, or asparagus."—Amelia Simmons, American Cookery, 1796

Mint Sauce

Take fresh young spearmint leaves; wash and dry thoroughly. Chop them very fine. Put in a sauce boat. For every 3 tablespoons mint leaves add 2 tablespoons white sugar and 6 tablespoons good cider vinegar. Make up early in the day so the flavors will mellow. Serve with roasted spring lamb.

Wild Duckling

1 onion
1 cup water
2 oven-ready wild ducks
2 slices bacon
Salt and pepper to taste
Bundle of sweet herbs (bay leaf,
    chervil or parsley, and tarragon
    or rosemary)

2 tablespoons lemon juice
1 tablespoon mushroom catsup
    (available in specialty food
    stores)
2 teaspoons cornstarch dissolved
    in ¼ cup water
½ cup dry sherry

Chop onion in the bottom of roasting pan. Add water. Place ducks on top of the onion with a thin slice of bacon over the breast of each duck. Add salt and pepper. Roast at 400°, basting frequently until done, about 1 hour. Remove ducks, strain, and skim fat from broth, returning broth to pan. Add bundle of herbs, lemon juice, and mushroom catsup. Simmer for 10 minutes, adding additional water if necessary. Meanwhile, carve duck into serving pieces and arrange on a large platter. Remove herbs from broth, thicken with cornstarch dissolved in water, add sherry, and bring to a boil. Pour this gravy over the duck, garnish with parsley and toast points, and serve with a steaming bowl of rice. Serves 6.

(Adapted from Mary H. Freeman, *Colonial Receipts*)

A Georgia Fete

In 1791, two years after he was inaugurated, President George Washington made a tour through the South in order to inspect the land and meet the citizens of the newly formed United States. When he reached Georgia, a group of the state's most influential citizens, including Governor Edward Telfair, met the presidential party on the road and escorted it to Augusta. As Governor's wife, Sarah Telfair was first to entertain the President with dinner at four, a tea with "many well dressed ladies," and finally an evening ball. For the next two days George Washington was feted and entertained by the people of Augusta.

    Since there is no historical record of Sarah Telfair's menu for dinner, this menu is an attempt to capture the distinctive culinary heritage of Georgia.

Plantation Dinner and Ball

HONORING
George Washington, President of the United States
GIVEN BY
Governor and Mrs. Edward Telfair
THE GROVE, AUGUSTA, GEORGIA
May 18, 1791

OYSTER BISQUE

OGEECHEE SHAD WITH ROE

WILD DUCKLING

ROASTED SPRING LAMB

FRESH ASPARAGUS   MINT SAUCE

WATERCRESS AND HEARTS OF PALMETTO

SWEET POTATO SOUFFLÉ   PLANTATION RICE

BATH BUNS

FRESH STRAWBERRIES   CURD MOLD

SCUPPERNOG WINE   MADEIRA

Roots and Vegetables

Jambalaya

Every Georgia cook had her own receipt for Jambalaya, which is essentially a rice pilau with local ingredients added as available. The following is a basic receipt; modern cooks should feel free to experiment with other meat and vegetable combinations.

1 onion, chopped
1 cup rice
2 tablespoons melted butter
2 cups tomatoes, peeled
2 cups water
1 teaspoon sweet basil

1 red pepper pod, crumbled or,
    healthy dash of Tabasco sauce
1 teaspoon salt
Pepper to taste
1 cup ham, cubed
1 cup shrimp

Lightly brown onions and rice in melted butter, stirring constantly to prevent burning. Add tomatoes, cut in large pieces (canned tomatoes can be used), water, and seasonings. Cover tightly and simmer over low heat until the rice is tender, about ½ hour. Add ham and shrimp. If frozen shrimp are used, thaw them quickly in hot water; then add to Jambalaya and cook for only a few minutes until barely done. Too much cooking toughens the shrimp. Serves 6.

Jambalaya is an easy dish to cook in a Dutch oven in an open fireplace. The variations are endless—brown a chicken in melted butter, then add the onions, rice, and tomatoes. Fresh oysters, dropped in just before serving, are a delicious addition. Okra, fresh peas, and even black-eyed peas add variety. Many cooks use chicken broth or beef bouillon instead of water.

Plantation Rice

Georgia colonists found the lowlands along the Savannah River excellently suited to the growing of rice. In the eighteenth century rice, rather than cotton, was Georgia's major agricultural product.

4 tablespoons butter	¼ cup unsalted pistachio nuts, blanched
¼ cup pignoli nuts	1 teaspoon mace
2 cups hot cooked rice, salted	

In a skillet melt butter until foamy. Add pignoli nuts and sauté over low heat until golden, stirring constantly. Add the hot rice and stir to blend. Add the pistachio nuts and sprinkle with mace.

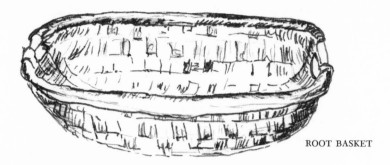

ROOT BASKET

Sweet Potato Soufflé

2 cups hot sweet potatoes,
  mashed
½ cup hot milk
6 tablespoons butter
¼ cup dry sherry
Dash of cayenne

½ teaspoon grated nutmeg
1 teaspoon grated lemon rind
½ teaspoon salt
4 eggs, separated and beaten
  separately

In a bowl beat together the sweet potatoes, milk, butter, and sherry. Add the pepper, nutmeg, lemon rind, and salt and blend well. Beat in the egg yolks; then fold in the stiffly beaten egg whites. Butter a soufflé dish and transfer the batter. Bake at 400° until the soufflé just begins to brown. Serve promptly to 6. This goes nicely with wild duck, turkey, or baked ham.

Watercress and Hearts of Palmetto

To clear Georgia's land for cultivation, colonists chopped down endless numbers of palmetto trees. Perhaps in doing so they learned that the tender heart of the tree's terminal bud was edible. Today, canned hearts of palm are available in many areas. This elegant salad is presented for the modern cook.

1 can hearts of palm
1 small jar pimento

French dressing
Large bunch fresh watercress

Slice hearts of palm in ¼-inch slices as you would celery. Mix with chopped and drained pimento and marinate in French dressing freshly made with olive oil and vinegar. Wash watercress and drain thoroughly. Arrange on salad plates. Just before serving, scatter the hearts of palm and pimento over the watercress. Serves 8.

Pickles and Preserves

Peach Chutney

6 large peaches	2 tablespoons preserved ginger,
6 large tomatoes	chopped
1 large green pepper, cut coarsley	2 teaspoons powdered ginger
6 small onions, cut coasely	2 teaspoons salt
½ cup raisins	⅛ teaspoon cayenne
1 cup vinegar	Juice of 1 lemon
1 cup sugar	2 teaspoons chili powder

Rub fuzz from peaches, remove pits, and slice. Skin tomatoes and chop. Add pepper, onions, raisins, vinegar, sugar, and preserved ginger, and simmer very slowly in a heavy pan until thick, adding the last 5 ingredients a few minutes before taking from the fire. Seal in sterile jars.

Breadstuffs

Bath Buns

Sarah Telfair copied the receipt for this popular English bun into her cookbook. Her version, presented here, uses caraway seeds to flavor the batter; today's housewife is probably more familiar with another version of this receipt—the Hot Cross Bun. For this treat, add ½ teaspoon cinnamon and ¼ teaspoon nutmeg to the flour and fold in 1 cup currants or raisins. Omit caraway seeds. After baking, glaze with thin white frosting in the shape of a cross.

2 packages dry yeast	1½ cups milk, scalded
¼ cup water	½ cup sugar
¾ cup butter	3 eggs
6 cups flour, sifted	2 tablespoons caraway seeds
1 teaspoon salt	1 egg yolk for glazing

Dissolve yeast in ¼ cup warm water. With a pastry blender cut butter into flour mixed with salt until the mixture resembles fine meal. Add lukewarm milk, sugar, and dissolved yeast. Add caraway seeds, reserving a few to top each bun. Beat eggs and add to the flour mixture. The dough will be sticky. Turn onto a floured board and knead until smooth and elastic. Return to the buttered bowl. Cover and let rise until doubled in bulk, about 1½ hours. Shape into 24 round buns and place on greased cookie sheets. Brush with egg yolk beaten with 1 teaspoon water. "Every nice housewife will keep a clean feather for the purpose," noted Sarah Telfair. Top with caraway seeds. Cover with a cloth and let rise for 30 minutes. Bake at 375° for 25 minutes. Makes 24 buns.

(Adapted from the Telfair manuscript cookbook)

Pecan Cornsticks

2 eggs	3 teaspoons baking soda
1 cup buttermilk	1 teaspoon salt
2 cups corn flour, or	¼ cup sugar
cornmeal	¼ cup melted butter
1 cup white flour	¾ cup pecans, crushed

Beat eggs well. Add buttermilk. Sift together flour, baking soda, salt, and sugar and add to mixture with butter and pecans. Pour into oiled cornstick molds and bake in a fast oven (450°) for 12 to 15 minutes.

This batter may also be cooked over hot coals in a long-handled waffle iron or in an electric waffle iron. Be sure the waffle iron is hot and well oiled before pouring the batter into it. Serves 8.

Uncommon Cakes and Pies

Hospitality Thins

⅔ cup butter, softened	½ teaspoon salt
1 cup sugar	1 teaspoon vanilla extract
2 teaspoons grated lemon rind	1 egg
2 teaspoons ginger	3 tablespoons lemon juice
½ teaspoon baking soda	2 cups sifted flour

PINEAPPLE BUTTER STAMP

Cream butter and sugar together. Add lemon rind, ginger, baking soda, salt, and vanilla. Beat in egg and lemon juice. Stir in flour and mix well. Refrigerate dough for 2 hours or more. Shape into ¾-inch balls. Place 1½ inches apart on ungreased cookie sheets. Bake in preheated oven (400°) for 6 to 8 minutes until set but not hard. Flatten with a pineapple butter stamp as soon as they come from the oven. Makes 6 dozen.

Sarah Telfair's Brandied Cheesecake

"Put two quarts of new milk in a stew pan. Set it near the fire, and stir in two tablespoons full of rennet. Let it stand until it is set. This will take about an hour. Break it well with your hand. Let it remain half an hour longer. Pour off the whey and put the curd into a colander to drain. When quite dry, put it in a mortar and pound it quite smooth." Thus Sarah Telfair's receipt begins. Fortunately, today's cook can start with commercially prepared cottage cheese.

¼ cup currants
2 tablespoons brandy
4 eggs, separated
1 pound cottage cheese
¾ cup sugar

2 tablespoons flour
¼ teaspoon freshly
 grated nutmeg
1 teaspoon grated lemon
 rind

Soak currants in brandy. In a blender, blend egg yolks and cottage cheese until smooth. Add sugar, flour, nutmeg, and lemon rind. Beat egg whites until stiff and fold into the cheese mixture. Add brandy and currants.

Sarah baked this cheesecake in small tins lined with puff paste. Since the batter is so rich, however, a simple mixture of ½ cup dried bread crumbs and 1 tablespoon melted butter is sufficient for the crust. Pat into the bottom of an 8-inch springform pan; add cheese mixture. Bake at 350° for 45 minutes. Let cool in the oven.

(Adapted from the Telfair manuscript cookbook)

Sweet Dishes and Confections

Transparent Pudding in Puff-Paste Crust

4 eggs
2 cups sugar
8-inch puff-paste pie shell

1 cup butter
¼ teaspoon nutmeg

In a saucepan lightly beat the eggs. Add sugar and butter and cook over moderate heat, stirring constantly until mixture thickens. Remove from the heat and pour into puff-paste crust that has been cooked for 15 minutes at 400° (For a good crust, you may use the following receipt, which, however, yields enough pastry for 4 crusts.) Reduce oven heat to 350° and bake until center is set, about 30 minutes. One teaspoon grated orange rind or ¼ cup citron can be added to the filling before baking if desired.

(Adapted from the Telfair manuscript cookbook)

Puff Paste

1 pound butter, chilled
4 cups flour
1½ teaspoon salt

¾ to 1 cup water
Butter for spreading

Cut the cold butter into the flour mixed with the salt. Add enough water to make a stiff dough. Divide into 4 portions. On a well-floured board roll out the crust, spread with a layer of butter or lard, and fold and roll out again to the thickness of a "crown piece" (about ⅛ inch thick). The dough will be very rich and soft; tears may be mended by pressing edges together with fingers. Place in pie plate and flute the edges. Add desired filling or bake empty crust at 400° for 20 minutes until light brown. This receipt makes enough for 4 piecrusts. The pastry is very rich, crisp, and delicious.

(Adapted from the Telfair manuscript cookbook)

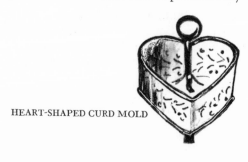

HEART-SHAPED CURD MOLD

Curd Mold

The heart-shaped curd mold in the Telfair kitchen was used for one of the most elegant yet simple desserts of the eighteenth century. Unfortunately, the modern cook cannot reproduce the eighteenth-century curd because pasteurized or homogenized milk will not produce the rich curd of fresh milk. For those who are fortunate enough to have a supply of fresh cow's milk, we include this receipt.

Allow 2 quarts of fresh cow's milk to sour. Turn this curdled milk (clabber) into a curd mold that has been set upon a large, flat receptacle for collecting the whey. Place the lid on the clabber. The weight of the lid will press the curds together, forcing the whey to drain through the slots in the side of the mold. Allow the mold to remain overnight in a cool place. To serve, unmold the curd onto a silver platter. Spread with thick sweet cream and sprinkle with nutmeg and brown sugar. Pass with a bowlful of fresh strawberries.

General Nathanael Greene, Washington's southern commander, whose military leadership was largely responsible for the defeat of the British, described the fruit grown on his Georgia plantation, Mulberry Hill: "We have in the same orchard apples, pears, peaches, apricots, nectarines, plums of different kinds, figs, pomegranites, and oranges, and we have strawberries which measure three inches around."—G. W. Greene, Life of Nathanael Greene

Baked Pears

4 firm baking pears	1 cup sugar
½ lemon, thinly sliced	1 small cinnamon stick
1 cup water	8 whole pieces of allspice

Pare, core, and quarter the pears. Arrange in a buttered casserole dish with a tightly fitting cover. Slice lemon with the rind and place these slices on the pears. Add water, sugar, cinnamon stick, and allspice. Cover tightly and bake at 325° for 2 hours. This dish is simple to prepare and elegant to serve either hot or cold. Serves 6.

Sarah Telfair's original receipt calls for cooking the pears "close together in a black tin saucepan, the insides of which is quite bright" for six hours in a very slow oven. This procedure gives a lovely red cast to the pears.

(Adapted from the Telfair manuscript cookbook)

Preserved Oranges with Filling

Georgia bears were "immoderately fond" of oranges, noted William Bar-
tram, "and both they and turkeys are made extremely fat and delicious, from
their feeding on the sweet acorns of the live oak."—William Bartram, Trav-
els Through North & South Carolina, Georgia, East & West Florida, *1791*

Take 4 oranges, cut in half, and squeeze out the juice. Put the rinds in
water and soak for 1 day. Drain, then add fresh water. Bring to a boil
and simmer until tender, between 30 and 45 minutes. Drain and cool.
When cool enough to handle, remove all membranes from the oranges
to clean the shell. Make a simple syrup to cover the oranges (2 parts
water to 1 part sugar). Poach orange shells in the syrup in a covered pot
over low heat until very tender, about 30 minutes. Baste frequently.
Cool in the syrup in the covered pot. Store orange shells in a wide-
mouthed jar and cover with the leftover syrup.

Filling

2 2¾-ounce packages day-old
   Naples biscuits (lady fingers)
¼ cup sugar
4 egg yolks, beaten
¼ pound butter, softened
¼ teaspoon almond extract

½ teaspoon orange extract
¼ cup syrup from preserved
   oranges
4 egg whites
⅓ cup sugar

Grate Naples biscuits into crumbs in a blender. Mix ¼ cup sugar with
the beaten yolks; then beat in the butter, almond extract, orange extract, and syrup from the oranges. Whip the egg whites into moist peaks.
Add ⅓ cup sugar and whip until stiff and glossy. Fold egg yolk mixture
and grated Naples biscuits into the egg whites. Fill the drained orange
shells. Place in muffin tins to prevent them from falling over and bake
for 1 hour in a slow oven (300°). The top will be puffy. Serve in small
sherbert glasses, or place on a galyx leaf on a small glass dessert dish.

(Adapted from *The American Domestic Cookery,* 1808)

Benne Brittle

Black cooks in Savannah used the flavorful benne (or sesame) seeds exten-
sively in breads, cookies, and candies.

1 cup sugar
½ cup benne seeds

¼ cup water
¼ cup vinegar

In a saucepan stir all ingredients together until a candy thermometer registers 265°, or until a drop of the mixture in cold water is quite brittle. Spread on a buttered cookie sheet or marble slab. When cool, crack into pieces and store in a tightly covered cannister.

(Adapted from a Kirk family receipt)

Apricot Leather

Wash 1 package dried apricots and put them in water to soak overnight. Next morning, bring apricots and water to a boil and simmer for 5 minutes. Remove from heat and drain thoroughly. (Be sure all the water has drained off.) Mash the apricots through a sieve, or blend in a blender until smooth. Measure pulp; return it to the saucepan and add 1 part sugar to every 3 parts pulp. Bring to a boil and boil for 2 minutes, stirring constantly (at this stage the mixture may burn easily, so stir carefully.) Let the mixture cool for 15 minutes; then spread almost paper thin on a large piece of glass, marble slab, or aluminum cookie sheet. Form a rectangular shape. Place in a warm, dry room (an attic is excellent) to dry for 1 to 2 days (it should be pliable enough to roll). Cut the leather into 3-inch squares, sprinkle with granulated sugar, and roll tightly into rolls about the size of a small pencil. Roll in granulated sugar and store in a tightly closed box. Children love these fruity delicacies, which are healthful as well as tasty.

(Adapted from a Kirk family receipt)

The Indians of Georgia, observed William Bartram in 1773, cultivated fields of corn, beans, and sweet potatoes. Surrounding these fields were groves of fruit or nut trees. Hickory nuts were a special favorite: "I have seen above an hundred bushels of these nuts belonging to one family. They pound them to pieces, and then cast them into boiling water, which, after passing through fine strainers, preserves the most oily part of the liquid: this they call by a name which signifies hiccory milk; it is as sweet and rich as fresh cream, and is an ingredient in most of their cookery, especially homony and corn cakes."—William Bartram, Travels Through North & South Carolina, Georgia, East & West Florida, *1791*

Drams and Punches

Chatham Artillery Punch

Organized in 1786, the Chatham Artillery is one of the oldest military organizations in the United States. George Washington greeted its officers when he visited Georgia in 1791.

1 pound green tea
2 gallons water
3 gallons Catawba wine
1 gallon St. Croix rum
1 gallon brandy
1 gallon rye whiskey

1 gallon gin
5 pounds brown sugar
2 quarts maraschino cherries
3 dozen oranges, sliced and seeded
3 dozen lemons, sliced and seeded
10 quarts champagne, or club soda

Steep tea in 2 gallons of cold water overnight. Next morning, strain tea through cheesecloth and add all the other ingredients except the champagne or club soda. Although the punch may be used at once, experienced Georgians insist that a superior flavor is produced by allowing this mixture to mellow for at least 2 weeks.

To serve, pour the punch over ice in a large punch bowl, adding 1 quart of champagne (or club soda) for every gallon of punch. Makes 12 gallons. Serves 200.

Inbibe with caution; this punch is aptly named an "artillery punch!"

Bibliography

The American Domestic Cookery, by a Lady. Hartford, Conn.: Andrus & Judd, 1833.

BARTRAM, WILLIAM. *Travels of William Bartram.* Philadelphia, 1791. Reprint ed., Mark Van Doren. New York: Dover Publications, 1955.

BIRKET, JAMES. *Some Cursory Remarks Made by James Birket in His Voyage to North America, 1750–1751.* New Haven, Conn.: Yale University Press, 1916.

BOWNE, ELIZA SOUTHGATE. *A Girl's Life Eighty Years Ago: Selections from the Letters of Eliza Southgate Bowne.* Ed., Clarence Cook. London: Chapman & Hall, 1888.

BRIGGS, RICHARD. *The New Art of Cookery According to Present Practice.* Philadelphia: H. & P. Rice, 1798.

BULLOCK, HELEN. *The Williamsburg Art of Cookery.* Williamsburg, Va.: Colonial Williamsburg, Inc., 1939.

BUTTERFIELD, LYMAN H., ed. *Diary and Autobiography of John Adams, 1755–1804.* 4 vols. Cambridge, Mass.: Harvard University Press, 1961.

———. *Adams Family Correspondence, 1761–1778.* 2 vols. Cambridge, Mass.: Harvard University Press, 1973.

CARSON, JANE. *Colonial Virginia Cookery.* Williamsburg, Va.: Colonial Williamsburg, Inc., 1968.

CARTER, CHARLES. *The Complete Practical Cook.* London, 1730.

CHANCE, E. B., and L. B. LOVELL. *Two Quaker Sisters.* New York: Liveright, 1937.

CHILD, LYDIA MARIA. *The American Frugal Housewife.* Boston: Carter Hendee & Co., 1833. Reprint ed., Alice M. Geffen. New York: Harper & Row, 1972.

The Cook's Oracle, Containing Receipts for Plain Cookery. 2d ed. Boston: Munroe & Francis, 1823. (From Mystic Seaport, Inc., Mystic, Conn.)

COULTER, E. MERTON. "Edward Telfair," *The Georgia Historical Quarterly,* **20** (1936), 99–124.

CREVECOEUR, J. HECTOR ST. JOHN DE. *Letters from an American Farmer and Sketches of Eighteenth-Century America, 1769–1783.* New York: New American Library, 1963.

CROLL, P. C. *The Keim Family*. In *Annals of the Oley Valley in Berks County, Pennsylvania*. Reading, Pa.: Reading Press, 1926.

DABOLL, NATHAN. *New England Almanack 1819*. New London, Conn.: Samuel Green, 1819.

DAVIS, CHESTER. *A Hidden Seed and Harvest*. Winston-Salem, N.C.: Wachovia Historical Society, 1973.

Delaware Historical Society, Wilmington. Cookbook of Mrs. Charles Henry Black, 1849.

————. Cookbook of Jane Wilson, 1828.

————. Ledger of Corbit receipts.

DROWNE, HENRY R. *The Story of Fraunces Tavern*. New York: Sons of the Revolution, 1966.

DUKE, JANE TAYLOR. *Kenmore and the Lewises*. Fredericksburg, Va.: The Kenmore Association, 1965.

The Experienced American Housekeeper, or Domestic Cookery, from Rundee's "New System of Domestic Cookery." New York: Johnstone & Van Norden, 1823.

FREEMAN, DOUGLAS SOUTHALL. *George Washington*. New York: Charles Scribner's Sons, 1948.

FREEMAN, MARY H. *Colonial Receipts and Remedies*. Savannah, Ga.: Historic Savannah Foundation, Inc., n.d.

FRIES, ADELAID L. *The Road to Salem*. Chapel Hill: University of North Carolina Press, 1944.

GARDINER, ANNE GIBBONS. *Mrs. Gardiner's Receipts from 1763*. Hallowell, Me.: White, Horne & Co., 1938.

Georgia Historical Society, Savannah. Telfair receipt books, Ms. 290 and 291, n.d. Telfair Family Papers.

GIBBONS, PHEBE E. *The Pennsylvania Dutch*. Philadelphia: J. B. Lippincott, 1872.

GLASSE, HANNAH. *The Art of Cookery Made Plain and Easy*. Alexandria, Va.: Cotton & Stewart, 1812.

GOOLRICK, JOHN T. *Fredericksburg and the Cavalier Country*. Richmond, Va.: Garrett & Massie, 1935.

GREENE, GEORGE WASHINGTON. *Life of Nathanael Greene*. Boston: C. C. Little & J. Brown, 1846.

GRUND, FRANCIS J. *Aristocracy in America*. New York: Harper & Row, 1959. (First published by Richard Bentley, London, 1839.)

HARRISON, SARAH. *The House-Keeper's Pocket-Book, and Compleat Family Cook*. London, 1755.

HEDRICK, U. P. *A History of Horticulture in America to 1860*. New York: Oxford University Press, 1950.

HENDERSON, ARCHIBALD. *Washington's Southern Tour, 1791*. Boston: Houghton Mifflin, 1923.

HOTCHKISS, HORACE L., JR. "The Corbit-Sharp House, Family Circle, 1818–1845," *Winterthur Portfolio 1*. Ed., Milo M. Naeve. Winterthur, Del.: Henry Francis du Pont Winterthur Museum, 1964.

KALM, PETER. *Travels in North America, 1750.* Ed., Adolf B. Benson. New York: Wilson-Erickson, 1937.

Kenmore Association, Fredericksburg, Va. Betty Washington Lewis Manuscripts.

KIMBALL, MARIE, ed. *Thomas Jefferson's Cook Book.* Richmond, Va.: Garrett & Massie, 1949.

LAPHAM, LEAH INMAN. *A Rhode Island Rule Book* (kept by LeValley A. Inman). Providence, R.I.: Oxford Press, 1950.

LESLIE, ELIZA. *Seventy-five Receipts for Pastry, Cakes, and Sweetmeats.* New York: C. S. Frances, 1835.

Maryland Historical Society, Baltimore. The Letterbooks of Charles Carroll, Barrister, 1764–1768. Filed under Dr. Charles Carroll of Annapolis, Ms. 208.

————. Coale Family Receipts, 1800–1860, Ms. 248.

MITCHELL, STEWART, ed. *New Letters of Abigail Adams, 1788–1801.* Boston: Houghton Mifflin, 1947.

Montclair Historical Society. Research papers prepared by Junior League of Montclair, N.J., 1968.

Mystic Seaport, Inc., Mystic, Conn. Letter to Charlotte T. W. Gilbert from her friend C. D. Waters, 1829.

————. Cookbook of Caroline Hastings, Nashua, N.H., 1820

National Society of the Colonial Dames of America in the State of Maryland. "Some of Mrs. Carroll's Favorite Receipts, Mount Clare Mansion." n.d.

New Hampshire Historical Society, Concord. McClure papers, 1778–1812.

————. Moffatt-Whipple papers.

A New System of Domestic Cookery Formed upon Principles of Economy and Adapted to the Use of Private Families, by a Lady. Exeter, N.H.: Norris & Sawyer, 1808.

New-York Historical Society. Item 1253: Scotch and American cookbook from the family of David Moffatt, born in Edinburgh and came to America in 1819.

NIEMCEWICZ, JULIAN. *Under Their Vine and Fig Tree, 1797–99.* Elizabeth, N.J.: Grassman, 1965.

OLIVER, ANDREW. *Portraits of John and Abigail Adams.* Cambridge, Mass.: Harvard University Press, 1967.

PELL, CLAIBORNE B. "Rochambeau in Rhode Island." Address delivered January 28, 1955. Pamphlet at the Newport Historical Society.

PHIPPS, FRANCES. *Colonial Kitchens, Their Furnishings and Their Gardens.* New York: Hawthorne, 1972.

RANDOLPH, MARY. *The Virginia Housewife.* Philadelphia: E. H. Butler, 1846.

"Receipts of Eliza Lucas Pinckney, 1756, Charleston Museum," *Antiques* **47** (April 1970), 564.

Records of the Moravians in North Carolina. Trans., Adelaide L. Fries. 5 vols. Winston-Salem: North Carolina Historical Commission.

RICE, HOWARD C., JR., ed. *Travels in North America in the Years 1780, 1781, and 1782 by the Marquis de Chastellux.* Chapel Hill: University of North Carolina Press, 1963.

RICE, HOWARD C., JR., and ANNE S. K. BROWN, eds. *The American Campaigns of Rochambeau's Army, 1780, 1781, 1782, and 1783.* 2 vols. Princeton, N.J., and Providence, R.I.: Princeton University Press and Brown University Press, 1972.

ROGERS, GEORGE C., JR. *Charleston in the Age of the Pinckneys.* Norman: University of Oklahoma Press, 1969.

RUTLEDGE, SARAH. *The Carolina Housewife, by a Lady of Charleston.* Charleston, S.C.: John Russell, 1847 (3d ed. 1855).

SCHOEPF, JOHANN DAVID. *Travels in the Confederation, 1783–84.* Trans. and ed., Alfred J. Morrison. Philadelphia: W. J. Campbell, 1911

SIMMONS, AMELIA. *American Cookery.* Hartford, Conn.: Hudson & Goodwin, 1796. Facsimile ed., New York: Oxford University Press, 1958.

SINGLETON, ESTHER. *Social New York Under the Georges, 1714–1776.* New York: D. Appleton, 1902.

SMITH, ELIZA. *The Compleat Housewife, or Accomplish't Gentlewoman's Companion.* Williamsburg, Va.: William Parks, 1742.

SPARKS, ELIZABETH HEDGECOCK. *North Carolina and Old Salem Cookery.* Charlotte, N.C.: Dowd Press, 1955.

STANARD, MARY MANN PAGE. *Colonial Virginia: Its People and Customs.* Philadelphia: J. B. Lippincott, 1917.

SWEENEY, JOHN A. H. *Grandeur on the Appoquinimink: The House of William Corbit at Odessa, Delaware.* Winterthur Series Book. Newark: University of Delaware Press, 1959.

TAYLOR, E. *The Lady's, Housewife's and Cookmaid's Art of Cookery.* London, 1778.

TOWNSEND, GRACE. *Dining Room and Kitchen.* Chicago: Monarch, 1894.

Index of Receipts

257

The Northern Colonies

CATHERINE MOFFATT WHIPPLE OF NEW HAMPSHIRE

1734–1821

❖•❖

ABIGAIL ADAMS OF MASSACHUSETTS

1744–1818

❖•❖

POLLY WANTON LYMAN OF RHODE ISLAND

1763–1822

❖•❖

LYDIA WATROUS BUCKINGHAM OF CONNECTICUT

1753–1833

The Middle Colonies

SAMUEL FRAUNCES OF NEW YORK

1722–1795

❖•❖

FANNY PIERSON CRANE OF NEW JERSEY

1773–1826

❖•❖

MAGDELENA HOCH KEIM OF PENNSYLVANIA

1730–1804

❖•❖

MARY COWGILL CORBIT OF DELAWARE

1761–1845

The Southern Colonies

MARGARET TILGHMAN CARROLL OF MARYLAND

1742–1817

———◆◆———

BETTY WASHINGTON LEWIS OF VIRGINIA

1733–1797

———◆◆———

HENRIETTA MIKSCH OF NORTH CAROLINA

1741–1818

———◆◆———

ELIZABETH HEYWARD OF SOUTH CAROLINA

1750–1782

———◆◆———

SARAH GIBBONS TELFAIR OF GEORGIA

1758–1827